MW00576100

OH
BOY!

Masculinities and Popular Music

EDITED BY
FREYA JARMAN-IVENS
UNIVERSITY OF LIVERPOOL

JAN 23 2012

PROPERTY OF
SENECA COLLEGE
LIBRARIES
KING CAMPUS

 Routledge
Taylor & Francis Group
New York   London

Routledge
Taylor & Francis Group
270 Madison Avenue
New York, NY 10016

Routledge
Taylor & Francis Group
2 Park Square
Milton Park, Abingdon
Oxon OX14 4RN

© 2007 by Taylor & Francis Group, LLC
Routledge is an imprint of Taylor & Francis Group, an Informa business

Printed in the United States of America on acid-free paper
10 9 8 7 6 5 4 3 2 1

International Standard Book Number-10: 0-415-97821-1 (Softcover) 0-415-97820-3 (Hardcover)
International Standard Book Number-13: 978-0-415-97821-7 (Softcover) 978-0-415-97820-0 (Hardcover)

No part of this book may be reprinted, reproduced, transmitted, or utilized in any form by any electronic, mechanical, or other means, now known or hereafter invented, including photocopying, microfilming, and recording, or in any information storage or retrieval system, without written permission from the publishers.

Trademark Notice: Product or corporate names may be trademarks or registered trademarks, and are used only for identification and explanation without intent to infringe.

Library of Congress Cataloging-in-Publication Data

Oh boy! : masculinities and popular music / edited by Freya Jarman-Ivens.
    p. cm.
  ISBN 0-415-97820-3 -- ISBN 0-415-97821-1
    1. Popular music--History and criticism. 2. Masculinity in music. 3. Gender
identity in music. I. Jarman-Ivens, Freya.

ML3470.O4 2007
781.63'081--dc22   2007001859

Visit the Taylor & Francis Web site at
http://www.taylorandfrancis.com

and the Routledge Web site at
http://www.routledge.com

Contents

Acknowledgments

The most credit and my first and deepest thanks must go to the contributors for their excellent work, as this collection would of course not exist without it. I would especially like to thank Ian Biddle of the International Centre for Music Studies at the University of Newcastle upon Tyne, for having agreed to make changes to his own chapter in order to coauthor the introduction with me. Hearty thanks also go to all those who assisted with securing copyright permission: Mark Butler and Stephin Merritt; Shana Goldin-Perschbacher and Merri Cyr; Henry Spiller and Doel Sumbang; and any others behind the scenes. On a personal level, Sophie, Gabriel, and Caspar collectively allowed me space to get the project well off the ground. Ian Biddle was a source of immeasurable support in the last few months of preparing the manuscript. Anahid, Leo, and Maral also provided support at crucial moments and in many ways. The project as a whole owes a great deal to all of these people, and I thank them from the bottom of my heart. Finally, whatever work here is mine to dedicate, I do for my own beautiful boys, Gabriel Jupiter and Caspar Mercury.

Introduction
Oh Boy! Making Masculinity in Popular Music

IAN BIDDLE AND FREYA JARMAN-IVENS

Fill in the gap: "I read the news today . . ."; "When you're with me . . ."; " . . . Only if I had you"; " . . . this must be love." "Oh boy!"—the exclamation that completes each lyric line—sparks off a series of cultural associations, many of which can be productively connected with the project of this collection. On an immediate level, it points to a sense that something is awry, out of place, not where it should be. It also, more specifically, belongs to that stereotyping of (U.S.) popular culture, perhaps slightly outmoded, seen in nostalgic representations such as *American Graffiti* (dir. George Lucas, 1973) and *Grease* (dir. Randall Kleiser, 1978). Although its usage can be traced back at least as far as 1917 (with the premiere of Jerome Kern's successful musical *Oh Boy!*), it has become cemented to the 1950s in the popular imagination. Indeed, it denotes a use of language connected more resolutely today with the conservatism of the 1950s than to the transgressive potential of that historical moment when youth culture first erupted into the mainstream. And yet, despite its resolutely outmoded tone, the expression's history points as much to a transgression—as expletive, exclamation, a kind of verbal spasm—as it does to clean-cut white America. Probably the most famous musical example was the song "Oh Boy!," released by Buddy Holly and the Crickets in 1957. It was also famously

1

used as a refrain throughout the Beatles' "A Day in the Life" ten years later. In these and other examples, "Oh boy!" points to a taxonomy of bodily states (surprise, titillation, enervation, anxiety, disgust) which not only outstrip the expressive potential of language but also exceed the subject's capacity for self-articulation. In relation to the present volume, the effect of this expletive—"Oh boy!"—is to hint not only at an ironic commentary on the gendered ideologies grounded in that historical moment, but also its continued implications within contemporary popular culture.

In Britain, the phrase was adopted—apparently inspired by the Crickets' song[2]—as the title of a prime-time popular music show that ran from 1958 to 1959, *Oh Boy!*, "Britain's first indispensable television pop show"[3] and a kind of precursor to *Top of the Pops*,[4] which debuted in 1964. *Oh Boy!* featured mostly male solo artists, although a group of 16 young women known as the Vernon's Girls were regulars on the show, appearing on every one of the thirty-eight shows. Anonymity framed the Vernon's Girls: that there were so many of them made for an avoidance of intimacy between the audience and the performers; and their name instantly defines them as a collective, as well as having associations of corporate ownership (as they were initially established as a publicity vehicle for Vernon's Pools). And because of this collective identity, it was easy enough to maintain a constant turnover of members: according to the *TV Times* in 1958, "Because girls leave to get married . . . dance director Leslie Cooper and their singing teacher, Peter Knight, often hold auditions at Vernon's."[5] The Vernon's Girls functioned as a collective in contrast to individual regular male stars, such as Cliff Richard, who appeared on twenty-eight of the 38 shows (with and without the Drifters). As a popular cultural forum, *Oh Boy!* allowed for gender codes to be constructed and enforced, where self-sufficient solo masculinity was juxtaposed with anonymous collective femininity. Similarities between Richard and Elvis Presley were noted, and the same kind of disapproval underpinned reviews of them both. The *NME* described Cliff Richard's pelvic gyrations: "His violent hip-swinging during an obvious attempt to copy Elvis Presley was revolting—hardly the kind of performance any parent could wish their children to witness."[6] Meanwhile, the Vernon's Girls' function was a supporting one, providing coordinated dance routines and backing vocals for the (male) stars. *Oh Boy!* regularly featured young upcoming male stars capable of captivating a predominantly female audience, and positioned women in an anonymous, corporately owned, and sexually objectified collective on a weekly basis.

It's a Man's World

This collection of essays sets out to explore the construction and representation of masculinity in popular music and thereby inevitably raises several questions, definitional and ontological, the first and most pressing of which is the question as to what masculinity "is." One aim of this introduction is to sketch out something of a working definition which can underpin the essays presented in the collection, although what emerges in the collection as a whole is more of a "working problematization," in which certain recurring themes related to an idea of masculinity are gradually drawn out alongside a series of problematics that must always be considered concurrently. Thus, we do not wish to start with some bold and distinct definition of "masculinity," but to allow an idea of how it functions culturally to materialize gradually throughout this introduction, and ultimately throughout the essays as a collection.

If we both presume and accept that, in no small degree, the study of masculinity involves the study of men (and some of the conditions of and exceptions to this presumption will be dealt with below), the range of interfaces between men, masculinity and popular music must be dealt with without seeking to avoid the problematic senses in which they operate. The masculine-dominated nature of the music industry is notorious, but this is not to say that male artists outstrip female artists in terms of sheer numbers (although quite possibly that is the case in the management of the industry and the musical production). Rather, it is to say that the dominant ideologies of gender are such that, in popular culture as a whole, that which is perceived and produced as "masculine" enjoys widespread hegemony over that which is described and produced as "feminine." One obvious example is that supposedly "masculine" genres such as rock musics are culturally privileged as "authentic" and "meaningful," in contrast to so-called feminine genres such as "teen-pop," which is widely perceived as being devoid of significant meaning.

This tendency to emphasize the "masculine" to the detriment of the "feminine" is also reflected in academy-mediated discourses on gender, and the impact of the study of men on the already precarious visibility of women needs some mention here. As Bryce Traister has eloquently shown, the interest in men as objects of study has had the effect of "[crowding] out the women and texts responsible for the rise of feminism . . . and [returning] the man to a humanity whose historicized particularity nonetheless shifts . . . cultural criticism, once again, in to the dominant study of malekind."[7] This remarginalization of the feminine, and the tendency in what Traister terms "phallocriticism" to uncritically represent heterosexual masculinity as the ground upon which all masculinities are built, has resulted, it would seem, from an uncritical and essentially narcissistic tendency in masculinity studies (especially, but not exclusively, studies of heterosexual men by heterosexual men) to reproduce the power relations that feminism in its most radical moments sought, and continues to seek, to overturn.

Nonetheless, we would like to suggest that there might be a problem with taking this caution at face value, timely and persuasive though it may be: if we accept the terms of Traister's caution as they stand, we are left marooned in the epistemological impossibility of talking *about* men as objects of scrutiny. Or, to put it another way, in order for men to emerge *as objects of scrutiny*, we must find ways of talking about them that are not prejudicial to feminist work, but which also nonetheless give room to a careful and critical assessment of masculinity *as a problematic*. We might see this, first of all, in terms which stake out an autochthonous set of needs and resources for masculinity studies: what feminist discourse has productively insisted on for women (put very crudely, that women be given access to the symbolic tools to intervene in discourse, and opportunities to form meaningful subject positions that are not thereby beholden to masculinist constructions of gender and that might even in some sense operate from another kind of discursive space) may be that very strategy we should strategically *reverse* for men because the material and political context of the one is radically different to that of the other. It may thus be a strategically sound move to place men under a certain amount of discursive pressure here, to wrest from them the technologies of discourse in an attempt to refigure them not as "subjects," but, in an admittedly vulgar Hegelian fashion, also as objects. We say this not because we want to prolong any "culture of difference," to cite Luce Irigaray's radical articulation,[8] but to find a way of *naming* men, of bringing them into existence as objects of discourse, as productively articulable beings whose claims to any kind of infinitely malleable (universal) subject position are radically contestable. In this sense, it is precisely that problem that feminists have sought to address, the problem of how to locate and operate the position of subject in discourse, which needs to be attenuated for men: the two genders cannot be simply "equalized"—what is good for the goose on this occasion is precisely *that which is not good* for the gander.

A number of texts have been produced that seek to redress the imbalance of at least the male domination—if not necessarily the *masculine* domination—of the perception of popular music, and of popular music historiography. Gillian Gaar's *She's A Rebel*[9] and Lucy O'Brien's *She-Bop*[10] both start from the premise that, like the Western art music canon, an Anglo-American popular music canon exists, and it is a male one. Gaar and O'Brien thus separately seek out histories (or, rather, herstories) of women in popular music with a view to quantifying the very real impact that female popular musicians have had throughout popular music history. What the present collection may *appear* to do, then, is to swing the imbalance back in favor of the implicitly dominant male artist and masculinity, suggesting perhaps that masculinity and maleness are synonymous. What must be made clear at the outset, then, is that this collection is not intended to be a history of men in popular music. Instead, it is founded on an underlying characteristic of masculinity, namely that it has a tendency "to define itself as nonperformative," and is commonly perceived and presented as "natural," "original," and absolute,[11] in contrast to what is called femininity, which has for some time now been understood as performative and constructed. Intellectually, we can easily enough identify the flaws in these male-centered perceptions, because, as Judith Butler has famously identified, "genders can be neither true nor false, but are only produced as the truth effects of a discourse of primary and stable identity."[12] That is to say, all gender formations are results of careful and sustained practice and are thus not simply *formations,* but "*per*-form-ations." Hegemonic gender formations enforce especially effectively the criteria to which the subject must conform if s/he desires the attendant privileges of a hegemonic gender identity. Moreover, stable gender formations (hegemonic or otherwise) require the repetition of a set of acts and the reiteration of signifiers, which point toward the gender formation being constructed. This logically leads the inquisitive reader of popular culture to seek the ways in which masculinity is constructed, just as femininity has long been accepted as performative. Of course, these acts and signifiers appear in musical texts just as they are found in fashion styles, language, physical gestures, and so on, and it is this that has led to the collection of the essays presented here.

You Think You're a Man, You Are Only a Boy

Although *Oh Boy!* the television show emphasizes a cultural division between "boys" and "girls," male and female, and specifically the sexualized consumption of each for the other, another significant division is implied in the single word "boy," between boys and men. The cultural position of the boy is something that contributes to the construction of the cultural position of men and of adult masculinity, and is as defused, pluralized, and subalternized as is "the feminine" in hegemonic constructions of masculinity. In a popular music context, one important connotation of the boy is that of the boy band,[13] which, as a spectacle, enacts and problematizes a number of important facets of not-yet-stabilized masculinity. The typical boy band is made up of four or five young men—boys on the brink of adulthood—each with distinct physical qualities and personalities, brought together into archetypes, which together make up something approximating a whole: the earnest "leader" of the pack (Gary Barlow of Take That; Ronan Keating of Boyzone); the "joker" in the pack (Robbie Williams of Take That; Brian Littrell of the Backstreet Boys); the cute "baby" (Mark Owen of Take That; Stephen Gateley of Boyzone); and maybe the "sexy" one (Keith Duffy of Boyzone; Howard Dwaine of the Backstreet Boys). Each archetype is designed to bring about some kind of desire on the part of the audience, be that a desire for friendship, a desire to "understand," a desire to "mother," a desire to be, a desire to have, and so on. Although individual boy band members are required to be physically attractive—according to convention, and arguably more than in most other musical arenas—as groups they are specifically *not* designed to bring about full sexual desire in the audience member. The majority of boy band members—both past and present—have been "cute," maybe a little "rugged," but their primary cultural function is merely to *awaken* desire in a young audience, not to bring sexual desire fully to the surface.[14]

What the boy band phenomenon illustrates effectively is the extent to which the boy as a cultural icon has to negotiate carefully the potential threat of masculinity.[15] The figure of the boy—specifically the adolescent boy—operates as a site of slippage, as he sits on the border between childhood and adulthood. His juvenility performs an important role in his sexualization, since he is man enough to be desired and desiring, and yet boy enough to be unthreatening. At the same time, the androgyny that underpins the boy's body—the hairlessness, his "pretty" face—also positions him at a point on the borderline between the sexes, and this borderline position is a dangerous one for the culture in which the boy operates. Androgyny disrupts the binarisms of sex and gender and upsets the structures of desire that are based on such binarisms. As such, it is quite often visibly important that the boys of the boy bands have normative masculinities maintained for them by their marketing machines: even as they operate in homosocial spaces, their masculinities are constructed primarily (but not exclusively) through bonds formed by the exchange of women, and their heterosexuality is thus assured.[16] Their heterosexuality is tenuous, of course, and this—combined with the boys' thoroughgoing borderline operations—is why boy bands are embroiled in slippages between discourses of effeminacy and homosexuality.[17]

In what could be described as an act of reclamation, and for the same reasons that "boy" allows for a slippage that operates along a homosocial-homosexual continuum, it has also been adopted as something of a gender identification by certain groups of young homosexual males. In fact, the sound-object *boi*[18] functions as a marker of antinormative gender identities across gay youth cultures. In the context of BDSM (Bondage and Discipline, Domination and Submission, Sadism and Masochism), the word "boi" refers to a sub—a submissive partner in a sexual scenario—and can refer to males or females of any age: in this sense the word is about a power dynamic between two or more people. The spelling "boi" especially is used by lesbians who seek to describe their masculinity without operating within the vocabulary of adult masculinity, of "man." These are women who identify with a sense of masculinity, though not necessarily of maleness, and the word may be placed in semantic alignment with the word "butch."[19] "Boi" can also then be positioned in contrast to "grrrl," in the sense of "riot grrrl," and undertakes a kind of political work for masculine women, especially lesbians. For male homosexuals, the term not only plays with the specific power relations gestured at in the man/boi binarism but also embraces a certain fluidity in gender designation. Verbal play in sexual scenarios often conflates the "boi" position with an overtly (unreconstructed, misogynist) hegemonic construction of "girl" as object par excellence: bo(y/i)/g(i/rr)rl is thus a fluidity that is performatively gestured at throughout the sexual victimization of the sub; the dom's masculinity is assured, natural(ized), and the sub's is always open to radical effacement. *Boi* as a sound-object thus sparks off multiple meanings—boy/girl; boy/man; boi/man; boi/grrl—and works like a point of zero gravity in which multiple gender identifications can be formed, and at which the most radicalized, disruptive, and performative object-positions are taken up.

Especially because of its function as a point of slippage between multiple gender identifications, *boi* invites particular recognition of the potential for female masculinity. As Judith Halberstam has observed, "masculinity does not belong to men [and] has not been produced only by men." Instead, and just as masculinity has been formed in part by juvenile male bodies as well as those of adult men, "what we call 'masculinity' has also been produced by masculine women, gender deviants, and often lesbians."[20] Halberstam also implies that "masculinity" as a notion is most effectively understood as an alteritous formation, understood in terms of what it "is not," or sites of excessive and/or insufficient masculinity: "Masculinity . . . becomes legible as masculinity where and when it leaves the white male middle-class body."[21] This collection seeks to offer musical ways of imagining this maxim. Although it has not been possible to include a chapter in this collection on explicit expressions of non-male masculinity, it is worth noting that—over the course of the collection—those places where masculinity becomes most legible are precisely those places where it leaves normatively "masculine" musical expression, when it ceases to be the music of self-assuredly normative "masculine" bodies. As such, vulnerability, multivocality, and falsetto are seen to be the stuff of "anti-masculine" musics, situated in a dialogic relationship with the traditional "cock-rock" canon, and thereby exposing something of what we perceive to be "masculinity" in musical expression.

Boi/Boy as Site of Contestation

The bo(y/i) matrix might be said to serve as a marker of a broader network of dissident masculinities that bring a certain pressure to bear on hegemonic masculinities by contesting their claims to occupy the exemplary subject position. Bo(y/i) works in particular to problematize any such claim other masculinities might make to occupy *ex officio* the position of wielder of discourse, father, *Herr*. And yet, this disturbance may not offer the kinds of emancipatory outcomes that some of its proponents would like to claim for it: Slavoj Žižek has shown how the contemporary fascination with BDSM, in which the bo(y/i) finds its most frequent articulation, is a marker not of disruption but of the need to put the symbolic order back to rights, to rethrone the absent father. Indeed, the needs of the sub, which are central to the sexual scenario of most BDSM encounters, are structured around this need in particular. The sadist (a particular instance of the mistress or master) "follows the logic of institution, of institutional power"[22] by overtly performing the operation of power in violence, a power the sub finds lacking in the symbolic order. It is this overt playing out of power that acts as a compensation and which puts the symbolic order back in place. As Žižek puts it, "it is the servant therefore who writes the screenplay . . . : he stages his own servitude."[23] As we have already suggested, it is those moments where the performativity of masculinity becomes legible that masculinity "itself" becomes legible: in the scenario where man/boi is played out, masculinity "as such" operates.

The bo(y/i) matrix, then, is undoubtedly a function of masochism which, as Suzanne R. Stewart has shown, does not necessarily mark the ceding of power to another agent but the consolidation of power already in place. Her suggestion that the "rise" of masochism, especially at the *fin de siècle* before this one, represented a strategy for holding on to male power under siege, is particularly useful here.[24] Indeed, the role of the bo(y/i) in articulating her or his own desire is crucial to the way in which masochistic scenarios operate, and the crucial object of desire in such scenarios is not the bo(y/i) of the mistress or master, but the voice as detached from the body giving pain. For Lacan, indeed, masochism is connected to the invocatory drive, that drive whose object of desire is the voice, a partial object, an *objet petit a:* it would seem that the ear as erogenous zone, connected to the voice, and structuring the masochistic dynamic, is what this is all about—for the masochist, it is that which functions as the object of desire par excellence. Pornographies (gay, straight, bi-, and so on) that play with domination scenarios make much of verbal abuse, and invariably insist on concentrating the gaze on the sex object (the "subject" of the mistress's or master's abuse) and on holding the mistress or master to the side of the frame such that her or his *acousmêtre* remains dislocated from the body that brings pain—in the beginning was the word. Indeed, "verbal" (that is verbal abuse from the mistress or master) is one of the most common sites of erotic recall after the event, and it is here that the event takes its place in the symbolic order. In this sense, the bo(y/i) is wielder of desire—she or he searches for the voice of the mistress or master—and the giver of pain fades as little more than a cipher into the background of the scenario, an emptied out acoustic avatar where a body once stood.

To recognize the bo(y/i)-voice relationship here as key is to understand something crucial about some of the ways in which song might come to constitute a site for the articulation of gender: masochism, that state of performative "as if" as Žižek terms it,[25] is resolutely connected to pleasure and the performance of pleasure, to an enacting of being taken up by another's will. One might observe here something of the explicitly masochistic positioning of the listener's relation to the voice in song. The *acousmêtre* of popular song invariably asks the listener to take up a position that is in some senses masochistic: write out, construct the scenario for yourself and then resubmit to it. Indeed, the thematization of that scenario is ubiquitous in popular song: where voice enters, so a series of enactments of the subject in chains ensue—"Rescue Me," "Prisoner of Love," "I'm in Chains," "It Hurts So Good," "Lovin' Chains," "Chained To You," "Chained (To Your Love)."

Masculinity at Large

In popular music, gendered operations occur on the levels of visual and aural signifiers, the latter of which includes verbal and nonverbal signifiers. Crucially, musical genres are gendered spaces and operate according to highly codified conventions. Genres create gender formations by creating *points de capiton* ("quilting points") within their space between signifiers and gendered meaning. To use Franco Fabbri's terminology, the semiotic, social, and ideological rules of musical genres in particular are sites for gendered identities to be (per)formed:[26] semiotic rules include lyric content and "gestural-mimic" codes; social and ideological rules include (crucially) conventions about the participants of a given musical event. Yet so much more than these nonmusical codes is at work in the gendering of musical genres, since most of the "rules" that Fabbri identifies have the capacity to perform gendered work in specifically musical ways.[27] Of technical rules, different technical aspects become coded as performing gender in different ways: in punk, for instance, a lack of technical skill performs a cohering function within a (sub)culture of disenfranchized delinquent male youth, whereas in heavy metal, virtuosic guitar-playing ability contributes to the construction of "genius" and "artist," concepts which already draw on a history of male (and masculine) excellence.[28] In terms of the semiotic rules of genre, instruments can also become gendered operators. Similarly, the production and placement of the voice has densely gendered connotations. The electric guitar, for instance, has significant implications of maleness and masculinity, as Mavis Bayton notes.[29] Vocally, the sense of intimacy generated by a front-mixed, unprocessed, close-mic'd voice—associated in genre terms with crooning or easy-listening—performs a gendered work very different from an imprecisely pitched, half-shouted voice that seems to come from a large space, such as is favored in various rock musics. With regard to social and ideological rules, Fabbri cites the division of labor as one manifestation. The distinction between sexes on the basis of vocal performance in contemporary R&B music, for example, is a useful example of this, as much of this music pits female singing against male rapping, reinscribing a longstanding (and unhelpfully binaristic) stereotyping of music as feminine, concerned with senses, and of language as masculine, a rational structure.[30]

Considering musical genres as gendered spaces illustrates the extent to which the observations made by Susan McClary in *Feminine Endings* were never confined (or indeed intended to be confined) to the Western art music canon.[31] This is not to say that the same semiotic system that McClary explores in that book applies to all musics, or even all Western musics. The value of McClary's book lies instead in the example it offers of ways of unpacking the politics of musical forms and content and in that it paved the way for the kind of work being undertaken in the present volume. Of course, musical codes are not so immutable that they always mean only one thing, even when the codes are contained within one musical space. Indeed, McClary herself notes the limitations of musical coding: countering a traditionalist analysis of a Chopin polonaise, in which the emphasis on the "weak" second beat is blamed for a "limping," antimasculine quality, McClary asserts that it is precisely that emphasis on the "weak" beat that "gives the polonaise its arrogant swagger."[32] It must be made quite clear, then, that no "absolute" gendered-ness can be ascribed to any single musical gesture or moment, be it a form, a melodic gesture, a cadence, the choice of instrument, or any other piece of aural information presented to the listener. Rather, sonic gestures *become* codified, having gendered meanings ascribed to them over a period of time and generated through discursive networks, and those meanings are mutable according to the cultural, historical, and musical context of those gestures, and the subsequent contexts into which they are constantly reinscribed. Clearly, there are multiple ways in which genders are constructed, formed, performed, problematized, and negotiated within and between music genres, taking into consideration visual and aural, verbal and nonverbal coding of genders.

As one example, where elaborate vocal melismas may be used to express Lucia's madness—her excessively "feminine" insanity—in Donizetti's opera, intricate virtuosic performances on the electric guitar are used to validate the myth of masculine genius in heavy metal and hard rock music. Of course, these differences of gendered coding are explicable to a certain extent through a number of discourses underpinning the formation of cultural artefacts. In the first of these two cases, on a very broad level, relevant factors include the nineteenth-century intensification of articulations of "the madwoman" as a cultural figure, and contemporaneous anxieties concerning the unified "modern" subject. Analogously, formations of "mad men" have tended either toward the trope of the "village idiot" or toward that of the genius eccentric, "touched by God."[33] Perhaps it is at this discursive level that the musical connection starts to take clearer shape: a similar set of musical gestures is used as the foundation for two different gendered expressions, both of which have some roots in anxieties concerning sanity and morality.

Despite the potential for similar musical gestures to be afforded radically different gendered meanings—despite the distinct lack, that is, of fixity of gendered-ness in musics, and the way in which "gendered-ness" is always already inscribed onto the text from outside the text (even as those external discourses may be factored into the production of the text)—there is a sense in which the logic governing the gendering of sonic objects exposes the underlying logic of gender formations. That is to say, to trace the reasoning behind ascribing gendered meaning to musical material is simultaneously to reveal something about the perceived qualities of genders. In accordance with what Sherry B. Ortner calls the "universal devaluation of women,"[34] binarisms are mapped onto each other in ways that equate the female and the feminine with the negative. In musical terms, this tends to mean that notions of authenticity, originality, and skill are constructed as masculine musical expressions. An anecdote recounted by Paul Théberge makes a useful starting point for the illustration of this point:

I am reminded . . . of an interview with a noted rock guitarist that I once saw on television: as the conversation turned to issues of synthesizers and sampling in pop music, the guitarist rose from his seat, looked directly into the camera, and, pointing to his guitar, defiantly declared: "This is a *real* instrument." With that single gesture and statement, he seemed to mobilize all the ideological assumptions that have been used to support the notion that rock music is more "authentic," more genuine, than "synthetic" pop.[35]

This statement engages a number of negotiations between technologies: essentially, the guitar is conceived of as less "technological" than the synthesizer, and therefore more "authentic," "real," "masculine," because (as we have noted earlier) femininity has long been understood to be synonymous with "artifice," whereas masculinity constructs itself precisely as "unconstructed" and works hard to naturalize itself. Théberge's point is specifically about the index of technological visibility, but since value judgments are made about both technologies and systems of gender, we can also suggest that such negotiations inform the gendered meaning ascribed to different modes of musical practice. That is to say, whenever guitar-based rock music is figured as normatively "masculine" (and even at the same time as certain social and practical factors may inform the male-dominance of the genre[36]), it is at the same time understood to be implicitly less "technological" than synthesizer-based musics, which are often dance-oriented and figured as less robustly "masculine": "The mind/body-masculine/feminine problem places dance decisively on the side of the 'feminine' body rather than with the objective 'masculine' intellect. It is for this reason that dance music in general usually is dismissed by music critics, even by "serious" rock critics."[37]

It is something of a circular process that is at work in the gendering of music: an instrument (or musical form, or genre . . .) is discursively constructed in gendered terms because the technologies have their own already ascribed gendered meanings; and the gendered-ness of technologies is grounded by the already ascribed gendered-ness of the instrument (or form, or genre . . .). This circularity can be usefully understood in terms of what Pierre Bourdieu calls "somatization,"[38] a process in which we as cultural subjects believe ideals and ideologies to be "natural" and internally generated, whereas they are more accurately described as external processes that impact on the subject. It must be noted that Bourdieu does not intend for this to imply that such a thing as a "presomatized" subject exists: it is not the case that subjects are ever "pure," un-acted-on by cultural forces. Rather, the process of embedding external forces within ourselves as subjects has *always already* occurred: we are *always already* in a state of somatization. This process occurs in a similar way in musical objects and discourses. Even as the gendered meanings ascribed to musical moments and sonic objects may be fluid, shifting and morphing between cultural and historical locations, their ascription—the fact that they are ascribed at all—has always already occurred.

I Need a Hero

If cultural forces work in such a way as to naturalize gender formations, and in ways which exscribe their own work, one must question the extent to which such a thing as "masculinity" can be defined. Thus, we return to the problem with which this introduction started, namely what masculinity "is." In a sense, as we have already suggested, the idea of "masculinity"—particularly normative masculinity—arises primarily as an alteritous formation, in contrast to antinormative masculinities and to ideas of femininity (which, in turn, emerge on the basis of what "femininity" is "not"). Gender formations are thus extremely tenuous, brittle structures always prone to being brought down. And yet normative gender formations somehow manage to sustain themselves in some kind of robust form, naturalizing themselves such that they close themselves off to question.

A notion that may be helpful in unpacking the cultural work performed by masculinity—as well as the cultural work on which "masculinity" is dependent—is that of the hero. There are two senses in which this notion operates with respect to masculinities: first, the most exalted varieties of masculinity are typically "heroic" masculinities (or, often, precisely "antiheroic" masculinities); and second, those exalted brands of masculinity are themselves held up as the heroes of gendered operations. Slavoj Žižek's schematization of four types of ethical agent is particularly helpful in understanding both of these operations (see Figure 0.1).[39]

Žižek describes the positions of the two "vertical" agents thus: "the saint is ethical (he does not compromise his desire) and moral (he considers the Good of others), whereas the scoundrel is immoral (he violates moral norms) and unethical (what he is after is not desire but pleasures and profits, so he lacks any firm principles)."[40] The superego is positioned by Žižek as "the very opposite of the hero, an unethical moral Law, a Law in which an obscene enjoyment sticks to obedience to the moral norms."[41] Thus, the hero is described as "immoral, yet ethical—that is to say, he violates (or rather, suspends the validity of) existing explicit moral norms in the name of a higher ethics of life, historical Necessity, and so on."[42] So, what might this mean for masculinity, as we have started to construct it in this introduction? Žižek's construction of the Hero is, in effect, of an uncompromisingly self-serving figure, one who strives for his own preeminence. And it is indeed this kind of formation of the masculine which is culturally reified: those figures exalted as heroes (certainly by Western cultures) are characterized by their "drive," their "single-mindedness," but not (typically) by their commitment to the "Good of others." Even those figures who may be described as "antiheroes"—Kurt Cobain, for example—are understood to be concerned primarily with their own status (although this

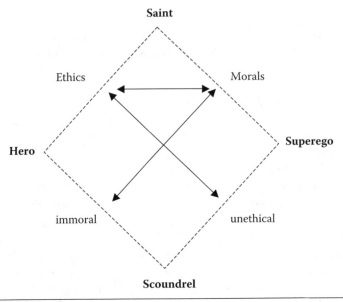

Figure 0.1: Žižek's schematization of the matrix of "ethical attitudes."

is not to suggest that they strive for success in the usual sense), as opposed to their potential benefit to others. And, logically, the "fallen hero" may be the hero who ceases to dedicate himself to one of the causes (morality or ethics). Moreover, masculinity in and of itself operates in the manner of a hero, insofar as "'heroic masculinities' depend absolutely on the subordination of alternative masculinities."[43] That is to say, normative ("heroic") masculinity *per se* is entirely and only committed to the project of sustaining its own normativity and "natural" status as synonymous with the white, middle-class, male body.

If we can say anything about masculinity, it is that, like all gender (per)formations, its ontology is radically malleable. To say such a thing, however, is not to say that its operability is indeterminate or that definitional questions are always already impossible. On the contrary, the radical malleability of masculinity as a "field," "territory," discursive space, cultural effect, identity or ethical frame points to the effectiveness of gender in intervening in cultural practices at all levels and the question as to *what* masculinity might *be* becomes ever more fascinating, ever more urgent: like Freud's partial objects, masculinity's malleability is what motivates the ontological question in the first place.

In this light, it should come as no surprise that masculinity occasions a bewildering array of scholarly approaches, ranging from the most empirical studies to the most hermeneutically inclined readings of cultural forms.

In this sense at least, masculinity might be said to constitute something like what Lacan has termed the *sinthôme,* that core of the subject that is not subjective, an operative field that effaces itself as it operates. Conversely, it may be that masculinity *only* becomes visible precisely because it refuses to map precisely onto the male body, precisely because it draws attention to the tension between culturalist and biologically determinist constructions of the human. It is, we suggest, in this very refusal that the very possibility of naming masculinity is grounded.

Masculinity's relation to popular music in particular is center-stage in this book: that relationship, however contested, however malleable, engages an extraordinary range of cultural materials, operates as one of the dominant sites for the working through of masculine identities and, in particular, might be said to be the primary site at which vernacular masculinities are rhetoricized. Indeed, we might say that this relationship is one of the most intensely operative fields in the contemporary Western imagination of gender and that a book of this nature is quite timely.

Notes

1. Kern's musical was made into a silent film by the same name (dir. Albert Capellani, 1919).
2. David Oswell, "A Question of Belonging: Television, Youth and the Domestic," in *Cool Places: Geographies of Youth Cultures,* ed. Tracey Skelton (London: Routledge, 1998), 35–49 (42).
3. Mark Paytress, *Bolan: The Rise and Fall of a 20th Century Superstar* (London: Omnibus Press, 2002), 15.
4. BBC1, 1964–present.
5. David Griffiths, "Oh Girls! Sigh *Oh Boy!* Fans," *TV Times* (October 12, 1958), http://www.fortunecity.com/greenfield/wolf/31/id33.htm.
6. Author unknown, "*Oh Boy!* Attacked by the Alley Cat," *NME* (December 12, 1958), http://www.fortunecity.com/greenfield/wolf/31/id48.htm.
7. Bryce Traister, "Academic Viagra: The Rise of American Masculinity Studies," *American Quarterly* 52, no. 2 (June 2000): 274–304 (276).
8. Luce Irigaray, *Je, Tu, Nous: Toward a Culture of Difference,* trans. Alison Martin (London and New York: Routledge, 1993).
9. Gillian G. Gaar, *She's a Rebel: The History of Women in Rock & Roll* (London: Blandford, 1993).
10. Lucy O'Brien, *She-Bop: The Definitive History of Women in Rock, Pop and Soul* (London: Penguin, 1995).
11. Judith Halberstam, *Female Masculinity* (London and Durham, NC: Duke University Press, 1998), 236.
12. Judith Butler, *Gender Trouble: Feminism and the Subversion of Identity* (London and New York: Routledge, 1999 [1990]), 174.

13. It is worth recognizing the various ways in which "boy band" is represented in writing: "boy band," "boy-band," and "boyband" are all commonly used. Might this graphic complexity in some way gesture toward the cultural complexities of the phenomenon?

14. What we are talking about here, of course, is the explicitly hegemonic work of many boy bands such as those mentioned. Other groups, which might include East 17, run counter to these propositions, not least because they draw on working-class and/or racially "other" musical and visual subcultural resources. The work of such bands is much more disruptive of masculine hegemony.

15. See Germaine Greer, *The Boy* (London: Thames & Hudson, 2003).

16. This reading is of course indebted to Eve Kosofsky Sedgwick's *Between Men: English Literature and Male Homosocial Desire* (New York: Columbia University Press, 1985).

17. Such slippages are further complicated, or at least brought into the foreground, by boy band members revealing themselves to be gay, such as Stephen Gateley (formerly of Boyzone) or Mark Feehily (of Westlife).

18. This is the phonetic spelling of the sound-object.

19. For some current definitions of the word "boi" see http://www.urbandictionary.com/define.php?term=boi&defid=1201968&page=1.

20. Halberstam, *Female*, 241.

21. Ibid., 2.

22. Slavoj Žižek, *The Metastases of Enjoyment: Six Essays on Woman and Causality* (London and New York: Verso, 1994), 91.

23. Ibid., 92.

24. Suzanne R. Stewart, *Sublime Surrender: Male Masochism at the Fin-de-Siècle* (Ithaca, NY and London: Cornell University Press, 1998).

25. Žižek, *Metastases*, 91.

26. Franco Fabbri, "A Theory of Musical Genres: Two Applications," *Popular Music Perspectives*, ed. David Horn and Philip Tagg (Göteborg and Exeter: International Association for the Study of Popular Music, 1981), 52–81 (56–59).

27. It is interesting to note that the English language is unusual in that it distinguishes between "genre" and "gender": most languages use the same word for each concept.

28. On punk, see Dave Laing, *One Chord Wonders: Power and Meaning in Punk Rock* (Milton Keynes: Open University Press, 1985). On the virtuoso in heavy metal, see Robert Walser, *Running With the Devil: Power, Gender, and Madness in Heavy Metal Music* (Hanover, NH: University Press of New England, 1993).

29. Mavis Bayton, "Women and the Electric Guitar," in *Sexing the Groove: Popular Music and Gender*, ed. Sheila Whiteley (London and New York: Routledge, 1997), 37–49.

30. See, for example, "Favorite Things" (by Big Brovaz, 2003), "Always On Time" (by Ja Rule and Ashanti, 2002), or "I'll Be Missing You" (by Puff Daddy, featuring Faith Evans, 1997). City High's "What Would You Do" (2001) is a particularly interesting example, because the male rapper speaks a chorus previously sung several times by a female vocalist. Thanks are due to Toby Haslam for helping find these examples.

31. Susan McClary, *Feminine Endings: Music, Gender, and Sexuality* (Minneapolis: University of Minnesota Press, 1991).
32. Ibid., 10.
33. Philip Martin, *Mad Women in Romantic Writing* (Brighton: Harvester Press, 1987), 14–15.
34. Sherry B. Ortner, "From 'Is Female to Male as Nature is to Culture?'," in *Gender*, ed. Carol C. Gould (Atlantic Highlands, NJ: Humanities Press, 1997), 16–24 (17).
35. Paul Théberge, "Technologies," in *Key Terms in Popular Music and Culture*, ed. Bruce Horner and Thomas Swiss (Malden, MA and Oxford: Blackwell, 1999), 209–224 (211).
36. See Bayton, "Women."
37. McClary, *Feminine*, 153.
38. Pierre Bourdieu, *Masculine Domination* (Stanford, CA: Stanford University Press, 2001).
39. Further reading of this diagram follows in Chapter 6 of this volume.
40. Žižek, *Metastases*, 67.
41. Ibid., 67.
42. Ibid., 67.
43. Halberstam, *Female*, 1.

Boys, Boys, Boys: Male Bonds, Masculine Connections

1

Which Freddie?

Constructions of Masculinity in Freddie Mercury and Justin Hawkins

SHEILA WHITELEY

As a popular musicologist, I find myself increasingly irritated by tabloid pop journalism, whether on television or in the press. Clearly there are notable exceptions, and I am an avid fan of *The Guardian*'s Michael Bracewell, whose insights into such artists as Patti Smith and Björk have informed my own writing; but all too often there is an emphasis on the three s's of sensationalism, stereotyping, and stitching-up. Generally the spotlight falls on image, but when critiques include new releases, these are tethered by clichéd references to genres or past bands, and are all too often underresearched. As such, listening is tempered by a constricted interpretation.

This is evidenced by reviews of the Darkness ("Retro camp rock . . . comedy panto rock . . . they mimic the clothes and riffs of the ghosts of metal past"), which both situate and confuse (metal, rock). The problem is further compounded by snapshot journalism that situates the band as "hair metal," "mock rock," "glam rock," "vintage ass rock" without analysis of the musical text. Certainly the Darkness invite intertextual comparisons—there are definite nods to past heroes such as AC/DC, early Judas Priest, or Led Zeppelin—and, as such, their music constructs a certain nostalgia. The band has a similar lineup to Led Zeppelin, with the guitars detuned to a drop D, at least one electric guitar, a bass guitar, drums, lead vocals, and backing vocals. Energetic drumming and guitar-based songs focused around a central riff or motif, often doubled by the bass, which is also heard as a grounding pedal or playing a counter-melody, reinforce this impression. It is, however, lead singer Justin Hawkins who attracts the most attention, whose camp posturing and falsetto invite a comparison with Freddie Mercury, not least those evocative hooks. But am I falling into the journalistic trap? Returning to Queen's albums and videos, questions are raised as to "Which Freddie" informs the performative displays of Hawkins: to what extent is Hawkins retro-rock; and is this pastiche or parody?

While it is somewhat of a cliché to observe that listeners identify with performers, finding a sense of their own identity confirmed, modified or constructed in the process, as Richard Middleton points out, "there is nothing simple here,"[1] not least when considerations of sexuality and gender are taken into account. Two questions are raised: *Can* music (pop in particular) express, represent or construct sexual feelings, pleasures, behavior, identities, and, if so, how? If it can, how are these qualities mapped onto gender positions and relationships?

Simon Frith provides one route into these teasing questions by exploring three levels of performance: the persona created in interpreting the particular song; the image of the performer as performer (the star's personality); and the individual physically present (a "site of desire"). As he argues, a performer can move between these, as it were commenting on them. Moreover, they can seem to slide together (or move apart).[2] My exploration of Freddie Mercury and Justin Hawkins draws on this model, raising questions as to whether their performing persona and sexual identities converge; and the extent to which they are constructed and stylized—so confusing the three levels through a sequence of "poses."

Innuendo

I have always been an avid fan of Queen and still cry when I hear "Love of My Life," or listen to their final album, *Made in Heaven*. Freddie Mercury's death overshadows so much of his earlier output that it becomes difficult to listen with the innocent ear that accompanied such releases as "Radio Ga-Ga" or "We Are the Champions." A recent NorthOne production for Channel 5's documentary *Freddie's Lovers* (July 14, 2004) confirmed my feelings. His songs contributed to his self-realization as an individual and relate not only to his numerous lovers but also to his emerging presence as gay. At the time, this was only hinted at, and his fans largely considered his performances theatrical camp.[3]

Early examples of his wit and innuendo can be found in "My Fairy King" and "The Fairy Feller's Masterstroke," in which the titles and use of falsetto implied an underlying sexual ambiguity. Characteristic of many glam rock acts, his androgyneity, which fused with campness, stood in sharp contrast to the vigorous heterosexuality of mainstream rock. The use of Zandra Rhodes silks, nail varnish, and makeup all contributed to a sense of "otherness," but Fleet Street's obsession with sexuality, "Who do you sleep with Freddie?" and his bantering response, "Girls, Boys and Cats,"[4] kept his performances salacious but his private life at arm's length. Although this is, as they say, no big revelation, it is salutary to remember why Janis Joplin kept her bisexuality hidden from the public gaze[5] and why Dusty Springfield fled to Los Angeles to escape the scrutiny of an always zealous press.[6] The Homosexual Reform Act (1967) may have seemed a step in the right direction, but the current climate was unforgiving of outed homosexuals and lesbians alike. The tremors surrounding Jeremy Thorpe, former leader of the Liberal Party, shook the walls of the establishment in 1975. Accused of having a homosexual relationship with Norman Scott, who claimed to have been threatened by Thorpe after the end of their affair, he was subsequently one of four defendants in a court case, but was acquitted of attempted murder. The ensuing scandal ruined his parliamentary career, and the animosity and hysteria directed at him by the media was a timely reminder that it was better to stay in the closet.

The paradox of legality/persecution is reflected in Queen's 1974 album, *Sheer Heart Attack* which contained the single "Killer Queen." Written by Mercury and notable for its studio mix and feel for narrative, it gave Queen its first American Top Twenty hit and became the gay anthem for the winter of 1974, aptly gaining an Ivor Novello award for Mercury. The album cover was particularly striking, with a photograph of the band collapsed in a heap, Mercury's trousers undone, and black nail varnish on his left hand. Framed against a black background with gaudy red lettering, the imagery reinforced the ambiguities already surrounding Mercury's persona, blending showmanship with high camp. This was heightened by his adoption of the Union Jack, which was often emblazoned on his jackets or draped around his shoulders, and his wearing of a crown and ermine-trimmed robes, which led to mass singing of "God Save the Queen" even before the band recorded a version of it in 1975.

"Killer Queen" is set at a deceptively fast tempo (dotted crotchet = 113 bpm), which is propelled by the drums and bass. The song is about a high-class call girl[7] (known as a Killer Queen), but the vocal nuancing and provocative mic gestures in live performances[8] suggest both campness and an affirmation of gay aesthetics. The opening bars (falsetto[9] plus piano) provide autobiographical detail in the references to "Moët & Chandon" and "caviar,"[10] while the "she" ("she's out to get you . . . what a drag") surely needs inverted commas, so providing the ironic connotations, whereby "she," (the "willing" and "playful pussy cat" of the song) are "dragged" into association with Mercury's Queen-like persona. The audacious video heightens the connotations, suggesting an audiovisual love call to the gay community and, as such, the release of "Bohemian Rhapsody," a signature track from Queen's 1975 album, *A Night at the Opera*, provides an intriguing insight into Mercury's private life at the time, the song's three separate acts reflecting three separate turmoils, all, it seems, underpinned by Catholic guilt.

The title draws strongly on contemporary rock ideology, the emphasis on creativity legitimizing the individualism of the *bohemian* artists' world, with *rhapsody* affirming the romantic ideals of art rock,[11] as an epic narrative related to the heroic, with ecstatic or emotional overtones. Like all good stories, the opening starts with a sense of tension and enigma. The multitracked voices are unusually situated at the opening of the piece, the rhythm following the natural inflection of the words, the block chords and lack of foreground melody creating an underlying ambiguity—who is speaking, who is the promised epic hero? This sense of uncertainty is heightened by the harmonic change from B♭6 to C[7] in bars 1 and 2: the boundaries between "the real life" and "fantasy" are marked by instability, and "caught in a landslide," the octave unison at the end of bar 3 propels the listener into the next phrase. Here, "no escape from reality" provides a clue to the underlying turmoil, but the piano arpeggios in bars 5–6 and the stabilizing effect of the harmonic progression, anchored this time by the root of the chords, shift the mode of address: "open your eyes."

The introduction of the central character is marked by a restatement of the rhythmic motif in its realigned position in the lead vocal and piano. Underpinned by the vocal harmonies, there is a sense of pathos that is interrupted by a chromatic movement in the first inversion block chords of the voices and piano (bars 10–11, "Easy come, Easy go") before the confessional of "Mama, just killed a man." Here, the affected warmth of the vocal and the underlying arpeggios on piano suggest an intimate scenario. It is both confessional and affirmative of the nurturant and life-giving force of the feminine and the need for absolution. The emotional quality is given a particular resonance in bars 21–24. Framed by a lingering "Ma-ma," the melody opens out, the vocal rising to a falsetto register only to fall dramatically downward at the end of bar 23. Underpinned by chromatic movement in the bass, there is an underlying mood of desperation ("If I'm not back again this time tomorrow"), which is opened out in bars 25–31, as the melodic phrases fragment, "carry on . . . as if nothing really matters."

1975 was somewhat of a turning point in Freddie Mercury's personal life. He had been living with Mary Austin, manager of the London boutique Biba, for seven years, but had just embarked on his first gay love affair with David Minns. Aware of the constant surveillance by Fleet Street, Mary accompanied him when dining out with his new boyfriend. It was apparently a very romantic affair, one that lasted until 1978, but the tugs between security (Mary), escape (David), and an acknowledgment of his sexuality are there. The confessional of "Bohemian Rhapsody," the intimate address to "Mama" provides an initial insight into Mercury's emotional state at the time: living with Mary ("Mama"), wanting to break away ("Mama mia, let me go," bars 88–89). Bars 80–85, in particular, provide an emotional setting for the dialectic interplay between the masculine and feminine voices. The heavy timbres of the lower voices, underpinned by the phallic backbeat of the drums and tonic pedal, traditionally connote the masculine ("We will not let you go"), while the shrill, higher voices in first inversion chords imply the feminine "Other"[12] ("Let me go"). They signal entrapment and the plea for release.

The heightened sense of urgency seems to resonate with Mercury's inner turmoil, leaving the security of Mary Austin (who, in fact, remained a close friend throughout his life), coming to terms with gay life ("Easy come, easy go"), and living with a man ("So you think you can stone me and spit in my eye"). Mary was, however, more perceptive than the song implies. At the time, Freddie had asked her if she thought he was bisexual. Her reply—"I don't think you're bisexual. I think you're gay"—provides an insight into their relationship and her continuing support. Even so, the "just gotta get out" provides a metaphor for desperation as it moves toward the climax, the guitar supported by an aggressive drum beat, before the emergence of the piano at bar 120. The return to the opening tempo thus suggests a release of tension, the outbursts are over and the final "Nothing really matters to me," where the voice is cradled by light piano arpeggios, suggests both resignation (minor tonalities) and a new sense of freedom in the wide vocal span.[13]

Queen's career, from now on, was marked by expensive and expansive albums, which were drawn from a carefully marketed succession of hit singles and extravagantly produced shows. *A Day at the Races* (1976) provides an insight into the extravaganza of high camp, this time with an increasing commitment to gay culture. "We Are the Champions" became a gay anthem, whereas "Somebody to Love" (both UK No. 2 hit singles) provides an insight into Mercury's continuing search for true love. As *Freddie's Lovers* points out, "He could have anyone he wanted sexually," evidenced, perhaps, by his latest conquest, Joe Liza Fanelli (the affair lasted from 1978–1979), a naive sou-chef who soon found that he couldn't exist in the hedonistic climate of Freddie's world. Extravagantly decadent parties fed the myth of theatricality, high camp and sexual freedom. At one, he paid half the fee for the use of prostitutes specially brought in for his friends.

They shared company with an assembly of high camp antics, including ending up naked in the in-house swimming pool, the mood enhanced by a generous supply of cocaine.

The search for that "Crazy Little Thing Called Love" (*The Game,* 1980) then moved across to the Los Angeles gay biker scene, where his music took on the aura of a macho-rock tribute to Elvis, grease and motorbikes: "It's not rockabilly exactly, but it did have that early Elvis feel."[14] Although the LA scene was one building block in Freddie's more butch appearance, Queen's return to New York, to play at Madison Square Garden, was another. Post Stonewall (1969)—where gays, drag queens, and butch lesbians had engaged in a weekend riot against the NYPD's raid on the Stonewall Inn, Christopher Street—Greenwich Village had acquired the status of a gay Mecca, albeit tempered by the emerging news about AIDS, which hung like a pall over its newly acquired freedoms. As such, the video for "I Want to Break Free" provides a somewhat misjudged excursion into Freddie's sense of personal liberty and outrage. It was the ultimate fantasy video, but the seeming flippancy of including straight members of the band in its cross-dressed scenario almost severed him from the New York scene. It suggested camp posturing rather than a serious engagement with personal freedom.

The successful comeback of the band, resulting from their performance of "Radio Ga-Ga" for Live Aid (1985), "It's a Kind of Magic" (1986, from the soundtrack for the $20 million film, *Highlander*) and a series of massive open-air UK concerts, culminated in the December release of *Live Magic.* The following year, the single, "Barcelona" (1987), with Spanish opera singer, Montserrat Caballé, reached the UK Top Ten. 1985–1987 was reputedly Mercury's happiest period and is given a musical focus in "These Are the Days of Our Lives" (*Innuendo,* 1991). Having moved into Garden Lodge with lover Jim Hutton, he was joined by Mary Austin (controller of the budget), ex-partner Joe (chef), with Freddie as Queen Mother. It was his functioning Royal Residence, and coincided with the release of "The Great Pretender"/ "Exercises in Free Love," but by 1987 Mercury was concealing the fact that he had contracted AIDS.[15] *Innuendo* was released on February 4, 1991 and once completed, Mercury was insistent that the band commence recording as much new material as possible. Previous albums had often taken more than a year to record and *Made in Heaven* was not released until four years after his death. "It's a Beautiful Day" (intro and outro) was not completed; "My Life Has Been Saved" is a reworked version of a Queen B-side single ("Scandal," 1986). "I Was Born to Love You" and "Made in Heaven" featured on previous releases, the former on *Mr. Bad Guy,* the second on Roger Taylor's solo project with his band The Cross, entitled "Shove It." Although there have been other posthumous album releases, this was the first instance in which the artist was fully aware of the project and its looming sense of finality. *Made in Heaven* "was not a case of an artist simply working right up to his death, but a unique example of an acceptance of fate and determination to see a project through to completion—rare enough in ordinary life but here captured on vinyl and CD."[16]

Dedicated to "the immortal spirit of Freddie Mercury," the opening track "It's a Beautiful Day" is touchingly optimistic. The string pad, which fades in gradually over 36 seconds, evokes memories of "Who Wants to Live Forever?" from Queen's 1985 album, *A Kind of Magic*.[17] Moving slowly into D major arpeggios on piano and bass guitar, combined with samples of bird song, the rising line creates a moment of optimism, which is given additional weight by the opening lyrics, "It's a beautiful day, the sun is shining, I feel good and no-one's gonna stop me now," the last phrase providing a momentary reference to the 1979 song, "Don't Stop Me Now." It is, however, the introduction of "Mama" that provides a knowing nod to Mercury's audience. Evoking memories of "Bohemian Rhapsody" it seems also a reference to his lifelong friend, Mary Austin. This time, however, the escape to pastures new is overcast by a falling phrase. "No-one's gonna stop me now" implies resignation. The mood is maintained in the vocal line "Sometimes I feel so sad, so sad, so bad" and the change from full voice to falsetto on the word "hopeless" ("It's hopeless, so hopeless, to even try"), over the Gm and Cm chords (vi and ii of B♭). The aural effect is an imperfect cadence (inferring a modulation to Gm via chords I, iv, and Vadd9), so providing a feeling of incompletion. This comes with the next song, which begins in Gm "I'm taking my ride with destiny" ("Made in Heaven"). Freddie died in Joe's arms on November 24, 1991, and it is not too improbable that the sixth track on the album, "I Was Born to Love You" is a tribute to his steadfastness and love. Mercury had been in show business for 23 years and, as his funeral demonstrated, his lovers were with him to the end.

It is apparent, I hope, from my brief analysis of his very extensive repertoire, that Mercury was a complex person, tough on the outside, soft inside, with a touching love for his friends and a resilience that allowed him to come to terms with AIDS and his death. As such, it is suggested that his songs and his personal life—including his sexuality—have an implicit resonance. They are not simply an over-the-top camp offering to his fans; rather, they relate to his persona and provide a particular insight into the way in which his performances (both live and "on record") express, represent, and construct sexual feelings and how these are mapped onto sexuality.

A Thing Called Love

So where does this leave Justin Hawkins? It is, perhaps, no coincidence that he performed "Bohemian Rhapsody" at a karaoke competition on Millennium eve, acting out every line and doing spectacular star jumps[18] before joining brother Dan (guitarist), Ed Graham (drummer), and Frankie Poullain (bass)[19] as vocalist, guitarist, and synth player for the Darkness. As frontman, his flamboyant vocals (characterized by an agile falsetto), leaps, and splits (borrowed, it seems, from David Lee Roth), and a rock style strongly influenced by the now defunct heavy metal band The Commander,[20] it is apparent that his performing style is highly eclectic. There are echoes of Mercury and Sparks and his decidedly retro-glam style is heightened by swishy hair and glitzy cat suits. The Darkness have also been compared with AC/DC, Aerosmith, Kiss, early Van Halen, and Thin Lizzy—again a postmodern eclectic mix—and spent two years on the London pub circuit before releasing their debut EP, *I Believe in a Thing Called Love* through independent Must Destroy Music. Their credibility as a performing band was underpinned by securing opening slots with Deep Purple and Def Leppard, and the release of their "Keep Your Hands Off My Woman" single (February 2002) and subsequent signing of a major-label contract with Atlantic Records in March drew increasing attention from the press. Presaged by a series of festival appearances, *Permission to Land* debuted at the top of the British charts in 2003.[21] Reputedly, Sir Brian May (Queen) claimed he would buy every copy of the Darkness's album in order to "propel it to the number one position on the charts, proving once and for all that the public will no longer stand for the TV manipulation of those purveyors of pre-wrapped garbage of the *Pop Idol* variety."[22] His feelings were apparently shared by UK Prime Minister Tony Blair, who told a group of schoolchildren he loved listening to the band,[23] possibly not an enthusiasm to share when the CD has a parental guidance sticker. They are certainly entertaining, but the lyrics are extreme cock rock: hard, heavy, and dirty, albeit tempered by an ironic humor.

Opening with "Black Shuck," the listener is propelled into a hard-rock AC/DC feel, not least when the band moves into a whirling frenzy of guitar lead pyrotechnics (which owe more than a little to Angus Young). It is, however, the agility of Hawkins's vocal delivery that impels the song's corporeal drive. The lyrics are colored by stabs of falsetto ("the parishioners were *visited upon* by a curious beast") and an Ozzy Osbourne growl that inflects the narrative of the predatory one-eyed dog with an appropriate Sabbath feel, before climaxing in a falsetto octave jump *down* into the chorus. Here, the vocal gymnastics, the octave plus fifth leaps, create an aural analogy with his high scissor jump, challenging and often outstripping brother Dan's bravura rock guitar. This is given dramatic focus in the final chorus, where the guitar rises in formulaic rock style, heightening the sense of climax, only to retreat downwards as Hawkins takes on the call and response "(Black Dog) that dog don't give a fuck, Black Shuck" with an acrobatic agility and power that compels audience participation. It's a crowd sing along and in live performance provides an immediate connection between band and audience that is heightened by Hawkins's powerful falsetto and tempered by the final "woof," which provides the first indication of his ironic humor.

The AC/DC inflections are also there in "Get Your Hands Off My Woman" where "mother-fucker" invites a raucous call and response in live performances. This is macho rock, with hard driving rhythms, soaring guitars, colorful language and audience interaction. It is apparent, however, that Hawkins's seeming spontaneity is underpinned by a quite remarkable feel for pitch, dramatic range, and precision. The 16-bar introduction (which has more than a passing nod to Billy Idol's "White Wedding") is interrupted at bar 8 with a swooping vocal glissando that drives the hard rock feel into the opening verse. The angularity and searing falsetto of the opening phrase, "You are drunk and you are surly," is, dare I say, remarkably like Kate Bush. There is a comparable sinuous and dramatic quality in the vocal range and a precision in pitch that underpins the emotion of the lyrics, coupled with a theatrical agility which is at its most dramatic in the final chorus. Here, the "off" ("Keep your hands off . . .") glissandos upwards,[24] the heavily punctuated "my woman" given added weight when the band drops out, creating a delayed sense of gratification before the final gliss—"Fuck-er"—where Hawkins's remarkable two-octave falsetto swoop is exposed to full dramatic effect.

It is, however, the hit single "I Believe in a Thing Called Love" that exemplifies most clearly the band's success formula. The heavily compressed guitars of the four-bar opening riff beg for volume and come into full blast for the answering phrase which lifts into the opening verse in characteristic rock style. The verse itself is pitched low, suggesting a light rock feel, reinforced by the omnipresent riff in the bass and lead guitar. It is, however, the theatricality of Hawkins's vocal delivery that dominates, opening out the narrative uncertainty of the lyrics ("Can't explain all the feelings . . . my heart's in overdrive") with deft syllabic punctuation, cutting through the thick, guitar driven melody before the evocative "Touching yoo-oo-oo" of the chorus, which again recalls Kate Bush in its angular intervals and high tessitura. This, however, is only the launching pad, and the song builds in excitement with the guitar playing a call and response riff in conjunction with the vocal line. By the final chorus, the drums are playing the classic rock back-beat and Hawkins takes on call ("Touching you") and response ("Touching me") through a skilful manipulation of his falsetto that assumes the role of both lead and backing vocals in what is nothing less than a bravura performance. Meanwhile, the guitars play the chords with a repeated quaver pattern, the bass doubling the root notes or adding passing notes before the final falsetto lift off, "I believe in a thing called love / Ooooooh," which climaxes into a final guitar solo underpinned, once again by the bass riff, before the archetypal arena rock ending.

The song is quintessential rock: hard, heavy, and fun. Its catchy riff is infectious, the lyrics lighthearted, and Hawkins's vocals are firmly tongue-in-cheek with more than a passing nod to his rock predecessors. Above all, there is a sense of interaction which is clearly enhanced by live performances. The well-honed choruses provide an opportunity for sing alongs and Hawkins's showmanship comes to the fore. As bass player, Frankie Poullain told the BBC, "Rock 'n' roll isn't about being cool—it's about breaking rules. And the biggest rule at the moment is that you have to be cool."[25] *Think:* Radiohead, Coldplay, Travis. *Contrast:* scissor kicks, spandex cat suits, long permed hair, and the flame tattoo that adorns his crotch, allied to an overarching campness, which, like Hawkins's falsetto, has provoked comparison with Freddie Mercury. Small wonder, then, that the band has been likened to Spinal Tap. Yet for its thousands of fans, the Darkness *is* cool in its evocation of the past. It is not so much the band's specific music that elicits praise; rather it is the kind of songs that clearly inspired them and the fact that they are undoubtedly musically aware.

It is apparent, too, that although the band pays unapologetic homage to past heroes, its nostalgic mood is "of the moment." Like the Scissor Sisters, "[They] . . . have tapped into a previously unhip genre and cherry picked the finest moments to crystalize them into something fresh and new without resorting to the cheap tricks and gimmicks of parody and caricature."[26] Both bands are also high camp, but whereas "the Scissor Sisters are filthy and gorgeous, bathed in nostalgia for a sexual nirvana where identity is in flux and sex is dangerous,"[27] there is no such sexual fluidity in Justin Hawkins. True, comparisons might be made on the shared campness, excess, and humor but the persona created by Hawkins in his flamboyant theatrics and vocal style carries no hint of gay sexuality. Rather, he embodies rock excess—the tongue-in-cheek swagger, charm, and dirty lyrics—and although his camp gestures and falsetto evoke memories of Mercury, there are also hints of other past heroes, Ian Gillan (Deep Purple), Jon Anderson (Yes), Thijs van Leer (Focus, not least in the hit single, "Hocus Pocus": compare the original with the Darkness's cover version), and Russell Maël (Sparks).[28]

Is it a case, then, of seeing "who we know" when confronted with Hawkins's larger-than-life stage presence? Is it because the ghosts of glam

rock, stadium rock, hair metal were suddenly resurrected to taunt the introspective cool of Coldplay that the Darkness became sufficiently significant
to attract the attention of Melvyn Bragg, who featured Justin Hawkins on
his prestigious TV series, *The South Bank Show*? Why is the media so fascinated by his private life and off-stage personality? (He is reputed to have
a body-piercing whenever he's miserable, including having his "manhood"
pierced as a punishment for cheating on girlfriend and band producer, Sue
Whitehouse; he is equally flamboyant on and off stage, wearing cat suits
for interviews, and courts press attention in his often vitriolic outbursts.)
The answer surely lies in Hawkins's exuberant personality and incredible
vocal agility. Together they provide the necessary sense of showmanship
characteristic of both stadium rock and hair metal. They make you want to
join in, jump around and take life a little less seriously.

Returning to Frith's performance model, it would thus appear that the
persona created by Hawkins in interpreting the songs (the camp gestures,
permed hair, spandex cat suits, body piercing, tattoos, scissor jumps, and
evocative falsetto), his image (as mediated by the press, TV, and the Internet in their constant comparisons with Mercury), and the individual physically present relate to the codes of camp performativity, "a way of seeing
the world as an aesthetic phenomenon, not in terms of beauty but in terms
of a degree of artifice, of stylization."[29] There is, however, a distinction
between being consciously camp (Hawkins) and being a Queen (Mercury)
and to explore this issue further I want finally to explore in more detail the
nature of their falsetto and how this relates to codes of masculinity.

Flying High: The Grain of the Voice

Although signification covers all the processes related to communication (meaning, expression, subjectivity), *signifiance* in song concerns the
"grain" of the voice, "where the melody really works at the language—not
at what it says, but the voluptuousness of its sound-signifiers . . . it is the
body in the voice as it sings."[30] It is an erotic process, in which the subject
is overwhelmed by *jouissance*.

The voice, the mark of character, of persona and of an individual body,
is inevitably heard as gendered. The falsetto, in particular, has a "feminine" quality; it entails a special method of voice production that extends
the upper limits of the male vocal range. In effect, it confuses gender distinctions. "It is a form of drag: a vocal masquerade. In this way, the falsetto voice challenges the authenticity of gender-assigned voices. When
voices are so strictly assigned to particular bodies, the falsetto becomes
transgendered—it moves between binaries of male and female."[31] Produced by relaxing the throat and using the diaphragm, "the suppression of

head and chest resonance creates a *sotto voce* (literally 'under the voice'), suggest(ing) a 'fourth voice,' a fourth sex, not properly housed in the body."[32] It is "unnatural," a sonic merge of male authority and feminine ambiguity, an acceptance and integration of male and female, suggesting that both gender and sexuality are transferable. By going beyond the so-called limits of the natural voice, it traverses sonic possibilities, vocalizing inadmissible sexualities and engaging with the erotics of risk and defiance, a desire for desire itself.[33] The falsetto thus creates a sense of trinity: he is she is he. As such, it could be argued that the falsetto voice invokes a queer sensibility, a fluidity that refuses gender-based constructions. However, although the vocal mannerisms connote a feminization of expression, it is arguably the case that the content of the song and its relationship to genre impact on its reception.[34] It can, in effect, shift the emphasis from straight to gay or, conversely, connote a campness that is parodic, aligned to the sense of burlesque inherent in, for example, music hall and pantomime. It is this distinction that, for me, underpins the difference between the Killer Queen anima of Mercury and the Black Dog antics of Hawkins.

Mercury's falsetto was colored by a theatricality that ranged from the English burlesque of "Good Company" (*A Night at the Opera*), stadium rock bravura ("We Are the Champions," "Radio Ga-Ga," "We Will Rock You"), Broadway end-of-show Big Number ("Let's Turn it On," *Mr. Bad Guy*), opera (*Barcelona*) and intimacy ("Love of My Life," *A Night at the Opera,* "It's a Beautiful Day," *A Kind of Magic*). His use of falsetto, albeit identifiably "Freddie," thus related to the distinctive mood of the song—enhancing the emotional content, suggesting pathos, anguish or an ecstatic high. There is also, as my discussion shows, a clear sense of personal narrative that moves the vocal gestures into often paradoxical realms, traversing campness, as a form of drag, to draw on his sensual feminine anima.

Clearly, this is not the key to analysis when it comes to the Darkness. Rather, it is the parodying of rock excess. Hawkins's camp gestures and acrobatic falsetto exaggerate the performative codes of rock within a heterosexual frame of reference—the dirty and often misogynistic lyrics, flaunting the earlier excesses of glam rock and hair metal in his tighter-than-tight cat suits and swishy hair—rather than resonating with a gay sexuality. Think, for example, of Freddie Mercury singing "Get Your Hands Off My Woman" and the distinction is, I believe, apparent. In effect, Hawkins both treads and parodies the well-worn paths of the cock-rock hero—raunchy, explicit, and often crude, in which the singer is both potent and attractive[35]—through an overtly camp delivery that draws heavily on the codes of glam rock (an emphasis on visual presentation, outrageous costumes, swishy hair). As one reviewer tellingly observed, it is "fist-pumping, groin bulging" rock,[36] albeit dressed in feather boas and spandex. As such, the sense of a fourth sex, as implied by Mercury's nuanced falsetto, his sexuality, and the plurality of subject positions (within the varied generic of his repertoire) are missing. Rather, Hawkins's masculinity merges with his falsetto and is defined by agility and power. It is the voice used to cut through the often dense rock textures, and has a distinctive "personality," which is evidenced in both its dramatic range (the characteristic octave plus swooping glissandos; the angularity of the high tessitura vocal lines; the tongue-in-cheek quality of his more "chirruping" hooks) and inflection (the sudden falsetto coloring that lifts the lyric line). Thus, it is only when his falsetto is allied to his over-the-top camp gestures that the doppelgänger of Mercury really comes to the fore.

Constructions of masculinity are, we know, socially and historically informed, and within popular music they provide a particular route into understanding and relating to different genres. This is not to impose a static frame of reference but, rather, to demonstrate pedigree and provide insights into where a band's coming from. Given the prestigious position of Queen as the Number One Stadium Rock band and the attraction of Freddie Mercury for anyone with a love of theatricality, it is not surprising that he is a strong influence on Hawkins. It is also evident that Hawkins wants the band's new album, *One Way Ticket to Hell . . . And Back* to have a similar emphasis on production values (its producer Roy Thomas Baker is also famous for bringing out the awesome vocals and guitar on Queen's first four albums). Reviews again draw parallels—most specifically to the humorous innuendos in "English Country Garden"—but essentially the album focuses attention on nostalgia and posturing. As my analysis of Hawkins has shown, he has a distinctive vocal style which is characterized by the precision of his falsetto and surely this is what takes him beyond the evocation of Mercury into what should be his own scenario.

Even so, the fact that the Darkness have made me relisten to bands that I have taken for granted for far too long, is no bad thing. The band may have their weaknesses—and current reviews of *One Way Ticket* situate it as a one way ticket to mediocrity—but there is little doubt that they have reignited the partylike atmosphere that has, for too long, been missing from rock. Whether they will go down as simply a short-lived novelty band is too early to assess. As such, it is salutary to end with a review of Queen who, by the late 1970s attracted this somewhat caustic comment:

> Queen are as good an example as any with which to approach the theory of the vacuum effect in rock: this states that when a top-flight, proven rock attraction withdraws into a period of inactivity, this void will be filled by substitute, usually lesser-talented acts. In 1973–74 Led Zeppelin and David Bowie were largely unavailable to British

audiences and along came . . . Queen [who] hedged their bets by sounding like an *ersatz* Zeppelin but kept one foot in the glam rock arena via the androgynous posturings of singer Freddie Mercury.[37]

Maybe, then, it takes time and determination to convert the past into a self-identified future.

Notes

1. Richard Middleton, *Popular Culture: Understanding Pop Music* (Milton Keynes: Open University Press, 1997), 62.
2. Simon Frith, *Performing Rites: On the Value of Popular Music* (Oxford: Oxford University Press, 1996), chapter 10.
3. Britain has a long heritage of camp performers, including pantomime dames, and contemporary audiences would have been used to television programs and films such as *Some Like It Hot* and *Are You Being Served?*, in which being camp is not necessarily the same as being gay. Even so, John Inman's famous catch phrase "I'm free" does suggest a certain camp cottaging.
4. NorthOne production for Channel 5's documentary *Freddie's Lovers* (July 14, 2004).
5. See Sheila Whiteley, *Women and Popular Music: Sexuality, Identity and Subjectivity* (London and New York: Routledge, 2000), 51–61.
6. Springfield created a decidedly queer persona while achieving popular success in a trendy milieu in which lesbianism, lacking the criminal status and thus the glamor of male homosexuality, remained invisible and unfashionable. She finally admitted to her lesbian sexuality in London's *Evening Standard* and relocated to Los Angles in 1972 to avoid the storm of controversy over her sexual revelation. Patricia Juliana Smith, "'You Don't Have to Say You Love Me': The Camp Masquerades of Dusty Springfield," in *The Queer Sixties*, ed. Patricia Juliana Smith (London and New York: Routledge, 1999), 105–126.
7. The 1963 Profumo affair, in which call girls Christine Keeler and Mandy Rice Davies had become somewhat of a notoriety, provided a telling insight into prostitution. These were women who enjoyed many of the privileges associated with the so-called high society, including ministers from the Conservative government of the time. Prostitution was shown to have its more glamorous associations, so removing it from the street corner, and the tabloid press floated between a love affair with the glamorous Christine and Mandy and a joyful outing of the hypocrisy of government ministers. The ruling Conservative Party was brought down and Harold Wilson's Labour government soon enacted sweeping legislative and social reforms, based on the premise that the most civilized and enlightened society is a permissive one. Film and stage censorship was diluted and the 1967 Sexual Offences Act decriminalized acts between consenting adult men. Meanwhile, "the *enfant terrible* of 1960s British drama, Joe Orton, became the embodiment of youthful, 'masculine' queer sensibility, an image that was to subsequently inform the gay culture of the 1970s. He was murdered by his lover, Kenneth Halliwell, a personification of the older 'homo' stereotype." Patricia

Juliana Smith, "Introduction," in *The Queer Sixties,* ed. Patricia Juliana Smith (London and New York: Routledge, 1999), xviii. Although it is speculative to draw on the Profumo affair as relating to the high society "killer queen," it is nevertheless suggested that the associated glamor relates to the "built in remedy for Kruschev and Kennedy" and the "well-versed in etiquette" of the song. The "lending" of Keeler to a Russian diplomat was a timely reminder of the fragility of relationships with Soviet Russia. Mercury's performance, while drawing on the topicality of the Profumo affair suggests, far more, the "youthful, masculine" of the Orton-inspired gay community, a reminder that they, too, enjoyed high-class rent boys "guaranteed to blow your mind, insatiable in appetite. Wanna try?"

8. The microphone has well-versed phallic connotations. Its shape and use by stars such as Mick Jagger invite associations with fellatio, or with exposure, as in the well-publicized shot of the black mic protruding from his partly unbuttoned trousers.

9. The sound of a single voice overdubbed is markedly different from separate voices singing the various parts of a given harmony. The distinctiveness of Freddie's impeccable intonation, not least in his falsetto range, was to become a fundamental part of the Queen sound.

10. Mercury was known for his love of the Ritz and a high life style. In turn, this contrasted with the more down-to-earth connotations of his seaside numbers, and the gay biker aesthetic of his time in New York.

11. The rhapsody was first introduced by the Bohemian composer, Jan Václav Tomášek in 1803.

12. "Bismallah!" ("In the name of Allah") was more widely "heard" by his fans as "Miss Miller."

13. I am indebted to Holly Marland, a former student on the BA (Hons) Popular Music and Recording, University of Salford, whose musical analysis of "Bohemian Rhapsody" both informed and supported my discussion. "The Five Codes and the Philosophy of S/Z," BA diss., University of Salford, 1997.

14. Roger Taylor, quoted in Ken Dean, *Queen: The New Visual Documentary* (London: Omnibus Press, 1991), 44. Elvis also exhibited an often camp sensibility as in, for example, the video for "Jailhouse Rock." An example of how Elvis might have sounded singing "Crazy Little Thing" can be found on *Return to Splendor* (2000), on which the song is sung by Elvis impersonator Jim "The King" Brown.

15. The day before his death, Freddie Mercury had issued a statement "for my friends and fans around the world," confirming he had AIDS and that he had "felt it correct to keep this information private to date in order to protect the privacy of those around me" (*The Independent*, November 26, 1991). Hundreds queued up at Garden Lodge to pay their respects. His funeral took place three days later at the Kensal Green Crematorium, attended only by close friends and family, and was conducted according to the Zoroastrian faith of his family. "Bohemian Rhapsody" was rereleased as a double A-side with "These Are the Days of Our Lives" on December 9, and returned to the top of the charts; the royalties were donated to the HIV and AIDS charity the Terrence Higgins Trust. Other tributes followed, including a concert at Wembley stadium on April 20, 1992, at which many major stars, including David Bowie, Elton John, and Liza Minnelli, performed.

16. John B. Smith, "Meaning in Music—An Analysis of *Made in Heaven,* the Final Album by Queen," MA diss., University of Salford, 1998. As Smith points out, many album reviewers have not realized that "the arrangements/ instrumentation of these tracks has been extensively reworked and even the lead vocals have been pitch-shifted/sampled in places in order to fit in with the new arrangements." This was to compensate for Mercury's voice at the time and is particularly evident in "Made in Heaven." Thank you John and for other insights gained from your work.

17. As John Smith notes, "The string pad is simply made up of one note, D, in unisons and octaves between the differing string timbres employed. A wide stereo separation, with slight chorus/delay effects maintain a level of interest, but it is the lack of any 3rd in this 'chord' which lends it the air of mystery." Smith, "Meaning."

18. http://www.thedarknessrock.com/biography/ (accessed April 30, 2006).

19. Replaced by Richie Edwards in 2005.

20. Credited on the Darkness's debut album *Permission to Land:* "your wish is my commander."

21. *Permission to Land* was shortlisted for the 2003 Mercury Music Prize. The band won three Brit Awards in 2004, including Best Group, Best Rock Group and Best Album and two *Kerrang!* awards for best live act and Best British Band. They opened Glastonbury (2003) and headlined the Carling Festival in Reading.

22. David Missio, "Bringing Rock Out of The Darkness: Review—The Darkness @ The Phoenix," *A&E* 131, no. 26 (January 16, 2004), http://www.queensjournal.ca/article.php?point=vol131/issue26/arts/lead1.

23. This seems another instance of Blair's attempt to woo young people, comparable to his earlier stated love of the rock band Oasis.

24. There is a guitarlike quality in Hawkins's glissando swoops. The top note is as difficult to pin down as the harmonics in Hendrix's improvisations and implies that Hawkins often uses his vocal agility to take on the guitar line. This is most evident when he plays and sings at the same time.

25. Christine Sams, "Breaking the Cool Rules," *The Sun Herald,* January 12, 2004, http://www.smh.com.au/articles/2004/01/11/1073769447200.html?from=storyrhs.

26. XFM Online, "Scissor Sisters—the Astoria, April 3, 2004," http://ixfm.fimc.net/Article.asp?id=22496.

27. Tara Brabazon, "Giving Scissors to the Sisters: Ana Matronic and Cutting up the Popular Cultural Landscape," *Meowpower Feminist Journal Online* 1, no. 4 (May 20, 2006), http://www.academinist.org/mp/current/a10mpm06.html.

28. In 2005, Justin Hawkins set up a solo project called British Whale. His debut single, "This Town Ain't Big Enough for Both of Us," a cover of the 1974 hit by Sparks, was released on August 15, 2005, and reached number six on the UK singles charts.

29. Susan Sontag quoted in Jon Savage, "The Enemy Within: Sex, Rock, and Identity," in *Facing the Music,* ed. Simon Frith (London: Mandarin, 1990), 131–172 (167).

30. Roland Barthes, "The Grain of the Voice," in *On Record: Rock, Pop, and the Written Word,* ed. Simon Frith and Andrew Goodwin (London and New York: Routledge, 1990 [1977]), 293–300 (295).

31. Edward D. Miller, "The Nonsensical Truth of the Falsetto Voice: Listening to Sigur Rós," *Popular Musicology Online* 2, http://www.popular-musicology-online.com/issues/02/miller.html.
32. Elizabeth Wood, "Sapphonics," in *Queering the Pitch: The New Gay and Lesbian Musicology,* ed. Phillip Brett, Elizabeth Wood, and Gary C. Thomas (London and New York: Routledge, 1994), 27–66 (31).
33. Wood, "Sapphonics," 33.
34. There is, for example, a distinction between the gospel-influenced traditions of soul/funk singers such as Marvin Gaye, Al Green, and Curtis Mayfield, in which the falsetto expresses emotions of love, longing, sexual desire, and political discontent and the falsetto of, for example, Robert Plant (Led Zeppelin), who forces his voice into a falsetto range at moments of great passion. Miller, "Nonsensical."
35. Simon Frith and Angela McRobbie, "Rock and Sexuality," in *On Record: Rock, Pop and the Written Word,* ed. Simon Frith and Andrew Goodwin (London and New York: Routledge, 1990 [1978]), 371–89 (374).
36. www.epinions.com, "The Darkness: A Modern Rehashing of Hair Metal," review of *Permission to Land,* September 18, 2003, http://www.epinions.com/content_113079586436.
37. Jim Miller, *The Rolling Stone Illustrated History of Rock and Roll* (New York: Random House, 1976), 189.

2

Negotiating Masculinity in an Indonesian Pop Song
Doel Sumbang's "Ronggeng"

HENRY SPILLER

Although its reggae rhythm, diatonic melody, and functional harmonic vocabulary give it an unabashedly global sound, Indonesian singer-songwriter Doel Sumbang's song "Ronggeng"[1] nevertheless relies on a local Sundanese[2] image of a *ronggeng* (professional female entertainer) for its impact. In this essay, I place Doel Sumbang's "Ronggeng" into its local cultural context by discussing how the *ronggeng* image in West Java provides a framework in which men can negotiate Sundanese masculinity; I then demonstrate how Doel Sumbang deploys the musical gestures of modern global pop to recreate the sensations that an encounter with a *ronggeng* is understood to initiate in a typical Sundanese man to create a song that addresses West Java's Sundanese past as well as its modern present in the ongoing negotiation of masculine identities.

Ronggeng

Professional female performers who sing and dance with men have long played a vital role in Sundanese performing arts. Such women have been called various names in different times and places; the term *ronggeng* is a typical designation in many parts of West Java. Whatever the name, these female performers are key players in a variety of performance genres in which they interact with male audience members; all participants dance to the accompaniment of music that features prominent drumming, accenting and supporting the dance movements. By most accounts, a *ronggeng*'s interaction with her male clients may extend to engaging in sexual acts with them; her status as a sex worker is an important part of her image. These "dance events" are more than entertainment; they provide an opportunity for the ongoing iteration of Sundanese gender ideology. I use the term "gender ideology" here to refer to a complex system of conventions, notions, and ideas that serve to differentiate gender identities based loosely on biological sex differences but which go far beyond biological dictates; the term refers as well to conventions that assign one gender primacy over the other(s) to produce gender asymmetry. Like all ideologies, gender ideology is most effective when it appears to be immutable and unchangeable—as the "natural" order of things.[3]

In my analysis, dance events serve a vital function in the construction of Sundanese gender ideology and provide an excellent window into Sundanese notions of gender. *Ronggeng* are a focus for male desire in such events and play a central role in the performance of Sundanese gender ideology. In recent years, however, the negative connotations of this role have become more prominent; as a result, there is presently a dearth of performers who call themselves *ronggeng*. In the popular Sundanese imagination, however, *any* female singer or dancer reminds the viewer of dance events and evokes what I call the "*ronggeng* image." This *ronggeng* image, in turn, succinctly evokes the associations, protocols, and meanings that surround dance events.

Aesthetics and Gender Ideology

Aesthetic judgments contribute to gender ideology by investing arbitrary artistic practices with the quality of "natural" beauty, enabling consumers to regard the power and status relationships these artistic conventions index as "natural" as well. Susan McClary has exemplified this process with what she calls the "climax-principle" of seventeenth-century European tonality; she equates the climax-principle with a form of violent eroticism connected to male domination, which, she writes, "has been transcendentalized to the status of a value-free universal of form."[4]

Gender differences and gender asymmetry are reproduced by assigning different qualities, attributes, and social roles to individuals based on their sex. Michael G. Peletz frames his study of gender identities and masculinity in Negeri Sembilan, Malaysia, with a dramatic binary opposition between *reason* and *passion*—two irreconcilable, contradictory characteristics that shape notions of masculinity.[5] This opposition is reflected in studies of Javanese gender ideology as well,[6] and, in my estimation, also is applicable to the Sundanese case. Passion—the unrestrained indulgence of desires—is a quality that humans seem to share with animals. Reason is associated with restraint, and is considered to be something that separates humans from animals; superior reason is associated with moral virtue and prestige.[7] The hegemonic Sundanese gender framework suggests that men have more restraint—more reason—whereas women are less able to control their passion. Several scholars have noted a contradictory discourse about reason and passion, however, that runs counter to this "official" discourse, in which men are portrayed as having more passion than women, creating a double-bind situation for men.[8]

In Sundanese culture, a common presumption is that men have more capacity for rational thought and control over desire than women because they are more likely to find an appropriate balance between reason and passion. At the same time, men are expected to be sexual athletes who can quench the unrestrained sexual desire of their wives; their success in controlling female desire is a source of status and power. Thus, male sexual potency is admired, but unrestrained sexual activity is not; where the line is actually drawn between these two extremes is, however, ambiguous. By virtue of their unrestrained sexual desire, women are regarded as having the dangerous capacity to overwhelm men's reason and lead them into temptation. As a consequence, women submit to a variety of constraints that rein in, but do not completely eliminate, their attractive power. For women, to incite desire in men is a positive quality because it gives men an opportunity to display their potency, but to be too publicly attractive invites scorn. Once again, the line between acceptable and unacceptable attractiveness is ambiguously drawn.

Naturalized boundaries between contradictory qualities are the stuff of which gender ideology is made. Sundanese individuals actively produce and reproduce gender ideology by somehow naturalizing these contradictions—making them seem noncontradictory—in dance events. The complex system of contradictions, double standards, and desires that constitute gender ideology is reproduced in dance event protocols. The events are enacted by men and for men, with the complicity of an archetypal woman—a *ronggeng*—in keeping in line with a fundamentally patriarchal gender status quo, which, like all patriarchies, is in large part created by the work of women.[9] The hyperfemininity of *ronggeng* brings the imagined oppositions of masculine and feminine, so vital to gender ideology, into sharp relief.

Ronggeng bind together the various elements of dance events by performing femininity in several sensory modes. Visually, *ronggeng* accentuate their feminine attributes through extraordinary dress and grooming.

Aurally, *ronggeng* voices incite desire through melody and poetry. Tactilely, *ronggeng* interact with men on a one-to-one basis, dancing in close proximity to—even touching—their partners. As objects of desire in multiple dimensions, *ronggeng* force the male participants to make a choice: either to indulge their desires or to transcend them.

The male participants, inspired by the *ronggeng,* dance at the boundary between reason and passion. Presented with an exaggerated version of femininity, men position themselves as masculine creatures within the matrix of reason and passion through their choice of partners, songs, movements, interaction with the *ronggeng* and other men, and their decision to pursue clandestine relations with the *ronggeng* outside the dance arena. The great variety of options allows each man to construct a nuanced identity for himself within the constraints of Sundanese masculinities. As far as the male dancers are concerned, they are simply engaging in an aesthetic display of dancing. By probing the boundaries between reason and passion, however, the participants in Sundanese dance events enact the contradictions that comprise Sundanese masculinities and femininities. By aestheticizing the contradictions, these performances smooth over the inconsistencies and make them appear natural—even beautiful. The ramifications of what they are doing are far-reaching; they are actively creating, refining, contesting, and affirming gender differences and gender identities—gender ideology—by iterating and naturalizing the contradictions inherent in gender identities.

The *Ronggeng* Image

Female performers who sing and dance and consort sexually with male clients—or give the appearance of doing so—are encountered throughout Southeast Asian history and may be considered "an ancient and indigenous Indonesian entertainment."[10] Legends and myths describing the origins of *ronggeng* suggest roots in agricultural and fertility rituals.[11] Stutterheim postulates a sacred Hindu origin for *ronggeng* in Indian *devadasi,* the female "servants of god" in Hindu temples who sing and dance for temple rituals.[12] Whatever the philosophical and theological details, dance events address the nature of, and the relationship between, masculinity and femininity and aestheticize patterns of gender interaction to aid men in accumulating spiritual and political power.

According to Benedict Anderson's explication of Javanese thought, power is something to be accumulated, concentrated, and preserved, but not exercised.[13] One way to acquire power is through ascetic exercise and self-discipline. Sexual desire represents a human quality that has long been figured as having dangerous potential. One means, then, to accumulate power and status is to transcend sexual urges. Anderson also suggests an alternative approach to accumulating power—through drunkenness and sexual excess: "systematic indulgence of the sensual passions in their most extreme form was believed to exhaust these passions, and therefore allow a man's Power to be concentrated without further hindrance."[14] In a sense, then, the arena of sexual relations represents a win-win proposition for the men, who can gain status either by gratifying or denying their sexual urges. Brenner presents this win-win situation as follows: "the positive associations of sexual potency and of generally 'manly' behavior offset any shame that might accompany their inability to exercise self-control."[15]

Female performers operate within the hegemonic framework of the patriarchy. Nancy Cooper's discussion of the role of female singers in rural central Java parallels my own ideas about Sundanese *ronggeng*, suggesting that their primary function is to assist men in acquiring spiritual power:

> . . . women, through their attractive power, help men transform their
> exuberant power into constructive spiritual potency. . . . [Female
> singers], through singing, . . . suppress the signs of their embodied
> power in favor of men's spiritual and social potency.[16]

In contrast to the win-win situation of the male participants, dance events are a lose-lose proposition for female participants—they deploy their own substantial power mainly to strengthen their male clients' positions. Dance events provide a forum for men to gather, refine, and give evidence of their power; the female participants willingly submerge their own subjectivity in the service of this process. Their willing participation in dance events may net them some short-term measure of power, money, and status; in the long run, however, *ronggeng* behaviors contribute to asymmetrical gender relationships.

These notions of power are predicated on particular ideals of masculine and feminine qualities and behaviors. *Ronggeng* provide a pole of feminine energy against which masculine power can be enhanced and/or opposed. In dance events, the relationship between *ronggeng* and the men with whom they dance is not a personal relationship; *ronggeng* are not spouses or mates, but rather resources that provide vital feminine energy to be shared among men in their quest for power. Femininity is developed in dance events as it relates to a hegemonic masculinity. The status quo in a patriarchal society is maintained by controlling and assimilating women's power; feminine energy can never be wholly masculinized, however, because to do so, ironically, would deprive it of its potency. The appeal of Sundanese femininity lies in its apparent uncontrollability. Gender ideology is rooted in a fundamental contradiction: to possess women's uncontrollable power is to render it controllable—thus stripping away its power and desirability. It must, then, remain in the hands of women.

Ronggeng aestheticize this contradiction by dancing *and* singing; a *ronggeng's* dancing implies submission to control, while a *ronggeng's* singing suggests uncontrollability. *Ronggeng* dance is relatively simple; one *ronggeng* active in the 1950s summarized her movement vocabulary as simply "movements of the rear end and walking."[17] These simple movements are tied to the regular, quadratic structure of the accompanying music and enforced by the drum patterns to which the men also dance. By dancing within these constraints, *ronggeng* acknowledge that they submit to the same controls that the men do. It is *ronggeng* singing, however, that men find most irresistible. Present-day styles of female singing in West Java are characterized by a beguiling elasticity of rhythm. Although the accompaniment for much vocal music is cast in a regular quadratic meter, with a regular pulse, and characterized by cycles marked with binary subdivisions, the vocal part floats over this regular background. It is as if a female singer were deliberately resisting the rhythmic demands of the accompaniment; her phrases spill provocatively over the edges of the rhythmic structures set up by the musicians. A female performer's dance movements embody the very rhythmic structures her singing subverts; through song and dance a *ronggeng* simultaneously resists and submits. *Ronggeng* arouse visual desire through their flamboyant dress and makeup that enhance body parts associated with female attractiveness; their dance movements, such as *goyang* (a sensual swaying of the rear end) further call attention to these attributes. *Ronggeng* also bypass the subtle economic relationships that characterize male-female relationships by demanding immediate monetary recompense for their services. A man's desire for the *ronggeng* as a physical, sexual being obscures his attraction to and desire for the feminine power she symbolizes. *Ronggeng* stand in for all women and their feminine power by essentializing the fundamental contradictions of femininity.

A *ronggeng* is a personification of male desire by dint of her flamboyant appearance, beguiling voice, and willingness to indulge men's sexual urges. However, she also defies normative moral standards—she flaunts her physicality and is sexually loose. The notion of femininity as something simultaneously desirable and revilable, at once attractive and repellent, is quite fragile, owing to the contradictions inherent in it; however, it also is vital to Sundanese gender ideology. Although ordinary women cover up this contradiction, *ronggeng* flaunt it. By being both of these things simultaneously, a *ronggeng* makes it appear that this contradiction is not only possible, but natural; *ronggeng* provide a mechanism to ensure that the foundations of Sundanese gender identities are not called into question.

It is not *ronggeng* alone who accomplish this sleight of hand; they perform within a web of protocols and conventions that govern who dances with whom, when dancing occurs, and how and where sex may take place. Such contexts—dance events—provide a special place in which participants can construct and naturalize gender identities. The events model ideas of desire and gender division through music and dance performance, and provide a context for men to position themselves vis-à-vis one another via aesthetic engagement. It is, however, the *ronggeng*—or more precisely, the *ronggeng* image—that most neatly capsulizes the whole process.

Ronggeng Image in Contemporary Dance Events

Ronggeng's role as a focus of male desire has always carried with it some negative connotations. In recent years, these negative connotations have intensified; as a result, entertainers who call themselves *ronggeng* are rare, as are performers who sing and dance at the same time. The *ronggeng* image persists, however, inscribed onto other kinds of female performers. Sarah Weiss contrasts a "traditional" perspective on dance events, which "represents participation by men in . . . activities of drinking, dancing, and sex as a duty" with a "more modern perspective [which] regards these activities as immoral under any circumstances."[18] In other words, dance events were once privileged as a context where ordinary rules were temporarily suspended. The suspension of morals at dance events would seem on the surface to be contrary to the tenets of Islam, which has been a dominant ethical code in Java since the sixteenth century. Why, then, would a change in dance events occur only around the turn of the twentieth century? Benedict Anderson points out that, until the late nineteenth century, Javanese Islam linked existing conceptions of power with Islamic ideas without substantially affecting underlying political or social paradigms.[19] Stronger Islamic orthodoxy in the twentieth century is only one reason why the moral contradictions of dance events were called into question. Similar revisions of morals were promulgated by Indonesian nationalists, who sought to align Indonesian standards with those of other "modern" nations. Such revisionist approaches gained strength during Suharto's New Order regime, when, according to Tom Boellstorff, "the family principle *(azas kekeluargaan)* . . . [set] forth narrow visions of masculinity and femininity as the foundations of society"[20] and "the nuclear, middle-class family [became a] metonym for the nation."[21] The kinship of dance events to prostitution—a practice prohibited in most "modern" nations—made them the subject of increasing scrutiny. The events always had "negative" connotations—the possibility of untamed feminine power is, I have argued, central to the meaning of dance events. What became increasingly unacceptable in the face of a globalized definition of prostitution was the notion that it is a "duty" to grapple with feminine power in the form of forbidden sexual relations.

Quite a few developments in Sundanese performing arts are the direct result of attempts to attenuate those aspects of *ronggeng* behavior seen as immoral in the twentieth century. Efforts to tone down the *ronggeng* often involved separating the duties of singing and dancing. A common trope is that it makes sense to appreciate *ronggeng* "art" without approving of their "bad" behavior, by which is meant sexual contact with patrons. To clean up the aristocratic Sundanese dance parties called *tayuban* in the early decades of the twentieth century, for example, the *ronggeng* were made to sit with the musicians and only sing. A name change was another approach to minimizing the negative associations of the *ronggeng* image. K. S. Kost concludes that patrons of Sundanese arts should insist on more respectful names such as *juru kawih* or *juru sekar* ("melody artisan") to raise the level of respectability in the Sundanese arts in general.[22]

The implications of the *ronggeng* image are so enduring that they continue to color perceptions of all female dancers and dancing—even recently created "classical" dances (*tari klasik*) intended as high-art showcases of Sundanese cultural identity. According to Irawati Durban Arjo, "the connotations of sexuality which adhere to this singer-dancer role still make it difficult for any woman to dance in public."[23] First steps toward making dancing respectable for women were made by the *Badan Kesenian Indonesia* (BKI: Indonesian Arts Group) in the 1940s and 1950s.[24] The leaders of the BKI tried to disassociate their young dancers from the *ronggeng* image by *staging* their dances, which effectively erected a barrier between the dancers and male audience members, removing any opportunities for the latter to join in. They also chose themes for their choreographed dances, such as animals or epic stories, that were not associated with *ronggeng* dancing. Finally, they presented their dances in contexts, such as receptions at the president's palace, in which the Sundaneseness of the presentation overshadowed any other subtexts. Accompaniments for these "respectable" female dances typically do not include any female voices, further removing these productions from the *ronggeng* image. Choreographers have succeeded in standardizing a formal performance context in which these *klasik* dances can be presented without any men from the audience getting up to dance; men still feel free to comment on the female dancers' appearance, however.

Regardless of terminology, and regardless of whether a female entertainer sings and/or dances, I argue that the *ronggeng* image is projected onto any female performer who either sings *or* dances. Female performers continue to evoke the associations I have discussed previously, primarily through continued association with the other elements of the dance events—music and amateur male dancers.

Doel Sumbang's "Ronggeng"

The persistence of the *ronggeng* image in West Java can be demonstrated not only by the way in which Sundanese audiences regard modern female performers, but also by the frequency with which the *ronggeng* image shows up in contemporary media. It has provided the inspiration for novels (e.g., Ahmad Tohari's *Ronggeng Dukuh Paruk*[25]), films (e.g., *Nyi Ronggeng,* dir. Alam Surawidjaya, 1969), and even a symphonic work (Yazeed Djamin's *Nyi Ronggeng*[26]). When invoked, the *ronggeng* image indexes a context for engaging with the whole complex of Sundanese gender ideology. Doel Sumbang's song "Ronggeng" is an excellent example of this phenomenon; in addition, I find the song to contain compelling clues about what the notion of *ronggeng* means to modern, urban Sundanese men.

Doel Sumbang,[27] a popular Sundanese singer-songwriter, writes songs both in Sundanese and Indonesian languages. He is well known for the wit of his lyrics as well as for their biting political satire.[28] Doel Sumbang told me that he was inspired to write "Ronggeng" when he attended a dance event in the early 1980s. He was struck by how the female performers seemed to satisfy such an important need in making the experience meaningful for the male participants; he also realized that such female performers were increasingly rare. The song, then, was an attempt to capture the kinds of feelings that a man dancing with a *ronggeng* might have—feelings that Doel Sumbang felt were of vital interest and continuing relevance to his audience.[29] Sumbang considers his style to be eclectic.[30] He has some background and a continuing interest in Sundanese traditional music; he incorporates self-consciously Sundanese or other "traditional" musical materials into his more recent work.[31] He remarked that *campursari* (a style combining popular elements with gamelan and other "traditional" sounds that became popular in Central Java in the late 1990s) was nothing new for him.[32] His primary idiom, however, is "international"—that of a synthesizer-playing singer-songwriter, who unself-consciously deploys whatever materials strike his fancy, whether they be global or local in scope, in his songs.

In his current work, Doel Sumbang prefers to use the Sundanese language because of the richness of expression it affords. When he recorded "Ronggeng" in 1984, however, he was pursuing a wider audience than the Sundanese-speaking population would provide, making the Indonesian language a preferable medium. "Ronggeng" is cast in a simple pop-rock idiom with mostly synthesized accompaniment. A bass, trap drum set, and keyboard lay down the basic grooves for the song, and a few synthesized instrumental lines provide countermelodies to the vocal line. The song is set in a minor key, with a i-VI-V chord progression for some sections and a i-VII-VI-I (or -V) chord progression for the other section. These chord progressions are typical of *pop Sunda*[33] and work especially well for harmonizing melodies in the Sundanese *sorog* scale[34]; however, the melody for "Ronggeng" is clearly modal/diatonic and not particularly evocative of *sorog*. The chord progressions thus indirectly cite "traditional" Sundanese music while maintaining an international, modern feel—effectively merging the "local" (the *ronggeng* image) with the "global" (an international style).

Figure 2.1 contains a transcription and translation[35] of the song's text. Each verse is set to one of three musical phrases, which are labeled "A," "B," and "C." The appropriate melodic phrase (A, B, or C) for each text verse is indicated in Figure 2.1; musical notation for the three musical phrases will appear in later figures.

The lyrics describe an encounter with a woman whom the protagonist calls "Nyi Ronggeng" (i.e., Miss Ronggeng). Doel Sumbang sings his song in an intimate, suggestive voice, which can be interpreted either as whispering in Miss Ronggeng's ear or else as talking to himself. Similarly, there are no markers to tell us when or where the encounter is occurring (or will occur). He could be describing a nightclub in Bandung as easily as a dance event in a remote village.

In my analysis, the song creates three different "registers,"[36] delineated by the three different melodic phrases and their accompanying chord progressions, as well as by contrasting poetic voices for each phrase. In the first register, the song's protagonist speaks in a voice of interaction with the *ronggeng*. The second register is the protagonist's own voice of reason, while the third is his own voice of passion—of surrender, introspection, and embodiment. These three registers portray the mixture of feelings a man might experience during an encounter with a *ronggeng*. First, he interacts with her as a fantasy object of desire. He cannot completely erase the vision of her as an invented creature and himself as ridiculous for finding her attractive, however, so in the second register he questions the rationality of his involvement with her. Finally, in the third register, he experiences his dance partner on a purely physical level, where he can shut out the other two more loquacious registers and wallow in the sensuality of the moment.

The use of different speech registers to characterize *ronggeng* is part and parcel of the *ronggeng* image, as illustrated by a conversation I once had with several Sundanese men. I asked about their perceptions of *ronggeng*. One man's first reaction was to enumerate quite methodically their negative characteristics—they engage in inappropriate, extramarital sexual behavior and they always ask for money. Why then, I asked, do *ronggeng*

A:

Sudah sekian minggu lamanya kita tak jumpa	It has been a few weeks since we've met
rinduku menyesap dada	my desire wells up in my breast
O Nyi Ronggeng	O Miss Ronggeng

Malam ini marilah bercumbu tumpah	Tonight let's flirt
'kan rindu 'kan ku buka bajuku	passions will spill, I will open my shirt
dan bukalah bajumu	and you please open yours

B:

Masih ingatkah engkau Nyi Ronggeng	Do you still remember, Miss Ronggeng,
sekian minggu yang telah lalu	from several weeks ago
ketika kita berdua seperti	when the two of us were together like
bocah ingusan yang tak tahu malu	inexperienced teens who know no shame

C:

Oh! Tubuhku, tubuhmu, sama tidak berbaju	My body, your body, together without clothes/shirts
dan marilah malam ini kita ulangi itu	and let's do it again tonight

A:

Atas nama Iblis malam ini	In the name of the Devil tonight
aku ajak kau untuk berolahraga gulat	I invite you to "play wrestling"
Atas nama Iblis malam ini	In the name of the Devil tonight
aku ajak kau untuk sama mandi keringat	I invite you to "bathe in sweat" with me

A:

Marilah Nyi Ronggeng	Let's go, Miss Ronggeng
tak perlu kau ragu dan malu	there is no need to be hesitant and embarrassed
juga jangan pura-pura tak mau	and do not pretend to "not want to"

Figure 2.1. Lyrics and translation of Doel Sumbang's "Ronggeng."

continue to capture men's imaginations? This question did not elicit a methodical answer; instead, the men shifted into a bantering register, making vague statements about the charms of female bodies and the ines-

Jika saja kau tak bisa berolahraga gulat	If you cannot "play wrestling"
Berenang gaya katakpun… bolehlah	Then swim like a frog… if you like

B:

Yang penting gerak biar badan segar	What is important is that the movements feel good
ayolah jangan bengong melulu	come on, do not be expressionless
Mari saling sekap dan saling piting	Let's imprison each other and hold each other
tapi jangan sampai saling benting	but not go so far as to throw each other around

C:

Nyi Ronggeng majulah	Miss Ronggeng, please come forward
rubuhkanlah/runtuhkanlah aku	make me collapse!
Jangan lupa hormat pada Iblis	Do not forget to pay homage to the Devil
yang jadi wasit kita	who is our referee

A: Atas nama iblis… berolahraga gulat; Atas nama… mandi keringat

A: Marilah Nyi… pura-pura tak mau; Jika saja… bolehlah

B: Yang penting… segar; Mari saling… banting

C: Nyi Ronggeng majulah… aku; Jangan lupa… wasit kita

B: Masih ingatkah… lalu; Ketika kita berdua… tak tahu malu

C: Tubuhku,… sama tidak berbaju; Dan marilah… ulangi itu (whispered: ya mari)

B: Yang penting… segar; Mari saling… banting

C: Nyi Ronggeng majulah

Figure 2.1 (continued)

capable desires of all men; relating anecdotes of questionable provenance; and searching for double meanings in each others' statements that could be twisted to suggest an admission of sexual contact between the speaker and a *ronggeng*. The men agreed that *ronggeng* employ magic of various sorts[37] to cloud men's judgment and to provoke sexual urges—in effect, to shift them into a purely physical register. The themes raised in this conversation effectively mirror the registers in Doel Sumbang's song.

The three musical phrases have slightly different characteristics that contribute to the creation of three different registers of emotional and intellectual involvement in the song, mirrored in the text. A generalized model of the "A" phrase is notated in Figure 2.2; it is characterized by an even rhythm of mostly eighth notes. Its gently falling strains are echoed by the descending "passacaglia" chord progression.

The text set to the first phrase is mostly fantasy talk directed to the *ronggeng.* In these phrases, the protagonist tells the *ronggeng* what he wants from her, how he feels about her, and describes activities in which the pair might engage.

Among the various "A" phrases in the song, the sexual charge of the words is proportional to the density of syllables and irregularity of rhythm in the text. For example, an expository line with little sexual charge such as "Malam ini marilah bercumbu tumpah 'kan rindu" ("Tonight let's flirt, passions will spill") snugly fits trochaic feet to the phrase template's regular eighth-notes, while the more highly charged and tongue-twisting "'kan ku buka bajuku dan bukalah bajumu" ("I'll open my shirt and you please open yours"), has an irregular, complicated rhythm, with extra unaccented syllables squeezed into the melody (see Figure 2.3).

This text rhythm, as well as the quick succession of explosive "k" and "b" consonants, effectively portrays the sort of tongue-tied, awkward self-

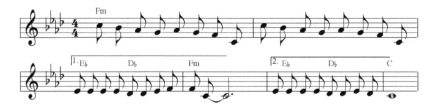

Figure 2.2 Generalized "A" phrase from Doel Sumbang's "Ronggeng."

Figure 2.3 "A" phrase from "Ronggeng" with "extra" syllables.

consciousness that a young man might have about such erotically charged talk with a strange woman. It also evokes the beguilingly elastic rhythm of a *ronggeng*'s singing style. Doel Sumbang's voice is often whispered or very quiet for these phrases. At one point, he imitates the *ronggeng*'s voice when he tells her "don't pretend to not want to." Although this might be interpreted as an acknowledgment of the *ronggeng*'s own subjectivity, such a sudden change of heart on the *ronggeng*'s part might be better considered a component of the *ronggeng* image—it conflates two qualities considered to be "feminine," namely wantonness and unpredictability. In any case, the protagonist is putting words into the *ronggeng*'s mouth, preventing her from speaking for herself.

Figure 2.4 is a generalization of the "B" phrase, which includes many sixteenth notes and begins with a dramatic leap up a sixth into the VI harmony. The melody continues to oscillate up and down, and the harmony alternates between VI and i. The initial leap of a sixth suggests a sudden leap into reality, and Doel Sumbang belts out these sections in full voice.

And, indeed, in these verses the protagonist adopts a more analytical frame of mind; he drops any pretense that his relationship with the *ronggeng* is real. He describes their previous encounter in stilted language ("the two of us were together like inexperienced preteens") and rhetorically asks the *ronggeng* to do her part to make her pretenses of desire seem real. The protagonist seems to be setting ground rules and specifying limits regarding how far he wants his fantasy to go; he requests that the *ronggeng* not get too carried away—"but not go so far as to throw each other around." This is perhaps the closest the song comes to acknowledging the *ronggeng*'s subjectivity—it hints that there is the possibility that the *ronggeng* can ruin the encounter by violating the conventions that enable the entire process. In any case, it expresses the protagonist's own voice of reason.

The "C" phrase (see Figure 2.5) is strikingly contrastive; it moves almost exclusively in slow quarter notes. There is less harmonic variety, just a simple alternation between two minor triads—the subdominant and the tonic. The last two measures of the phrase, however, move to the dominant harmony (via a VI/iv/V progression) and the melodic density increases.

The "C" phrase texts are more experiential than the other verses, as if the protagonist were surrendering completely to the physical sensations of interacting with the *ronggeng*. Sumbang's ecstatic delivery of the lines "tubuhku, tubuhmu, sama tidak berbaju" is extremely affecting; the syllables are drawn out, disconnected, barely uttered, as if minimizing words and language to enhance the physicality of the memory. The text's alliteration, assonance, and internal rhyme heighten the sense of physicality, and conjure the image of the protagonist closing his eyes and savoring the memory of the feeling, the physical imprint of skin against skin. The short

Figure 2.4 "B" phrase from Doel Sumbang's "Ronggeng."

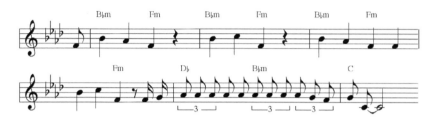

Figure 2.5 "C" phrase from Doel Sumbang's "Ronggeng."

utterances and the long note values suggest a retreat from the verbal into the realm of the sensual. The increase in scansion and harmonic tension at the end of each iteration of the phrase, as exemplified by the transcription in Figure 2.6, however, breaks the spell of this retreat into the physical, just as the dominant harmony at the "C" phrase's end returns ineluctably to the more cerebral first and second phrases. If the "B" phrase expresses the protagonist's voice of reason, this "C" section paints his passion.

The preceding paragraphs described three registers in which the protagonist speaks in the song, as manifest in the melody, harmony, and text. The first register ("A") is the protagonist's interaction with the *ronggeng*. The second register ("B") represents the protagonist's own rational inner voice of reason. The third register ("C") evokes his suspending rational thought and giving in to his passion and the physical sensations of the experience.

The way that the song deploys these three registers provides a clue to how modern Sundanese men use the *ronggeng* image in their own ongoing projects of constructing masculine identities. The "A" phrase, in which the protagonist interacts with the *ronggeng,* appears only at the beginning of the song. The last part of the song consists of alternating "B" and "C" phrases, leaving the "A" section out entirely (see the lyrics in Figure 2.1). It is as if the protagonist had stopped interacting with the *ronggeng* and was

Figure 2.6 End of "C" phrase from Doel Sumbang's "Ronggeng."

now engaged exclusively in an inner dialogue with himself. These two registers—the intellectual observation of the ridiculousness of his behavior ("B") and the surrender to the blissful physical sensations of the moment ("C")—represent the ultimate conflict encapsulated in all *ronggeng* encounters as well as the ultimate contradiction of masculinity. It is a dialogue between sense and sensation, between respectability and desire, and between reason and passion. In this light, it is significant that the song ends in the middle of the "C" section, leaving off the part that leads to the dominant harmony and thus back to "reality," as if, in the protagonist's inner conflict, the physical side—his passion—eventually triumphed over his reason.

The lyrics implicitly reference a variety of the hallmarks of the *ronggeng* image. The *ronggeng* is addressed by a title—Nyi Ronggeng—rather than a personal name. In this portrayal a *ronggeng* is an essentialized female presence. Her facelessness is reinforced by her "generic" name. It is important to him, however, that her movements seem "real" or "sincere" somehow, and he specifically pleads with her not to be "expressionless." In other words, he wants her to pretend to be an individual, attentive to him as an individual. He is fully aware, however, that any appearances of emotional attachment are performed and not sincere; although he treats her as an object, he fears her subjectivity and relies on her complicity (which is bought with money in most exchanges with *ronggeng*) to erase her own identity.

The lyrics are ambiguous with regard to exactly how sexual the activities are. *Buka baju* might mean "open a shirt" or "remove clothing"; *tidak berbaju* can mean "shirtless" or "unclothed." Doel Sumbang evokes a taboo sexual fantasy but deemphasizes actual sexual intercourse; the potential for sex is more significant than the act itself. His other suggestions for activities are whimsically coarse ("play wrestling," "swim like a frog") but similarly ambiguous. He emphasizes his guilelessness by comparing these acts to something "inexperienced teens" might do.

The song suggests that a *ronggeng* is an appropriate medium for focusing sexual desire, even for modern, urban Sundanese men. The ground of the *ronggeng* image provides Doel Sumbang with a canvas on which to paint his own interpretations of the essential contradictions of Sundanese masculinity—sense and sensation, respectability and desire, and reason and passion. The absence of a specific time frame might be interpreted as indicating the timelessness of the notion of a *ronggeng;* the fantasy aspect of the song speaks to the fantasy-figure status of *ronggeng.* The *ronggeng* image can evoke and provide a framework for reconciling, or at least coming to accept as natural, all of these contradictory feelings.

Conclusion

This *ronggeng* image persists, in myriad manifestations, into a present that is not home to very many actual *ronggeng*. A few characteristics of female performers are particularly emblematic of *ronggeng* and comprise what I call the *ronggeng* image. The tropes of objectifying beauty, sexual availability, and free-metered singing with fixed-meter dancing provide a common background over which these various types of contemporary female performers operate. In all cases, they provide a ground on which men can negotiate their own individual balance between reason and passion.

Together, a *ronggeng*'s free-flowing voice and her rhythmically constrained movements translate the contradictions of femininity into an aesthetic realm of music and dance and contribute to a context in which the whole edifice of gender ideology can be performed. *Ronggeng* represent an exaggeration of everything that a man's desire says women ought to be in private—beautiful, sexually available, and responsive—and are thus irresistible despite, or perhaps because of, their being everything his head says they should not be in public—promiscuous, greedy, vain, and uncontrollable. By exaggerating the symbols of femininity, *ronggeng* represent female power. By submerging their own subjectivity, they enact the exploitation of female power in service of a patriarchy. In performing the contradictions of femininity, *ronggeng* reconcile the contradictions of masculinity and provide a foil for the masculine clash between reason and passion.

In the present, the *ronggeng* image, excised from the complete context of dance events, continues to facilitate explorations of gender ideology. Doel Sumbang's song "Ronggeng" traces the same territory covered by the dance events to which it refers—the iteration of Sundanese gender ideology—while making it relevant to modern Sundanese listeners through its use of global musical gestures. The end result is a song that simulates the internal conflicts that characterize a contemporary, Sundanese approach to masculinity.

Notes

1. Doel Sumbang, *Lagu-lagu Kocak vol. 2* (Harpa Records HR 0031), 1984.
2. Sundanese is Indonesia's second-largest language and ethnic group (after Javanese); Sundanese language and culture are roughly coterminous with the modern province of West Java.
3. My notion of "gender ideology" draws heavily from what Judith Butler calls the "heterosexual matrix," which she defines as "that grid of cultural intelligibility through which bodies, genders, and desires are naturalized," and what R. W. Connell characterizes as "gender projects," which are "dynamic processes of configuring practice through time, which transform their starting points in gender structures." Judith Butler, *Gender Trouble: Feminism and the Subversion of Identity* (London and New York: Routledge, 1990),

151. R. W. Connell, *The Men and the Boys* (Berkeley: University of California Press, 2000), 28. My notion also derives from Barthes, who associates ideology with "myth," which "has the task of giving an historical intention a natural justification, and making contingency appear eternal." Roland Barthes, *Mythologies*, trans. Annette Lavers (New York: Hill and Wang, 1972), 142.

4. Susan McClary, *Feminine Endings: Music, Gender, and Sexuality* (Minneapolis: University of Minnesota Press, 1991), 130.

5. Michael G. Peletz, *Reason and Passion: Representations of Gender in a Malay Society* (Berkeley: University of California, 1996).

6. Suzanne A. Brenner, "Why Women Rule the Roost: Rethinking Javanese Ideologies of Gender and Self-Control," *Bewitching Women, Pious Men: Gender and Body Politics in Southeast Asia,* ed. A. Ong and M. G. Peletz (Berkeley: University of California Press, 1995), 31; Ward Keeler, "Speaking of Gender in Java," *Power and Difference: Gender in Island Southeast Asia,* ed. J. M. Atkinson and S. Errington (Stanford, CA: Stanford University Press, 1990).

7. Cf. Peletz, *Reason,* 222.

8. Brenner, "Why," 31; Keeler, "Speaking," 128; Peletz, *Reason,* 255.

9. Cf. Connell, *Men,* 21.

10. Clara Brakel-Papenhuyzen, "Javanese Talèdhèk and Chinese Tayuban," *Bijdragen tot de taal-, land- en volkenkunde* 151, no. 4 (1995): 545–569 (545).

11. Brakel-Papenhuyzen, "Javanese," 568; Kathy Foley, "Of Gender and Dance in Southeast Asia: From Goddess to Go-Go Girl," *Proceedings of the 20th Anniversary CORD Conference*; Robert W. Hefner "The Politics of Popular Art: Tayuban Dance and Culture Change in East Java," *Indonesia* 43 (1987): 75–96 (85–86); Ben Suharto, *Tayub: Pengamatan dari segi tari pergaulan serta kaitannya dengan unsur upacara kesuburan* (Yogyakarta: ASTI, 1980), 71.

12. W. F. Stutterheim, "A Thousand Years Old Profession in the Princely Courts on Java," *Studies in Indonesian Archaeology,* ed. W. F. Stutterheim (The Hague: Martinus Nijhoff, 1956), 100.

13. Benedict R. O'G. Anderson, "The Idea of Power in Javanese Culture," *Culture and Politics in Indonesia,* ed. C. Holt (Ithaca, NY: Cornell University, 1972), 8. There has been scant research about how these Javanese ideas apply to Sundanese notions; my own sense is that Javanese and Sundanese ideas of power and status are comparable.

14. Anderson, "Idea," 10.

15. Brenner, "Why," 35.

16. Nancy I. Cooper, "Singing and Silences: Transformations of Power through Javanese Seduction Scenarios," *American Ethnologist* 27, no. 3 (2000): 609–644 (609).

17. Turyati, *Ketuk tilu gaya kaleran* (Bandung: STSI Bandung, 1996).

18. Nugroho Notosusanto and Sarah Weiss, "Tayuban," *RIMA* 29, nos. 1 and 2 (1995): 119–124 (119).

19. Anderson, "Idea," 58–59.

20. Tom Boellstorff, "The Emergence of Political Homophobia in Indonesia: Masculinity and National Belonging," *Ethnos* 69, no. 4 (2004): 437–444 (470).

21. Tom Boellstorff "The Perfect Path: Gay Men, Marriage, Indonesia," *GLQ: A*

Journal of Gay and Lesbian Studies 5, no. 4 (1999): 475–510 (492).

22. K. S. Kost, "Dari ronggeng sampai jurukawih," *Kawit* 16 (IV-II): 11–13. For a thorough discussion of Sundanese terms for singing and singers, see Wim van Zanten, *Sundanese Music in the Cianjuran Style: Anthropological and Musicological Aspects of Tembang Sunda* (Dordrecht: Foris, 1989), 13–21.

23. Irawati Durban Arjo, "Women's Dance Among the Sundanese of West-Java, Indonesia," *Asian Theatre Journal* 6, no. 2 (1989): 168–178 (169).

24. Irawati Durban Ardjo, *Perkembangan tari Sunda* (Bandung: Masyarakat Seni Pertunjukan Indonesia, 1998); Arjo, "Women's Dance," 171–172.

25. Jakarta: Gramedia, 1982.

26. Cf. STE, "Indonesian Philharmonic Orchestra Embraces Ethnic Nuances," *Jakarta Post* (May 16, 1999): 9.

27. A pseudonym; his given name is Wahyu Affandi. Edwin Jurriëns, *Cultural Travel and Migrancy: The Artistic Representation of Globalization in the Electronic Media of West Java* (Leiden: KITLV, 2004), 129.

28. As Kompas Online points out, "His commercial name is 'sumbang' (n.b. an Indonesian word that means cynical, illicit, or out-of-tune), so cynical, too, is the tone of the criticism in his song lyrics." Anon., Nama dan peristiwa, Kompas Online, (May 4, 1998), http://www.kompas.co.id/9805/04/naper/nape16.htm (accessed April 30, 2006).

29. Personal communication, September 4, 2001.

30. Disctarra, *Doel Sumbang Konser Dua Dasawarsa di Jakarta & Bandung*, http://www.disctarra.com/tarra/news_info.asp?news_id=5014.

31. Cf. Jurriëns, *Cultural*.

32. Disctarra, *Doel Sumbang Latah Garap Music 'Campursari,'* http://www.disctarra.com/tarra/news_info.asp?news_id=1309.

33. Jonathan Hugh-Jones, "Karawitan Sunda: Tradition Newly Writ," *Recorded Sound* 82 (1982): 19–34; Jurriëns, *Cultural*; Sean Williams, "Current Developments in Sundanese Popular Music," *Asian Music* 21, no. 1 (1989): 105–136.

34. The diatonic equivalents of the *sorog* scale's five pitches (e.g., C-D-E♭-G-A♭), if considered as a subset of a minor scale, easily spell the i and VI triads; the interpolation of a single additional pitch (the leading tone) would complete a V triad as well. For information about *sorog* and other Sundanese scales, see: Simon Cook, "Indonesia: West Java," *New Grove Dictionary of Music and Musicians*, ed. S. Sadie (London: Macmillan, 2001); Max Leigh Harrell, "Some Aspects of Sundanese Music," *Selected Reports in Ethnomusicology* 2, no. 2 (1975): 81–101; Henry Spiller, *Gamelan: The Traditional Sounds of Indonesia* (Santa Barbara: ABC-CLIO, 2004); Andrew N. Weintraub, "Instruments of Power: Sundanese 'Multi-Laras' Gamelan in New Order Indonesia," *Ethnomusicology* 45, no. 2 (2001): 197–227.

35. Transcriptions of words and music, as well as the translation, are my own.

36. I use the term "register" here in the way that linguists use it: to identify a particular kind or variety of language that a speaker deploys in a specific social context.

37. Such as inserting *susuk* (a sliver of gold or diamond) under the skin around their eyes, lips, or buttocks to make these areas irresistible. Euis Suhaenah, *Ketuk tilu sebagai aset parawisata* (Bandung: ASTI/STSI Bandung, 1996), 14; Lilis Sumiati, "LilisTari Rakyat Jawa Barat," *Kapita selekta tari*, ed. A. S. Nalan (Bandung: STSI Press, 1996), 20.

3

Moshpit Menace
and Masculine Mayhem

JONATHAN GRUZELIER

Since its conception, the genre of heavy metal music has evolved and adapted in many ways to accommodate the constant flux of cultural and ideological changes as they have happened.[1] Schisms have occurred that have seen subgenres form, as well as combine, to create other subgenres, yet each evolutionary epoch still pays homage to the musical signifiers that were established by heavy metal patriarchs such as Black Sabbath and Judas Priest. That is to say, even though many subgenres feel the need to break away from the original cultural signifiers of heavy metal, they still rely on the initial sound and tactile energy of these musical visionaries to underpin their own stylistic innovations.

Accompanying the musical diversification of heavy metal, there has also been a significant evolution in the holiest of heavy metal communions: the live show. In recent years, heavy metal fans have tailored their physical gestures and spaces at live shows as a means of consolidating a series of cultural codes that pertain to the way a band perceives audience acceptance. Heavy metal fans throughout the 1970s and 1980s were seen to be supporting a live band by punching the air with their fists and head-banging in time with the music. Given the intensity of the music of those bands from that era, this form of expression seemed adequate enough as a means of connecting with the music as well as contributing to the solidarity of the heavy metal audience.[2] More significantly, it aided the construction of a male-dominated space within a genre of music, which was, by and large, synonymous with male subscription. Specifically, this is typically a young, white, working-class masculinity, which is shared by the participants.[3]

This bias toward male subscription is by no means a random coincidence. As a means of solidifying the subcultural codes of heavy metal, many values shared by concurrent genres had to be eschewed. This process included marginalizing any sexually ambiguous elements of popular culture:

> the heavy metal audience is more than just male; it is masculinist. That is, the heavy metal sub-culture, as a community with shared values, norms, and behaviours, highly esteems masculinity. Whereas other youth cultures and audiences, such as the early-1970s glam rock following that coalesced around David Bowie and the mid-1980s pop audience for Culture Club and Michael Jackson, countenanced play with gender, heavy metal fans are deadly earnest about the value of male identity.[4]

This valorization of masculine solidarity suggests that heavy metal, as a defining genre, tends to understand (and represent) itself as a haven of male homosocial interaction. When one examines Eve Kosofsky Sedgwick's study of homosociality, the initial concepts of the term become immediately pertinent to the masculinist code of heavy metal:

> "Homosocial" is a word occasionally used in history and the social sciences, where it describes social bonds between persons of the same sex; it is a neologism, obviously formed by analogy with "homosexual," and just as obviously meant to be distinguished from "homosexual."[5]

Whereas Sedgwick's studies have focused on homosociality in relation to English literature, the study of homosocial interaction in relation to heavy metal subcultures of past and present demands further consideration, especially when studying the evolution of the subcultural codes and the positioning of male-as-dominant in contemporary metal practices. To focus on this homosocial interaction it is necessary to examine the spaces where males demonstrate their adherence to subcultural codes in today's heavy metal epoch. The morphing of heavy metal throughout the 1990s, not least the violent "thrash" of such bands as Slayer and Anthrax, was accompanied by a reinvention of the physical spaces of audience/fan interaction. This was also evident in the adoption of borrowed gestures from other subgenres (such as punk) and contributed to an ever-evolving series of cultural codes that were being defined by the most influential bands at the time. The most prominent readjustment of audience space came about in the form of the moshpit, an area designated close to the stage where slam dancing (borrowed from punk rock) and moshing came into preva-

lence as the means of connecting with the music on new physical and emotional strata. The following descriptions of moshing as a dance form each
make some kind of connection between the practice and the music which
induces it as a phenomenon:

> Moshing is a ritualised and furious form of dancing combining very
> real violence with remarkable displays of emotion, life-and-death situ-
> ations, and the raw sex beat of rock 'n' roll. It induces euphoric displays
> of affection and hostility between its usually male participants.[6]

> The pushing and shoving/punching done during heavy metal, rock,
> and punk music.[7]

Although there are numerous definitions of moshing and descriptions
of how to mosh, it is important to realize that these descriptions are by
no means exhaustive. The emphasis on "violence," "pushing and shov-
ing/punching" suggests, however, that moshpit culture represents yet
another masculine dominant stereotype associated with the heavy metal
genre. This association between masculinity and moshing can be understood when one examines the male bias of the gender demographic and
the activity of a moshpit. Many of the gestures and "dance" moves appear
to be facsimiles of violent interaction, typically found in the antisocial
repertoires of drunken hooligans, whereas other gesticulations appear to
mimic existing dance moves in an overexaggerated and dangerous manner. Moreover, as much as the image of violence characterizes perceptions
of moshing, it does not understand itself to be an aggressive interaction,
or aim for hostility:

> Moshing is a hard skipping, more or less in time to the music, in a
> circular, counter clockwise pattern. Elbows are often extended and
> used as bumpers, along with the shoulders. The action is reminis-
> cent of bumper-car rides found at amusement parks. The ideal is a
> friendly jostling among those in the pit and between those in the pit
> and those located at its circumference.[8]

Either way, the behavior displayed by contemporary metal audiences presents a stark contrast to the comparatively tame activity of bygone heavy
metal shows. However, this marked difference in physical expression
still raises questions relating to the extent to which moshing serves as a
new area of male homosocial interaction in contemporary heavy metal.
More significantly, it is important to evaluate the extent to which masculine dominance is asserted through the moshpit and whether moshers
in this environment are aware of the atmosphere they are contributing
to. As such, the aim of this chapter is to discuss and examine some of

the most significant aspects of the moshpit in relation to contemporary heavy metal performances, and to compare and contrast these developing subcultural codes with those previously established by traditional heavy metal audiences.

Opening Up the Pit

Before discussing the "construction" of the moshpit, it is necessary to contextualize the bands referred to as contemporary heavy metal groups. The music media's fixation on pigeon-holing bands into specific categories, and their classification of bands under different subgenres, such as hardcore, metalcore, mathcore, New Wave of British Heavy Metal, doom metal, and so on, suggests a diversity of style that obscures the similarities of behavior in the moshpit. As such, although it is recognized that metal bands do not necessarily share all the same influences, ideals, or fans, or resemble each other sonically and artistically, the key element that links them together is that their music incites moshpit activity of varying degrees of intensity and varying degrees of male homosocial interaction.

Ideally, it would have been beneficial to make firsthand observations of moshpits in other countries, as I feel that certain key elements of moshpit culture are also affected by sociocultural factors relating to geographical differences. I have had to rely on certain texts, as well as the Internet, for a limited, yet nonetheless revealing view of non-UK moshpits. However, given the high volume of American bands featured in this chapter, it was hardly ever realistic to assume that the UK is the archetypal breeding ground of moshpit culture. Nevertheless, my use of firsthand observation has been my greatest aid, especially when one observes the paucity of academic texts on moshpit culture.

Of the concerts I have attended, artists such as Killswitch Engage, Machine Head, Sick of it All, Hatebreed, Fear Factory, Chimaira, Stuck Mojo, and Mastodon, to name a few, have been indispensable as reference material to my observations of contemporary moshpit behavior. Given that these bands do not belong to any of the archetypal genres such as New Wave of British Heavy Metal (Judas Priest, Iron Maiden, Saxon), Lite Metal[9] (Poison, Bon Jovi, Mötley Crüe), or Speed/Thrash Metal[10] (Suicidal Tendencies, Slayer, Nuclear Assault), they are grouped under the generic label "contemporary metal," thus allowing for some comparisons to be drawn between the developments in the behavior of the respective audience types from each era of heavy metal subculture.

On attending a contemporary metal show, an initial and obvious hint toward homosocial interaction can be perceived by the overwhelming number of male audience members. The percentage of males at the shows

I have attended have all seemed to equal approximately 70–75 percent. Of the females in attendance, a large proportion of these appeared to be girlfriends of the attending males. Apart from the couples, the rest of the male populace tend to gather in their respective friendship groups, drinking beer, and talking amongst themselves before the bands start to perform. In most cases, this traditional aspect of male bonding is observed throughout the heavy metal world and can be associated with previous observations of how males form social bonds:

> males, in contrast to females, tend to form bonding groups with members of their own sex. Writing in 1963, Jules Henry observed that in the United States "Boys flock. . . . Boys are dependent on masculine solidarity within a relatively large group. In boys' groups the emphasis is on masculine unity; in girls' cliques the purpose is to shut out other girls."[11]

When attending shows at smaller venues, where the crowd are more intimate, I have experienced a not unpleasant atmosphere of quiet calculation between the various groups of potential male moshers. It seems that the groups are determining which members of the crowd are most likely to present the most raucous members of the moshpit. By making themselves aware of these members, the individual males are more likely to assess the intensity of the moshpit, and furthermore, should they choose to mosh, they are able to tailor their moshpit moves to suit the space that will be delineated by the other moshers present. An example of this was presented to me at a show by New York hardcore band, Sick of it All, who were being supported by a then upcoming act called Bleeding Through. Given the relatively underground pedigree of Bleeding Through, it was expected that only their most hardcore fans would contribute to the moshpit. These fans were demonstrating their desire to become a part of the fray by positioning themselves in the crowd directly where the moshpit would begin. Added to this, their clothing and demeanor indicated their desire to represent their appreciation for the awaiting band. These particular moshers were significantly more muscular than the general crowd and tended to display more tattoos, either by removing their shirts or wearing tank tops, which revealed their arms. As they stalked the moshpit space, they could be seen to stretch and flex their limbs like athletes warming up for an event. Within seconds of the band starting their first number, the assembled moshers exploded with their repertoire of tailored moves, instantly creating and defining the perimeter of the moshpit. The initial reaction of the nonmoshers was to stand well away from the ruckus and observe the band and the moshpit from a safe distance. The moshpit moves on display had been tailored to complement the aural brutality of the band's performance, as well as conforming to the codes of audience appreciation that contemporary metal bands have come to expect. In this capacity, the moshers are utilizing their bodies and gestures in a metaphorical form of hypermasculine expression that reinforces the "male-as-dominant" perception of moshpit culture. Effectively, these moshers are suggesting that anyone not "man enough" to apply oneself to the fray is not worthy of a place in the moshpit. In this instance, the displays of masculine excess associated with heavy metal are directly related to the physical prowess of the males in attendance, thus limiting and confining any form of homosocial interaction. The perimeter of the moshpit represents a physical as well as a subcultural boundary for this interaction and becomes the transition point for other males to cross in order to contribute to the subcultural codes and homosocial atmosphere defined by the live show context.

However, from studying other moshpits, it is possible to find evidence that the above observation is an extreme example of a group of moshers who tend to represent a form of hardcore moshing ethics, which have evolved from a considerably more underground lineage, and therefore cannot be considered an empirical aspect of the contemporary metal community. Whereas this example is quite an intense representation of the homosocial interaction between moshers, there have been other instances at relatively larger shows, where I have noticed homosocial interaction take place on a more accepting level. This would appear to be a reflection on the commercial success of the band and the number of fans of that band who are willing to demonstrate their appreciation through moshing. In the case of Bleeding Through, only a small contingent of moshers defined the moshpit, effectively having to up the ante of their moshpit moves as a way of representing their appreciation for the band, yet at larger shows such as the Roadrunner Roadrage tour 2003,[12] the increase in audience numbers and commercial success of those bands meant that the moshpit energy could be spread among a larger body of fans, allowing the audience to enjoy a series of more communal moshpit activities such as the "wall of death"[13] and the "circle pit."[14]

While watching Chimaira's set on the Roadrage tour, I noticed that the moshpit resembled an initiation ground where moshers could prove their worth by entering the pit and testing their mettle against some rather heavy-set men. As the band was playing, I decided to throw caution to the wind and launch myself into the pit as a means of testing the outcome of this initiation. I became part of a group of initiates, effectively the smaller guys, who began charging at one another, pushing and shoving, throwing themselves at the big guys in waves and launching fearsome moshpit moves in an attempt to "become" the moshpit. This culmination of masculine energy in many ways played out established theories surrounding the perpetuation of homosocial interaction:

> This desire to unite powers with another man is one possible non-genital form of Eros, this desire and attraction creating the exaggerated impulse to homosociality. Sedgwick even describes the attraction as "intense and potent." Most men operate this way on occasion, though few are aware of it.[15]

Although the overt atmosphere was aggressive and violent, there also appeared to be an element of protection and acceptance that manifested itself whenever someone fell over or took a serious blow. This ability for moshers to take care of each other is a noble aspect of moshing that allows it to become a practice that does not disintegrate into mindless violence. Even though this practice is an unwritten rule of the subculture, it is evident in the sentiments of moshers throughout the world:

> When somebody falls down, you help him up. You don't stomp all over his head, chest and back! I won't go into a long discussion about this, because I'd like to think that it's just common sense while in the pit.[16]

> No personal vendettas. Slamming is a great way of transcending personal ego, getting a bash on the back of the head and returning it with a smile. If you want to get personal, that's a fight, not a dance. Take it down the block where you won't get the show shut down.[17]

> Always keep an eye out for a comrade who has fallen.[18]

The nature of these sentiments indicates that moshers are aware of the value of moshing etiquette in accordance with the codes of their subculture. Essentially, moshers adhere to these sentiments as a way of separating themselves from the negative value of violence that is often associated with other masculine-dominant practices. By doing this they are able to isolate the raw energy inherent of violent aggressive behavior and channel it as a means of expression relative to the tactile power of the music they are privy to. This is a form of subcultural solidarity that relates directly to Weinstein's observation of the heavy metal crowd:

> The audience must constitute itself as a community of comradeship, albeit a transient one. Using Tönnie's term, the members of the audience create a *gemeinschaft* [community]. Far from being calculating and suspicious, as participants in a *gesellschaft* [society] are, they behave in a manner closer to the ideal of philia, the "brotherly love" that was valued in the hippie counterculture.[19]

The "brotherly love" ideal that Weinstein describes relates closely to my own experience as a mosher. Of the moshpits I have participated in, each separate environment has involved significant male bonding rituals that serve to reinforce masculinist codes. There have been episodes where bare-chested male moshers have shared hugs and high fives while comparing cuts and bruises that they have recently inflicted upon each other. On a human level, this practice seems odd, yet equally endearing, and enacts a sportsmanlike attitude to physical competition—the handshake after a tennis match, the bow after a martial arts fight. Added to this, it allows for problematic aspects of the masculine ego to be transcended and reconstituted as a means of promoting subcultural unity. This process can only be achieved through the homosocial tendencies of male moshers, as it would be impossible for any form of catharsis through group physical interaction to exist unless all members of the subcultural unit are participating and accepting of the context in which the interaction takes place. One might surmise that males in this context are subconsciously aiding each other in the diffusion of tension, aggression and violence that may otherwise manifest itself in an environment outside of the context of the moshpit. From my experience of the contemporary metal community, this assumption would appear to explain the scarcity of violence between subcultural participants outside of the live show context.

Quite significantly, it is important to note that the various environs of the heavy metal live show demonstrate several examples of how the homosocial interaction between males is policed. It appears to me, as a mosher, that male heavy metal fans are happy to contextualize their homosocial interaction by delineating zones within a venue that require varying levels of social decorum. Obviously, the hub of the homosocial activity is in the moshpit, where male moshers are demonstrating an unabated yet largely unconscious frivolity toward homosocial behavior. Directly outside of the moshpit, the interaction between males reverts to a diminished state of potency, as the surrounding audience forces the male mosher to recontextualize his behavior so that he must become a part of the larger audience who are contributing through reduced kinesthetic means. A significant degree of homosociality is still maintained in this context; however, it corresponds more to the traditional form of heavy metal appreciation, whereby one's physical space is observed with respect. Essentially, within the four walls of the concert hall, homosocial interaction benefits from the contextual focus of the live music experience, allowing it to manifest itself freely while presenting an obvious gravity towards the moshpit. However, homosocial exchanges vary in intensity when one leaves the four walls of the concert hall, specifically in places such as the toilets, bar, or even the queue for admission outside the venue. These environments suffer from a lack of homosocial focus, as they are typically places where one cannot directly observe or appreciate a live band performance. This does not mean that immediate barriers are placed between the attendant males—in such circumstances men tend to adjust their manner to fit the social context, especially so in the case of the gents' toilets, the homosocial space in which intense performative work is required to assuage fears of homosexuality. Most significantly, moshing environments are a clear indication that for homosocial bonds to strengthen, a particular element must be objectified to unite masculine powers; whether that be sport, music, or women, groups of males must be provided with a focus to detract from any potential homosexual desires and suggestions. Evidently, the according behavior of males in each of the contextual zones of the heavy metal gig (moshpit, crowd, bar, toilet) demonstrates that male fans are subconsciously aware of the potency of their masculinity and the effect that it creates among other males.

Girls in the Pit

Although most of these observations have concerned the behavior of men at live shows, it is important to realize that moshpits are also shared by a determined yet notably smaller contingent of female moshers who wish to express their appreciation for the music via physical interaction. The participation of active female moshers at live shows represents one schism in the history of heavy metal that has allowed women, as fans of the music, to shrug off the stereotype of "sex object." However, the inclusion of females in the moshpit poses a series of issues that lead me to examine how the masculinist homosocial structure of the moshpit is affected by the inclusion of a female element.

There are numerous pasttimes and institutions in modern society that still work to segregate male and female roles apparently arbitrarily. Some of these institutions seem to separate the male and female roles for obvious reasons, such as in sporting teams, where ideals of fairness are upheld on the grounds of physical disadvantages between the two sexes. These boundaries are often upheld by both sexes as it seems to make the playing of certain games more logical if there is a consistency in potential ability between the players involved. Yet with popular music and its myriad of related subcultural machinations, there can be numerous instances found where male-female diversity and interaction is encouraged and celebrated on many levels. Whether it is the performance, production, or the appreciation of a musical genre, distinctions related to biological sex should play little or no part in the execution of any of the aforementioned aspects. However, there is clear evidence that particular musical subcultures create overt as well as covert gendered boundaries in order to reaffirm the values of their community.

With regard to heavy metal, female fans and performers alike have received a significant amount of attention as academics and the media have discussed their role in the construction of heavy metal subcultural codes. There is a variety of examples within heavy metal mythology that delineate women as objects of desire and of sexual service. Examples of this attitude are present in the art work, lyrical content, and music videos from artists as infamous as Mötley Crüe, W.A.S.P., and Whitesnake. There is even an instance described by Weinstein that serves to illustrate the tendency for traditional heavy metal bands to view women as sex objects:

> Some metal bands have developed an overtly sexist shtick as part of their performance. One such group is W.A.S.P. During the Chicago stop of its 1989 tour, Blackie Lawless, W.A.S.P.'s singer, introduced one of the band's most popular songs, "Animal (F**k Like a Beast)," which holds a place of honour near the top of the PMRC's hate list. In line with the code of heavy metal, the fans who were partial to the song, which in this case was most of the audience, stood up. A girl of about seventeen, sitting with another girl three rows in front of me, stood up and thrust out her hand in the classical appreciative salute during Blackie's introduction. This was one of her favourite songs. Then Blackie asked, as he leered and described a female figure with his hands: "Anyone here come to get some *pussy*?" As he said the last word very slowly and deliberately, the crowd roared its affirmative response. But before they did so, when the word was being uttered, the girl abruptly sat down. She obviously realized that it would be inappropriate for her to participate in this wild appreciation. It was fine to stand for the song itself, which did not exclude females from enjoying animal lust. It was the word "pussy" that labeled females as pure objects, not as pleasure-seeking or pleasure-obtaining subjects, that excluded her. The song then began and she stood up with the rest of the crowd to savour it.[20]

In this case, the objectification of females as sex objects has been perpetuated by the artist and no doubt supported by the largely male audience. Although this may represent a snapshot of the mind set of heavy metal in the 1980s, it does not necessarily relate to the global subcultural view of women in heavy metal, as Weinstein points out: "At the metal concert the emphasis is on relaxing constraint and de-sublimating, on being open to the performer's emotions."[21] With this in mind, it could be surmised that the heightened atmosphere of the live show induces behavior and opinions that are usually excluded or inhibited by the subcultural participants in attendance. Outside the context of the live show it appears that there is a hegemonic relationship between male and female fans that serves to uphold the masculinist preference of heavy metal:

> The distinction made by the metal sub-culture between women who dress and behave according to the masculine code and those who fit feminine stereotypes indicates that it is the culture of masculinity, not biological differences, that is of greatest significance.[22]

In many ways, this suggests that men are willing to allow female subscription to heavy metal but only on conditions set out by the masculinist codes of the genre. Notions of femininity could be seen as a means of usurping the masculinist code and diluting the validity of the genre and what it represents.

In the contemporary metal sphere, there is varying evidence that this hegemonic relationship still exists. Alongside the morphing state of gender politics from the 1980s, we have seen women carve their own identity into the musical and subcultural output of heavy metal. There is now an ever growing number of female performers and bands, which have to some extent increased the subscription of female fans into the contemporary metal world. This diversification represents one of the necessary schisms for which a music genre needs to evolve. However, contemporary practices such as moshing present an area of gender negotiation whereby males can be seen to enforce masculinist codes through their physical displays. The presence of female moshers could be perceived as a threat, especially when one considers that the inclusion of female moshers in a moshpit disrupts the homosocial interaction of the males. The homosocial interaction is dependent on the giving and receiving of varying degrees of potentially violent physical contact, with all male parties being aware of how this contact contributes to the subcultural codes. By adding females to the moshpit demographic, the males may become cautious of the intensity of their moshing as a means of avoiding inflicting serious injury on a female. Of the female moshers I have met, all of them have observed the potential risks of moshing and are willing to accept the consequences of their participation should they choose to mosh. Yet it appears that some factions of male moshers still observe women as a foreign body within the melee:

> A lot of the people who come out the worst from their pit experiences are women. Women can have a rough time out there. The unique solution is to go into the pit with your boyfriend and get him to protect you. If girls resort to this strategy they're flying in the face of pit theory, and they're missing out entirely on the thrills and spills.[23]

The females that I have encountered in the moshpit have been fearsome warriors who seem more than content to accept the potential risk of harm in order to contribute to the atmosphere of audience acceptance. It seems to me that women in moshpits are not trying to compete with men in terms of "owning" the moshpit. Rather, it seems that they wish to establish their right to appreciate the music to their full capacity without having to position themselves as sex objects "and occasionally allowing themselves to be used as 'coat racks' for the active males."[24] In many cases, it seems more apparent to me that while men may use the moshpit as a means of diffusing the negative elements of their sexual makeup, women have utilized it as a means of empowering their subcultural identity and eschewing their previously passive stereotype:

> One of the feminist points you might make in favour of the pit, a kind of riot grrrl punk argument, might be that the woman who can stand alone in there, not breaking down crying because she's essentially a wuss, has achieved something for herself as a woman. Whereas those fools being protected by their men are insisting on long forgotten privileges to do with being a woman. Half the fucking point of going into the pit is to be on your own, to reject the conventional society.[25]

Ideally, this view would serve as a healthy maxim for female moshers to observe. However, there have been unfortunate incidents within moshpits in the last ten years that have served to exemplify what can happen when the homosocial interaction of male moshers degrades into abuse. In particular, the Woodstock 99 event saw numerous cases of sexual abuse and violence that brought shame to the metal community. Most notably, Limp Bizkit, a successful nu-metal band of the time, was subject to a vehement lambasting as a result of their instigation of the crowd behavior. However, it is important to realize that many of Limp Bizkit's fans at that festival were males who were not part of the heavy metal subculture and had been attracted to the band primarily because of their MTV friendly reappropriation of rap-rock. These fans took the ethos of moshing at face value and misinterpreted it as a violent free for all:

> During Limp Bizkit, who have taken over rap and made it safe for Mid-western jocks, fans began to dismantle the barriers around MTV's broadcast towers and use them as platforms for crowd surfing. Singer Fred Durst told the pit that, "There are no rules" and ordered them to "smash stuff." Thus incited, the pit turned into a serious war zone where vicious guys began to kick the shit out of each other. Bodies on cardboard stretchers emerged from the audience at least twice during every song.[26]

In this case, the homosocial interaction related to moshing has disintegrated and been replaced with a group conscience that no longer seeks to conform to subcultural codes. The emphasis has now become placed on satiating the violent misgivings of the individual males. As the violence escalated, a new and ugly form of homosocial interaction was realized in the shape of sexual abuse toward the female members of the audience:

> David Schneider, a rehabilitation counsellor working as a volunteer told the *Washington Post* that he saw women being pulled into the pit and having their clothes removed before being assaulted and raped by the men in the crowd. "They were pushed in against their will and really raped," Schneider recalled. "From my vantage point it looked like initially there was a struggle and after that there were other people holding them down. It seemed like most of the crowd around were cheering them on."[27]

Naturally, this example is a disturbing anomaly in terms of moshpit culture and should serve as a reminder that not all aspects of male homosocial interaction are favorable. Luckily, evidence can be found that supports the moshpit community's stance on sexual abuse at shows and that also facilitates the realization of the subcultural goals of moshing:

> I don't go to a show and hop in the mosh pit to "feel up" cute girls. Sadly, this is what it seems to be today. Guys who have lost all synaptic activity and now think with their cocks have perverted the recreation of moshing.[28]

> The bottom line is that females must always be respected in the pit. Most women are already intimidated, so why make it more difficult?[29]

These opinions appear to uphold beliefs in a moshpit environment where sexual contact is neither tolerated nor entertained. However, there is evidence that certain forms of consensual sexual activity do occur within moshpits on a heterosexual and homosexual basis. Initially, this presents problems on a subcultural level as well as a homosocial level, mainly because moshpits are a dance environment largely devoid of posturing in the service of male-female pairing. Traditionally, heavy metal has never been considered as a courting ground for members of the opposite sex: "As a masculinist and overwhelmingly masculine grouping with an extreme heterosexist ideology, the heavy metal subculture stresses male bonding, not male-female pairing."[30]

Considering that the heavy metal code relies on masculine valorization, the concept of moshing as an environment for courtship suggests that any flirtatious activities serve to undermine the homosocial solidarity of the male moshers and disrupt the flow of physical interaction. The music of contemporary metal bands does not promote the act of male-female pairing and the moshpit environment seems like one of the least likely places to either impress one's subject of affection or lust, or try and make any form of initial conversation with them. Yet, it can be seen that the displays of masculine excess inherent in moshpits present a possible mode of erotic attraction. Some participants use the close confines of the moshpit to convey their desires, as one of Ambrose's female interviewees explains:

> I think it was up to the girls to make the first moves. You know . . . letting your hand drift accidentally across some guy's crotch. If he seemed to like it, as when he smiled back at you, you took it from there. I'd say I scored that way at least twice a month.[31]

A similar event happened to me when I was attending a show by Killswitch Engage. During the final song of the set, while in mid-sing along, I found myself being groped from behind. I immediately turned around assuming that it was my girlfriend playing a joke on me, yet I was surprised to find a pair of teenage girls smiling at me as one of them was withdrawing her hand from my backside. I took no offense to this, but found it surprising that anyone would choose to flirt with me, especially considering that my focus at the time was purely on the band and the entire musical moment, rather than trying to appear attractive to the opposite sex. One way of resolving this apparent paradox might be to suggest that sexual antics in the moshpit are being promoted through the unconscious posturing of male moshers, and that this posturing is created by a "raw" masculine display of energy conveyed in moshpit activity, coupled with the intensity of the live music.

Yet it is not just female participants who are susceptible to this display. Homoerotic suggestions concerning moshpits are rife, as the closely confined collection of bare-chested young men can easily be viewed as a playground for suppressed homosexual leanings. Some homosexual male moshers are willing to testify to their desire to enter this arena:

> So off I went down the front where all the sexy guys were. The next hour I had the time of my life slapping up against all these friendly men though I was very cautious. You know the way they go on about the homoerotic homophobic moshpit. They were happy enough about a little sweat touching sweat but I don't think they'd have been too happy about it going any further.[32]

For many people, the occurrence of homosexual desires stemming from the moshpit seems inevitable, especially when viewed on aesthetic levels, accompanied by stereotypes of sweaty, bare-chested tattooed men, rubbing up against each other. However, the concept of homoeroticism being harbored in the moshpit is anathema to the homosocial bonds formed by the masculinist codes of the subculture. Traces of this homophobic leaning can be found in the behavior of traditional heavy metal audiences:

> The masculinist element in metal sub-culture is not merely relevant to the attitudes toward and treatment of women. There is also an attitude of extreme intolerance toward male homosexuality. Heavy metal fans "are often vehemently opposed to other forms of music and to acts that display the slightest hint of ambisexuality. Headbangers are notoriously homophobic . . . and generally regard any act that does not go in for metal's much-macho posturing as beneath contempt."[33]

Although it would appear that contemporary metal fans have become more aware of and tolerant of homosexual diversity, the atmosphere and general ideology of the genre still remains an environment in which homosexuality is not celebrated or widely discussed. With this in mind, typical concepts of homosociality can be seen to have been altered due to the live music context that male moshers are interacting in. Most models of male homosocial behavior rely on the exchange of women as a means of securing heterosexual values between men. However, at the heavy metal concert, the exchange of women is virtually nonexistent, as it has already been noted that male-female pairing is not the prime concern of the audience. Personal observation of heavy metal audiences has shaped my view concerning this exchange and suggests that heterosexuality is secured through the aesthetic of heavy metal music. The overtly macho posturing and demeanor of many contemporary metal performers is enough to confirm to their audience that the primary aspects of the live show are concerning heterosexual aesthetics, which, in this particular context of gathered males, becomes the primary impetus towards male homosociality as manifested in the activities in the moshpit. It would appear that this attitude is used as a means of protecting the masculinist code of the genre, whereby the personal lives and particular opinions of each individual participant are disregarded at the live show in favor of concentrating on the task at hand: moshing and conforming to the codes of the subculture. The focused context of the live show serves to uphold the subculture and therefore cannot afford to waste time and energy by being an arena for topical debates that do not concern the valorization of the music.

Concluding Thoughts

It seems that moshing may serve as an underpinning subcultural requisite for the ever widening spectrum of contemporary metal. However, because of the undulating flux of stylistic elements in contemporary metal, it has become increasingly difficult to position moshing as a subcultural interaction that serves the same purpose for every participant. Unfortunately, it seems that through the eyes of the mainstream media, the act of moshing has now become synonymous with the appreciation of all forms of metal, and as a result, those members wishing to display outwardly their love of metal through their clothes or demeanor have been known to be referred to under the blanket title of "moshers." Such glib labeling only serves to compound the more progressively minded members of the contemporary metal community into blurring the edges of their subcultural boundaries. By doing so, they ultimately distance themselves from certain subculture stereotypes as well as those subcultural codes defined by the genre of heavy metal. Many of the bands I have mentioned demonstrate such a vast diversity of stylistic differences that it can be seen that the emerging generations of metal fans are following suit by happily reappropriating subcultural codes in an attempt to find their own identity within such a vital and unique parent culture. Although it can be seen that a variety of differing ideologies and clothing styles have been employed in this reappropriation, the act of moshing still seems to be the prevailing form of physical expression for these subcultural mavericks, and is still found in clubs and venues throughout the world.

In terms of homosocial interaction, it appears that male moshers are beginning to realize that the moshpit is capable of supporting a variety of subcultural goals and not just those that serve to reinforce masculinist codes. It can easily be argued that the diversification of the physical intensity of the moshpit has allowed a larger number of fans to appreciate the contemporary metal performance. The broadening demographic of contemporary metal fans are now able to use moshing as a means of demonstrating their appreciation of the aggression contained in the music, while not just having to address the masculine stigma attached to that aggression. In some ways this diversity may be perceived as a dilution of subcultural meaning—especially from the point of view of those hard-core moshers who uphold the typical macho mosher stereotype. Conversely, and in my opinion, the diversity of such a passionate form of expression can only be of benefit to a genre of music that is renowned for its solidarity and based on a subscription of proud pariahs.

Notes

1. Genre is defined as "a set of musical events (real or possible) whose course is governed by a definite set of socially accepted rules." Franco Fabbri, "A Theory of Musical Genres: Two Applications," *Popular Music Perspectives*,

ed. David Horn and Philip Tagg (Göteborg and Exeter: IASPM, 1982): 52–81 (52). See Fabbri for an explanation of how these rules may manifest themselves.

2. Deena Weinstein, *Heavy Metal: The Music and its Culture* (New York: Da Capo Press, 2000), 199.
3. Ibid., 99.
4. Ibid., 104.
5. Eve Kosofsky Sedgwick, *Between Men, English Literature and Male Homosocial Desire* (New York: Columbia University Press, 1985), 1.
6. Joe Ambrose, *The Violent World of Moshpit Culture* (London: Omnibus Press, 2001), 1.
7. http://www.urbandictionary.com/define.php?term=moshing.
8. Weinstein, *Heavy*, 228–229.
9. Ibid., 299.
10. Ibid., 299.
11. Ibid., 103.
12. The Roadrunner Roadrage tour has become an annual event featuring three of the top acts on the Roadrunner record label. The 2003 tour featured Chimaira, Ill Niño, and Spineshank.
13. The "wall of death" is a band-instigated event in which the vocalist orders the audience to divide into two approximately equal halves facing each other across the dance floor. On a specific cue given by the vocalist, the audience runs at each other and collide in a style resembling a medieval battle.
14. The "circle pit" refers to another band-instigated activity that involves audience members running en masse in an anticlockwise circle creating a large space in the dance floor. Eventually, the crowd members converge in the centre of the hole and resume moshing.
15. http://www.bu.edu/mzank/STR/tr-archive/tr7/Culbertson1.html.
16. Ibid.
17. http://www.pacificnews.org/jinn/stories/2.17/960812-moshing.html.
18. Ibid.
19. Weinstein, *Heavy*, 211.
20. Ibid., 222.
21. Ibid., 126.
22. Ibid., 105.
23. Ambrose, *Violent*, 98.
24. http://www.dangpow.com/~felixia/ws290.html.
25. Ambrose, *Violent*, 98–99.
26. Ibid., 20.
27. Ibid., 21.
28. http://www.fubarm.com/articles/jaysun/jaysun-nov99.htm.
29. http://www.altx.com/interzones/gangsta/mosh.html.
30. Weinstein, *Heavy*, 130.
31. Ambrose, *Violent*, 184.
32. Ibid., 188.
33. Weinstein, *Heavy*, 105.

4

To See Their Fathers' Eyes

Expressions of Ancestry through Yarrata among Yolŋu
Popular Bands from Arnhem Land, Australia[1]

AARON CORN

Ever wondered where you come from, who you are and where you've
been? Ever looked into the water just to see your father's eyes?[2]

The Sunrize Band, the Yugul Band, the Wirrinyga Band, the Gomu Band,
Soft Sands and the Dharrwar Band are names that very rarely figure in
accounts of the late twentieth-century internationalization of rock and
country styles. However, to the Indigenous communities of Arnhem Land
which, as shown in Figure 4.1, lies in the remote northeastern corner of
Australia's Northern Territory, the achievements and original repertoires
of these bands are legendary. Founded between 1966 and 1971 during a
period of newly won emancipation for Indigenous Australians from state
and mission authorities, these bands were established by teenaged boys
whose childhood fascination with shortwave radio had subverted the aus-
terity of the remote mission and government settlements on which they
had been raised.

They became the first musicians from Arnhem Land to emulate and
compose in the rock and country styles that they had loved since childhood, and they used their newfound freedoms of mobility and association
to engage with other musicians and wider audiences in the regional centers
of Katherine and Darwin. The legacy of popular bands from Arnhem Land
now includes national and international tours, original songs with lyrics in

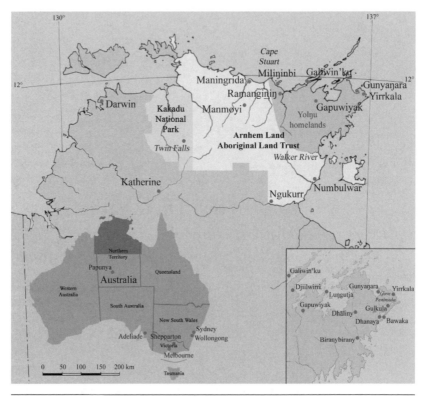

Figure 4.1 Locations within the Arnhem Land Aboriginal Land Trust.

the region's endangered Australian languages and studio albums that have charted worldwide. Moreover, their all but exclusively male members have established a new movement of musical creativity that blends the region's rich music and dance traditions with rock, country, reggae, and rap styles, and has fostered the current successes of Yothu Yindi, the Saltwater Band, the Nabarlek Band, and Yilila.[3]

This chapter demonstrates how the original repertoires of popular bands from Arnhem Land frequently incorporate traditional expressions of patrilineal ancestry and explores how their development has paralleled the changing social and ceremonial roles of local men within the past half century. Their endeavors have precipitated a unique convergence of adopted masculine tropes introduced through the imagery of rock, country, reggae, and rap with the venerated prowess of traditional male hunters, performers, artists, thinkers, theologians, and leaders. The chapter's primary focus is the creativity of Yolŋu musicians in the bands Soft Sands and Yothu Yindi from northeast Arnhem Land whose parallel work in broadcasting, education, philanthropy, and film has stimulated broad public dialogues

about contemporary tensions between traditional maintenance and inexo-
rable social change in Australia's remote Indigenous communities. Their
musically developed discourses about interculturalism have fostered new
sensibilities about race relations, legal pluralism and Indigenous sovereignty within Australia and beyond, and provide us with fresh insights to
the personal development of young men living in the remote Indigenous
communities of contemporary Australia.

My direct experience of musicians from Arnhem Land dates from 1996
when I first traveled there for field work towards my doctoral thesis on
tradition and innovation within the region's popular band movement.[4] It
was the unprecedented wave of international popularity enjoyed by Yothu
Yindi in the early 1990s that had piqued my interest in this topic, and I first
arrived in Arnhem Land at a time when the founders of the Sunrize Band
from Maningrida, the Yugul Band from Ngukurr, the Wirrinyga Band and
Gomu Band from Miliŋinbi, and Soft Sands and the Dharrwar Band from
Galiwin'ku were approaching the age of fifty.

With their traditional enthusiasm for the pursuit of knowledge and its
expression through traditional performance, they were eager to share personal insights to their original repertoires and reflections on their bands'
achievements. By 2001, I had identified the thirty-eight popular bands
listed in Figure 4.2, interviewed more than seventy of their musicians,
translated more than seventy of their original songs from Kriol and the
endangered Australian languages Yolŋu-Matha, Burarra, Wubuyu, and
Anindilyakwa, and assembled some one hundred recorded hours and five
hundred photographs of their rehearsals and performances.

In 2000, the University of Wollongong commissioned me to undertake
a study at Ngukurr in southeast Arnhem Land into the lifestyles of male
youths aged between fifteen and twenty-five.[5] Unlike the Yolŋu communities of Arnhem Land's northeast which, earlier in the twentieth century,
had been administered by liberal Methodist missionaries, the contemporaneous introduction of Anglicanism to Ngukurr all but eradicated
public expressions of traditional ceremonial conduct. Coupled with the
widespread inaccessibility of meaningful employment opportunities in
Ngukurr, the gross erosion of ceremonial performance as a traditional
mechanism for male self-expression and ascent to positions of community
leadership has rendered semiorganized football teams and popular bands
the only local activities through which male youths can experience personal mentoring and normative role-modeling from older men.[6]

Since 2001, I have worked extensively in bicultural contexts with Yolŋu
musicians from Soft Sands and Yothu Yindi in educating Indigenous and
other students at the University of Melbourne and the University of Sydney,
in presenting at scholarly fora and coauthoring scholarly writings,[7] in coor-

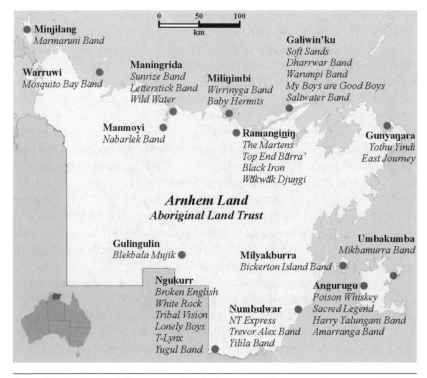

Figure 4.2 Popular bands from communities in Arnhem Land that were active between 1996 and 2001.

dinating the annual Symposium on Indigenous Performance at the Garma Festival of Traditional Culture in northeast Arnhem Land, in managing domestic and international tours for traditional performers, and in developing a National Recording Project for Indigenous Performance in Australia.[8] Outside work, we stay in each other's homes when traveling, participate in each other's ceremonies, and socialize with each other's families. In our common quest to deepen understanding between Indigenous and other Australians, we have laughed together, cried together, fought together, danced together, reveled together, sung together, and learned together.

Who Are the Yolŋu?

The Yolŋu (literally, "person," "human") are the Indigenous inhabitants and hereditary owners of northeast Arnhem Land. There are approximately seven thousand Yolŋu whose tropical homelands, as shown in Figure 4.1, extend from the Gove Peninsula in the northeast, west to Cape Stuart and southwest to the Walker River. The six major towns populated by Yolŋu within this area are Miliŋinbi, Yirrkala, Galiwin'ku and Ramanginiŋ, which were established as Methodist missions in 1923, 1934, 1942 and 1973, respectively, and Gapuwiyak and Gunyaŋara, which began as respective satellite outstations of Galiwin'ku and Yirrkala in the 1980s. The twenty-three Indigenous peoples who own and inhabit homelands in the remainder of Arnhem Land are the Burarra, Rembarrnga, Na-Kara, Dangbon, and Gun-Gurrgoni of the central north, the Kunibídji, Gunbarlang, Bininj, Amurdak, Mawng, Iwaidja, Gagadju, and Wuningangk of the northwest, the Jawoyn, Manangkari and Ngalkbon of the southwest, and the Alawa, Ngalakan, Marra, Ngandi, Waṉdarrang, Nunggubuyu, and Warnindilyakwa of the southeast.

Yolŋu society is an expansive network of more than sixty patrifilial groups that are known generically as *mala* (patrifilial groups; literally, "group"). Agnatic members of each *mala* share hereditary ownership in discrete physical estates or *wäŋa* (literally, "place," "home(land)," "country"), which constitute tracts of land, bodies of water and their natural resources. Seven mutually unintelligible Australian languages, known collectively as Yolŋu-Matha (literally, "people's tongues"), are spoken among the members of these *mala*. However, that each *mala* speaks its own patrilect or *matha* (literally, "tongue") with its own discrete lexicon of hereditary sacred *yäku* (names), is a decisive component of patrifilial identification among Yolŋu that holds binding legal ramifications for individual claims of ownership in *wäŋa* and other hereditary properties. Nancy Williams explains that:

> names comprise a category of a land-owning group's most important non-corporeal property and all names, including personal names, refer in some direct or indirect way to land. The importance of names lies in their relation to land: the group's most important real property. . . . To indicate that something possesses a name is tantamount to asserting that it is owned. . . . [9]

The Yolŋu have inhabited northeast Arnhem Land for countless millennia. They possess names and maintain knowledge for places far underwater that are known to have been above sea level some ten thousand years ago.[10] For centuries prior to the State Government of South Australia's unsolicited interventions in 1906, Yolŋu held extensive trade relations with Asian seafarers who were known to them as the Maŋatharra (Makassans).[11] Having sailed to Australia's northern coasts from the Indonesian port of Makassar on Sulawesi, the annual voyages of these visitors are recorded in hereditary canons of Yolŋu *yäku, manikay* (songs), *buŋgul* (dances), and *miny'tji* (designs) that survive to the present day. New evidence suggests that another foreign people of whom contemporary Yolŋu sing, the Bayini, were Chinese seafarers who landed in Arnhem Land while circumnavigating the globe as part of a marauding treasure fleet from 1421 to 1423.[12]

Michael Cooke records that, before the establishment of the first permanent missionary presence in northeast Arnhem Land at Miliŋinbi in 1923, the Yolŋu had already held an extensive knowledge of their Asian neighbors to the north for some five hundred years and had also been aware of Dutch colonization in Indonesia.[13] This information had been absorbed into Yolŋu canons of hereditary knowledge without displacing the intrinsic and durable logic of Yolŋu intellectual discourses.[14] Yolŋu intellectual traditions also withstood both the Northern Territory Administration's limitation of Indigenous people's freedoms of movement and association under the *Native Administration Ordinance Act* (Northern Territory Administration, 1940–1964), and the government-sanctioned administrative presence of Methodist missionaries in North-East Arnhem Land between 1923 and 1974.

As contemporary Yolŋu have continued to seek international recognition for their unbroken sovereignty over northeast Arnhem Land, they have remained observant of their rights and responsibilities as direct descendants through *yarraṯa* (literally, "string," "line") of the *waŋarr* (ancestral progenitors) who originally shaped, named and populated their hereditary estates there.[15] Through this birthright, Yolŋu identify as both the *wäŋa-waṯaŋu* (literally, "country-holders") and the *rom-waṯaŋu* (literally, "law-holders") of hereditary properties owned by the *mala* into which they are born. As *wäŋa-waṯaŋu*, they each share ownership in their *mala*'s hereditary *wäŋa* and, as *rom-waṯaŋu*, are charged with a duty to uphold the hereditary canons of *yäku, manikay, buŋgul,* and *miny'tji* that are incumbent with each.

Known collectively as *maḏayin* (sacra, all things sacred), these hereditary canons of *yäku, manikay, buŋgul,* and *miny'tji* codify the innate awesome beauty of each *wäŋa* as originally observed by *waŋarr* and passed to humans of their direct patrilineal descent within each owning *mala*. It is the responsibility of each individual to become accomplished in the ancestrally given precedents for *rom* (literally, "law," "culture," "correct practice," "the way") that *maḏayin* codify. Moreover, formal admission to traditional leadership roles in Yolŋu society and, in particular, the specifically male roles of the *djirrikaymirr* and *ḏalkarramirri* (literally, "powerful," "knowledgeable"), is largely predicated on a consummate knowledge and ability to perform one's hereditary *maḏayin*.

Footsteps on the Ground

Over the past two decades, increased access of globalized popular media and fashions, especially those associated with reggae and rap, has markedly changed the music and clothing favored by Yolŋu youths. Nonetheless, their communities remain inexorably isolated from greater Australia and, in fiscal terms, are endemically impoverished. They offer few options for fulltime work, access to public services is poor, imported goods and foodstuffs are sold at inflated prices, and incomes generally are very low. Like their counterparts in southeast Arnhem Land, meaningful employment opportunities are largely inaccessible to Yolŋu youths yet, by contrast, their continuing ownership in *wäŋa* and *maḏayin* through *yarraṯa* (patrilineage) remains central to their upbringings.

The skills and knowledges attained by men through the pursuit of *maḏayin* are central to their training in the traditional roles of hunter, warrior, politician, thinker, and performer. Following ceremonial initiation by *dhapi* (circumcision) at around the age of ten, males are permitted to access all three domains of sacred Yolŋu knowledge and practice: *garma* (public), *dhuni'* (ante-restricted), and *ŋärra'* (restricted). The most accessible of these is the *garma* domain that comprises all *manikay* series which are typically accompanied by *yiḏaki* (didjeridu), and their corresponding *buŋgul* choreography and figurative *miny'tji*. *Manikay* series and their *yiḏaki* accompaniments are performed exclusively by males while their corresponding *buŋgul* choreographies include roles for both males and females.[16] The ceremonial contexts in which they are performed include *dhapi,* extensive *bäpurru* (funeral) and posthumous purification rites, diplomatic delegations to other *mala* and the resolution of inter-*mala* disputes.[17]

Like the *yiḏaki* with its long hollow bore, the *bilma* (paired sticks) that male singers beat to accompany themselves and direct *manikay-buŋgul* (song-dance) performances exude both male and ancestral authority. Other accoutrements originally bestowed on Yolŋu by *waŋarr* include the *bulman* (spear-thrower) and matching *gara* (spears) that are first given as miniaturized gifts to young boys by their older male relatives and are traditionally carried by initiated men at most times. These too are quintessential icons of both male and ancestral agency.

Bulman and *gara* are designed as hunting tools and weapons of war but, when wielded by male dancers in ceremonial performance, they become things entirely other. They can become the tail of a fish in motion, the telescope of a Maŋgatharra sea captain, a wooden lance used to harvest wild honey from eucalypt trees, or the beating wings of a bird. Holding a *bulman* while dancing helps men keep their balance and, as such, most *buŋgul* choreography for males cannot be performed without one. The foundational skills practiced on the *buŋgul* ground are seamlessly transferable to the harvest, the hunt, the battle, and the negotiation, and are integral to knowing how to observe *rom* by following in the *luku* (footprints, steps) of *waŋarr*.[18]

Following *dhapi,* males are admitted to the *ŋärra'* domain of ceremonial knowledge and practice through which they will continue to receive deeply esoteric teachings and spiritual revelations throughout their lives. Djiniyini Gondarra,[19] a *djirrikaymirr* leader of the Golamala *mala,* describes the *ŋärra'* ceremony as an important Yolŋu legal chamber in which law is seriously discussed and binding legal decisions are made. Plans for all legal decisions made by men in *ŋärra'* contexts are open to public discussion beforehand within the all-inclusive *dhuni'* context of the *riyawarra* ground.[20] Men then withdraw to the *ŋärra'* ground in seclusion while their female and uninitiated male counterparts wait at the *riyawarra* (sacred tree on ante-restricted ceremony ground) ground. On the men's return, all are invited to join in a final purificatory act called the *wana-lupthun* (purification by immersion; literally, "arm-wash") in which all those gathered walk into a natural body of water together to demonstrate their assent to the legally binding decisions made at the *ŋärra'* ground.[21]

On the basis of their proven knowledge and demonstrable prowess in performing their hereditary canons of *madayin,* men are typically admitted by elders to positions of *djirrikaymirr* or *dalkarramirri* leadership in their forties. The chief role of a *djirrikaymirr* or *dalkarramirri* leader is to sing *dhuni'* invocations of their *mala*'s sacred *yäku* with *bilma, yidaki* and male chorus accompaniment. These invocations of *yäku* constitute the weightiest display of direct ancestral authority that can be executed outside *ŋärra'* contexts, and are typically performed to publicly confirm the legality of any ceremonial act whether it be a boy's *dhapi* or the culmination of a *ŋärra'* ceremony in *wana-lupthun.*

The process of becoming a *djirrikaymirr* or *dalkarramirri* leader and attaining the right to lead invocations of *yäku* is considered to be difficult and arduous.[22] Boys learn from a very young age the virtues of being *djambatj* (skillful, masterful, successful) at traditionally lauded tasks such as hunting, boating, fishing, dancing, and playing *yidaki.* Elders can reward the successes of young men with exposed *gakal* dances that utilize sacred *bathi* (baskets), the most significant artefacts of direct ancestral authority that can be revealed outside *ŋärra'* contexts, or by apprenticing them as *yidaki* players to master *manikay* singers. However, not all boyish exuberance and determination to be *djambatj* is expended on meeting with the approval of elders. The flamboyance and enthusiasm with which boys characteristically perform in ceremonial *buŋgul* has also found outlets historically in semi-improvised traditionalist music-dance styles such as *djatpaŋarri,* which, between 1934 and 1971, was highly popular among male youths living at Yirrkala.

The formation of the first popular bands in Arnhem Land between 1966 and 1971 afforded local young men even broader outlets for creative expression. *Djambatj* guitar, keyboard, and drum solos would now coexist alongside the traditional flamboyance of boys as *djatpaŋarri* dancers and *yidaki* players. The creative links between local youth styles such as *djatpaŋarri* and adopted popular styles such as rock are evident on albums by Yothu Yindi, which feature both original settings[23] and contemporized resettings[24] of historical *djatpaŋarri* items. Indeed, Yothu Yindi's second album, *Tribal Voice* (1992), is dedicated to three late *djatpaŋarri* masters of the Gumatj *mala.*

Voices on the Wind

The effective cessation of trade and cultural relations between Yolŋu and their Asian neighbors to the north by the State Government of South Australia in 1906 plunged northeast Arnhem Land into a period of dire isolation that was broken only by the establishment of Methodist missions there from 1923. It was not until shortwave radios became available for sale at local mission stores in the 1950s that Yolŋu would regain their ability to freely obtain news from the outside world. Moreover, it was this introduction of radio technology to Arnhem Land that, from the late 1960s, would inspire teenaged men of the region to form their own popular bands as a means of experiencing and exploring the world beyond the mission and government settlements on which they had been raised.

Djirrimbilpilwuy Garawirrtja is a founder of Soft Sands, which was established at Galiwin'ku in 1970. In 1982, Soft Sands became the first band from Arnhem Land to tour internationally and, in 1985, to record professionally. Its members have also inspired and directly guided the later musical successes of their close kin in Yothu Yindi and the Saltwater Band. Djirrimbilpilwuy was born at Galiwin'ku in 1950 where, from early childhood, he heard many new sounds on the shortwave radio that his father, Djupandawuy, bought from the local store.[25] With no dedicated radio service into Arnhem Land at that time, he became *djambatj* at intercepting international services and later, as a young man, worked as the telephoneless community's two-way radio receptionist. By the mid-1980s, he had become a pioneer of the Broadcasting for Remote Aboriginal Communities Scheme at Galiwin'ku and, in 1989, was a founder of the ambitious Top End Aboriginal Bush Broadcasting Association.

My early experience with listening to music was through short wave radio. There was no other radio communication but the transistor radio. . . . The only way we could pick up music and news was on a short wave radio, and we could listen to a lot of music. My favourite programme was listening to country 'n' western and it influenced me a lot. We picked up a lot of American stations and Asian stations and, in particular, I listened to the Indonesian and Filipino stations. Filipinos have a lot of music and lyrics that I've always loved, and I've always enjoyed them.[26]

By his early teens, Djirrimbilpilwuy had become a devotee of the program *Music By Request,* which was broadcast into Asia each weekday at 10 a.m. via the Australian Broadcasting Corporation's international radio station, Radio Australia.[27] It took more than a month for mail to travel from Arnhem Land to the show's presenters in Shepparton in Australia's southeast but the thrill of having a letter read and a request played on air against the odds was encouragement enough to keep listening.[28] Djirrimbilpilwuy also found ways to receive the mainwave broadcasts of 8DN from Darwin and, each Saturday evening, would strain to hear the popular music program *Party Time* over atrocious static.[29]

For its first fifteen years, Soft Sands remained faithful to its roots in the Melanesian gospel style that Methodist missionaries had first introduced to Yolŋu communities six decades earlier and in the radio-borne country 'n' western style that Djirrimbilpilwuy had enjoyed since childhood. The band's debut album, *Soft Sands,*[30] is a collection of original songs with predominantly Christian themes that draw on both of these formative styles. Even so, the band's *waŋarr* roots had always been apparent. The band's very name, Soft Sands, is a translation of the sacred *yäku, Munatha Yandhala,* which describes the fine soft sand that covers the beaches of Luŋgutja. Luŋgutja is the *wäŋa-ŋaraka* (literally, "bone-country"; "forefathers' country") of the Birrkili *mala* into which Djirrimbilpilwuy and the *wäwa* (brothers) with whom he founded Soft Sands were born and from which they trace their ultimate descent from *waŋarr* through *yarrata.*

It was through mentoring younger musicians that Soft Sands would have its most profound and lasting effect on the stylistic development of popular bands from Arnhem Land. Before forming Yothu Yindi at Yirrkala in 1986, Mandawuy Yunupiŋu had worked at Galiwin'ku as the assistant principal of Shepherdson College. It was there, in 1983, that he composed his very first song for popular band, "Djäpana: Sunset Dreaming,"[31] with coaching from an older *wäwa* in Soft Sands, the late Djati Yunupiŋu.[32] Yunupiŋu recalls how, one night, he and Djati worked on this new song into the early hours of the morning before rehearsing it for the first time with Soft Sands that following day.

> "Djäpana" is special for me. It was my first song and I wrote it one evening in 1983 while I was teaching as an Assistant Principal at Shepherdson College in Galiwin'ku. It was a Friday evening and I worked on it past midnight. Then, on the morning after, I played it for the first time with Soft Sands. My elder brother, Djati, had just toured North America with Soft Sands. . . . Writing "Djäpana" was very exciting for me and it set the pace, I guess, for my future involvement with Yothu Yindi. At the time I wrote "Djäpana," the Yolŋu side of my upbringing was starting to sink in. By then, I was in my late twenties and I was beginning to work out how to express myself using Gumatj *manikay*.[33]

"Djäpana: Sunset Dreaming" remains a highly innovative song that, in an unprecedented creative development, drew on *manikay* materials in which Mandawuy and Djati held ownership as agnates within the Gumatj *mala*. *Djäpana* is the yellow-red haze that spills across the clouds and horizon at sunset and is a subject in the Gumatj *manikay* series that recounts an ancestral visitation by Bayini marauders to the Gumatj homeland of Bawaka. Yolŋu history records that the Bayini had captured a woman named Djotarra and imprisoned her in the *yirrmala* (hull) of their boat. As the Bayini sailed away from the shores of Bawaka into the yellow-red haze of the *djäpana* sunset, their boat sank, drowning all aboard, and its wreckage remains eternally present there as the island Binhanhaŋay.

With the third verse of "Djäpana: Sunset Dreaming" warning Yolŋu to be cautious of Balanda (Europeanist) ways, the song's broader message is one of extolling cultural continuity amid foreign influences and intergenerational transition. The song itself serves to demonstrate how musical materials from outside Yolŋu culture can be imbued with themes and materials drawn from the *manikay* tradition to convey durable ideas that remain firmly grounded in Yolŋu thought and practice. "Djäpana: Sunset Dreaming" incorporates lyrics drawn from Gumatj *manikay* items on the subject of *djäpana* that, in their hereditary canonical settings, express *warwu* (sorrow, grief, worry) for Djotarra's loss and, in this new popular setting, also echo the longing felt by Mandawuy for his wife and daughters who remained at home in Yirrkala.

> You see, I was living there at Galiwin'ku on my own and I was really missing my family at Yirrkala. When *djäpana* is sung in our *manikay,* it's an expression of sadness for the departed or whoever you're thinking about at that particular moment. That time of day, when

the sun begins to set filling the clouds and the horizon with a yellow glow, makes you think about the past, the future and the present all in one. I picked *djäpana* as a subject for this song because we see the spectacle of *rräma* [yellow-red clouds at sunset] almost every day of our lives. In a true Yolŋu sense, it gave me a way of expressing just how much I missed my family at that time.[34]

Neparrŋa Gumbula, who became a member of Soft Sands as a teenager in 1971, is another musician whose mentoring by the band's older members led to his composition of original songs that would draw heavily on his hereditary knowledge of *maḏayin*. His earliest original song, "Guṉbirrtji," was composed with two of Djirrimbilpilwuy's *wäwa*, the late Biyarranydjarrwuy and Murrlanawuy Garawirrtja, and its hard rock style marked a radical disjuncture from the gospel and country influences in Soft Sands' established repertoire. The song was composed to celebrate the opening of a new general store at Galiwin'ku by the Arnhem Land Progress Association. However, like "Djäpana: Sunset Dreaming," its overriding message is one of cultural continuity through following the examples of ancestors who have gone before.

> The Guṉbirrtji were the traditional owners of Galiwin'ku. There was a group here called Guṉbirrtji but no longer are the Guṉbirrtji here. Djirrimbilpilwuy's father, Djupandawuy, was still alive during that time so I said to him, "I want to write a song called "Guṉbirrtji" for the opening of the store," which I did.[35]

Neparrŋa's own father, the late Djäwa, was an inspiration for his most ambitious composition, "Djiliwirri."[36] Before his death in 1983, Djäwa had been a long-serving leader of the Yolŋu community at Miliŋinbi and, in 1963, had led a Djaḻumbu (hollow log) ceremony for the final burial of his own father, Ŋarritjŋarritj, that was recorded by the Australian Institute of Aboriginal Studies for the film *Djalambu* [*sic. Djaḻumbu*] (dir. Holmes, 1964). When directing his companion music-video to "Djiliwirri," Neparrŋa juxtaposed historical footage from this ethnographic film against new ceremonial footage performed by Djäwa's descendants at Miliŋinbi in 1996 to demonstrate their unbroken intergenerational maintenance of *rom*.

The song itself is named after the *wäŋa-ŋaraka* of the Ḏaygurrgurr *mala* into which Neparrŋa was born and was composed in response to a *waŋarr*-induced revelation that he experienced there following his admittance by elders to *ḏalkarramirri* leadership in 1996. It begins with a striking *dhuni'* invocation of Ḏaygurrgurr *yäku* with male chorus, which echoes the ancestral bestowal of Djiliwirri on the Ḏaygurrgurr by the *waŋarr* *birrku<u>d</u>a* (bee). Although the remainder of the song is essentially a rock ballad, it also alludes to Djiliwirri and *birrku<u>d</u>a*'s links through *ma<u>d</u>ayin* to the ancestral *mokuy* (ghost), Murayana, and the ancestral Maŋgatharra *buŋgawa* (captain), Nuwa, after whom Neparrŋa's father's father's father was named.[37]

> My *waŋarr* is from the paper bark tree and I too am a honey bee. Djiliwirri is like a home. That's where we belonged in ancestral times before everything started. . . . I wouldn't have written this "Djiliwirri" twenty years ago, no. My father or my grandfather would have said, "No, this one will be done only on *bi<u>l</u>ma* and *yi<u>d</u>aki*, and it remains that way." This new "Djiliwirri" happened because of the needs of new generations and changing technologies. . . . We're giving it our own values so that our songs are educational. This is education to my people. They want to mix it up with other countries but I don't know what their beliefs are. My belief is that this is my country and that these are my belongings, and I'd like to share this with others around the world.[38]

Above all, it is the responsibility of *djirrikaymirr* and *<u>d</u>alkarramirri* leaders to ensure that *rom* is observed and that the young are properly instructed in their hereditary *ma<u>d</u>ayin*. Metaphysical *waŋarr* who remain eternally present and sentient in *wäŋa* recognize and care for the living on the basis of descendants' demonstrable knowledges of *ma<u>d</u>ayin*.[39] Following ancestral precedent, whether exemplified in the *ma<u>d</u>ayin* given by *waŋarr* or in the deeds of more immediate forebears known in life, is therefore a most profound Yolŋu virtue.[40] Within the past five years, Neparrŋa's own consummate knowledge of *ma<u>d</u>ayin*, enthusiasm for historical research and appointment as a Visiting Senior Fellow in Indigenous Australian Studies at the University of Melbourne has contributed greatly to the digital repatriation of rare ethnographic collections to the Galiwin'ku and Miliŋinbi communities.

Observing *rom* essentially ensures that hereditary canons of *ma<u>d</u>ayin* are correctly maintained and transmitted between generations. However, definitive historical episodes such as Djäwa's seminal engagement with film as a new medium for recording ceremony can also establish precedents for the extension of *ma<u>d</u>ayin* into new expressive forms on which leaders of descendant generations such as Neparrŋa can build. In this regard, "Djiliwirri," "Djäpana: Sunset Dreaming" and even the *yäku*-derivative name of Soft Sands constitute efforts by contemporary musicians from Arnhem Land to locate their respective *mala*'s continuing ownership in *ma<u>d</u>ayin* and *wäŋa* in their direct descent from *waŋarr* through *yarra<u>t</u>a*.

Reflections on the Water

Yolŋu traditionally believe that all things in creation, including people, countries, and their living ecologies, are physical consubstantiations of metaphysical ancestral forces that exist eternally on a *waŋarr* plane of reality[41] and that water is the transitional medium through which human *birrimbirr* (souls) migrate between the physical and metaphysical planes of existence.[42] As the epigraph to this chapter suggests, no reflection is ever just a reflection.[43] It is a *mali'* (shadow, reflection) of *waŋarr,* of every late human to have returned through hereditary waters to his or her metaphysical ancestral home, and of every dormant *birrimbirr* waiting to be (re)born in a living human from the very same waters. Water harbors transitional states that come into being only through the meeting of powerful yet interdependent forces and, in "Mainstream" by Yothu Yindi,[44] it is deployed as a salient metaphor for both intergenerational and intercultural exchanges of knowledge.

"Mainstream" is Mandawuy Yunupiŋu's third opus and was composed during his completion of the Bachelor of Arts in Education from Deakin University in 1986. From his early schooling by Methodist missionaries at Yirrkala in the early 1960s to his work as assistant principal at Shepherdson College in Galiwin'ku two decades later, Mandawuy had always been confronted by the underlying Anglocentric assimilationism of the school curricula that missions and the state had implemented in Yolŋu communities.[45] When taught of the assumed necessity of Anglocentric curricula for Indigenous schools at university, Mandawuy composed "Mainstream" and submitted it for assessment. This song essentially contends that *rom* has always been the *mainstream* intellectual discourse through which Yolŋu children are raised and educated and is as factually and pedagogically efficacious as Europeanist academic traditions. He was awarded a High Distinction for his efforts.[46]

The song's first verse refers to a yellow foam called *djikuŋgun* that is produced at *gaṉma* (brackish water) sites within the Gumatj and Wangurri *yapa* (sister) countries of Biranybirany and Dhäliny.[47] The meeting of saltwater and freshwater currents at these sites connotes the productive interaction of the Gumatj and Wangurri *mala* as two equal yet distinct political entities that cooperate in joint ceremonial performances without assimilating each other. The first verse also refers to Mandawuy's daughters. They too are Gumatj owners of Biranybirany and they enter his mind as he sees reflections in the water. The song's second verse introduces *maḏayin* imagery owned by their Rirratjiŋu mother thereby presenting a second model for inter-*mala* cooperation that is grounded in the prolific *yothu-yindi* (child-mother) relationship for which the band is named.

"Mainstream" culminates by projecting both the *ganma* and *yothu-yindi* models for inter-*mala* cooperation into its third verse to exemplify the equity and mutual respect that could exist between Indigenous and other Australians.[48]

Mandawuy's vision for bicultural learning quickly became the mainstay of Yolŋu school curricula.[49] Moreover, his theorization of collaborative social and intellectual spaces through songs such as "Mainstream" have since facilitated and legitimated the Yolŋu development of new intercultural dialogues such as those generated through the annual Garma Festival of Traditional Culture under the auspices of the Yothu Yindi Foundation. With Mandawuy as its founding secretary, this nonprofit organization was established in 1990 by elders of the Gumatj, Rirratjiŋu, Djapu', Gälpu and Wangurri *mala* to support and further the maintenance, development, teaching, and enterprise potential of Yolŋu culture.[50]

The Garma Festival of Traditional Culture was inaugurated at Gulkula in northeast Arnhem Land in 1999 and has since attracted thousands of Australian and international guests seeking to engage with Yolŋu culture firsthand, and participate in intercultural exchanges about education, health, law, performance, art, leadership, tourism, and the environment that have transpired at its annual key forum. In keeping with Yothu Yindi's own traversal of traditional Yolŋu and globalized popular styles, the festival offers both music workshops for young Indigenous Australian musicians with popular bands of their own and a Buŋgul Programme which, in 2005, extended Indigenous Australian participants an opportunity to share in A$15,000 of prize money for the best traditional group performances. Through my own work in coordinating the festival's annual Symposium of Indigenous Performance, I know many Yolŋu parents who view positive public performance experiences for their young to be the most important benefit to flow from this latter initiative.

The Yothu Yindi Foundation has also contributed substantially to widening public debates about the status of Indigenous youth in Australia through its coproduction of the motion picture *Yolŋu Boy* (dir. Johnson, 2001) with Burrundi Pictures in Darwin and the Australian Children's Television Foundation in Melbourne. Filmed on location around Yirrkala, at Twin Falls in Kakadu National Park and in Darwin, the film tells a fictionalized story of three teenaged Yolŋu boys from Yirrkala who undertake an epic journey over some six hundred kilometers to Darwin by dugout canoe, foot, speedboat, and automobile in the hope of preventing one of their number from returning to jail.

The three boys are named after *garma madayin* subjects. Lorrpu (Sulphur-Crested Cockatoo) and Botj (Ironwood Tree) are Gumatj and identify the guiding *waŋarr* from whom they trace their ultimate descent through *yarrata* as Maralitja (Saltwater Crocodile). Milika (Diamond Fish), who is most likely a son of their older sister, is Rirratjiŋu.[51] Their Rirratjiŋu-Gumatj *yothu-yindi* bond is modeled on Mandawuy Yunupiŋu's own relationship with his *waku* (sister's child) and Yothu Yindi cofounder Witiyana Marika.

Lorrpu is an idealist who believes in observing *rom* and follows the teachings of his elders. When the three boys become lost on their journey without food, water, and medicines, Lorrpu alone holds sufficient traditional skills and knowledge in navigation, hunting, and pharmacology to ensure their survival. Milika's key interests are listening to popular music, flirting with girls, and becoming a professional Australian Rules footballer. He appears to have absorbed little of his elders' traditional teachings and seems ambivalent about the relevance of *rom* to his future. The third boy, Botj has just returned home after serving time for petty crimes at Berrimah Gaol in Darwin. His actions have estranged him from his separated mother and younger siblings, and he can only find companionship in his childhood friends, Lorrpu and Milika, with whom he had been initiated some six years earlier.

Lorrpu and Milika soon find themselves unable to deter Botj from his appetite for recklessness and take flight. Abandoned and alone, Botj sniffs petrol to numb his alienation and, in his drug-affected state, breaks into a school classroom where he is confronted by a mural of the very same *bäru* (saltwater crocodile) design that was painted on his own chest for his *dhapi*. Faced with this reminder of his former self as a child of nine years who had shown great potential and excelled beyond Lorrpu in traditional skills, Botj assails the painting and, in his rage, unwittingly sets the room alight. Lorrpu is naively adamant that Botj can be guided back to *rom* by the Gumatj elder Dawu (Banyan Tree) who is away on business in Darwin. Their gambit to reach Dawu before the police can find Botj sets the three boys on their long journey.

Yolŋu Boy presents a clever dramatization of the complex contemporary expectations and challenges that young Yolŋu men face. To affirm the continuing relevance of *rom* to the young, the film's associate producers, Mandawuy Yunupiŋu and his older brother Galarrwuy, draw on their masterful knowledge of *madayin* to orchestrate gripping portrayals of the boys' *dhapi* and revelatory encounters with the *waŋarr* Maralitja.

The scene in which Maralitja emerges from the sea and dances over Botj's badly burnt arm demonstrates the agency of *waŋarr* in protecting and healing their living descendants. In the script, Lorrpu explains that Maralitja "is justice and the law with the power to protect us and the power to heal lost souls." Still, *Yolŋu Boy* offers audiences no easy answers. The boys' arrival in Darwin reveals the root of Botj's psychological problems to be that he is effectively fatherless. He locates his long-estranged father only to discover an alcoholic who is incapable of recognizing his own son. Despite the self-confidence regained by Botj through his travels, he once again turns to petrol sniffing in abject desolation and suicides.

To See Their Fathers' Eyes

> When the old people walked through the land, they made the rocks and trees. They made fire; everything we need. I had to walk like them. Be part of the land. This was my test. If I failed, we had nothing.
>
> "Lorrpu" in *Yolŋu Boy.*

As he deftly stalks a goanna to feed his famished and exhausted friends, it is these words that run through Lorrpu's mind. He must draw on the collective knowledge and strength of all ancestors who have gone before him, and follow in their *luku* to ensure his party's survival. In this sense, Lorrpu's plight is no different from that of contemporary Yolŋu culture itself: succeed and continue as a living consubstantiation of the eternal ancestral journey or fade into memory. Although portrayed as separate characters, the shared story of Lorrpu, Milika, and Botj represents the palpable tensions that contemporary Yolŋu commonly experience when the benefits of the new must be reconciled with an unbroken ancestral covenant to observe *rom,* and when hopes for the future are eclipsed by the endemic hardships of community life.

Any Yolŋu male could be Lorrpu, Milika, or Botj at different stages of his life. *Yolŋu Boy* poignantly exemplifies that trust in oneself, a caring family, worthy role models, supportive peers, and rewards for success will help most pull through but not all, yet also offers audiences a very frank critique by Burrundi Pictures, the Australian Children's Television Foundation, and the Yothu Yindi Foundation of the harsh realities experienced by males raised in the remote communities of northeast Arnhem Land.

This chapter has shown how performance traditions are used by Yolŋu leaders to build transferable skills and self-confidence in the young, to reward success and devotion to their teachings, and to prepare their descendants for positions of responsibility and community leadership. It has also shown how music and dance have traditionally served as expressive outlets for the exuberance, flamboyance, and creative potential of male youths. More importantly, this chapter has shown how the relatively new institution of the popular band in Arnhem Land has broadened creative possibilities for young men in ways that give them unprecedented scope and new reasons, as well as old, to learn and express the histories of their father figures and their fathers' fathers back to the *waŋarr* from whom all in their *yarraṯa* trace common descent. The importance of worthy role models to younger males, whether they be inspirational father figures or supportive peers, has been demonstrated as has the social and psychological dysfunction that can fester in their absence.

It has been shown how salient insights to the efficacy and durability of *rom* as a way of thinking and as a means of learning have been generated through the composition of original repertoires for popular bands from Arnhem Land, and how the introduction of bicultural curricula to Yolŋu schools and the development by Yolŋu leaders of new intercultural dialogues have been stimulated in turn. It is therefore in the spirit of widening intercultural discourses with Yolŋu hunters, performers, artists, thinkers, theologians, and leaders that, in conclusion, I posit to readers the very same questions put forward in this chapter's epigraph. Have you ever wondered where you come from, who you are and where you've been? Have you ever looked into the water just to see your father's eyes?

Glossary

biḻma	paired sticks
birrimbirr	soul
birrkuḏa	bee
buŋgul	dance, ceremony
bulman	spear-thrower
ḏalkarramirri	powerful, knowledgeable
dhapi	circumcision, foreskin
dhuni'	sheltered, ante-restricted
djambatj	skilful, masterful, successful
djirrikaymirr	powerful, knowledgeable
gaṉma	brackish water
gara	spear
garma	public
ḻuku	footprint, step, root, foundation
maḏayin	sacra, all things sacred
mala	group, patrifilial group
manikay	song
Maŋgatharra	Makassan
maralitja	saltwater crocodile
miny'tji	color, design
ŋärra'	restricted
rom	law, culture, correct practice, the way
riyawarra	sacred ante-restricted tree

rom-waṯaŋu	law-holder
waṉa-ḻupthun	arm-wash, purification by immersion
wäŋa	place, home(land), country
wäŋa-ŋaraka	bone-country, forefathers' country
wäŋa-waṯaŋu	country-holder
waŋarr	ancestral progenitor
wäwa	brother
yäku	name
yarraṯa	string, line, patrilineage
yiḏaki	didjeridu
Yolŋu	person, human
Yolŋu-Matha	people's tongues
yothu-yindi	child-mother

Notes

1. Spellings for Yolŋu-Matha words in this chapter follow the orthographic conventions prescribed by Zorc and Charles Darwin University. R. David Zorc, *Yolŋu-Matha Dictionary,* reprint (Batchelor: Batchelor College, 1996). Charles Darwin University, *Charles Darwin University Yolŋu Studies,* http://learnline.cdu.edu.au/yolngustudies/index.htm.
2. Yothu Yindi, "Track 4" *Garma* (Mushroom MUSH332822), 2000.
3. http://www.yothuyindi.com. Skinnyfish Music "Indigenous Roots Menu," http://www.skinnyfishmusic.com.au/indigenous_roots/index.html, http://www.yilila.com.
4. Aaron Corn, "*Burr-Gi Wargugu ngu-Ninya Rrawa:* The Letterstick Band and Hereditary Ties to Estate through Song," *Musicology Australia,* 25 (2002): 76–101. Aaron Corn, "*Dreamtime Wisdom, Modern Time Vision:* Tradition and Innovation in the Popular Band Movement of Arnhem Land, Australia," Ph.D. diss., University of Melbourne, 2003.
5. Aaron Corn, "Ngukurr Crying: Male Youth in a Remote Indigenous Community," Southeast Arnhem Land Collaborative Research Project Working Paper, No. 2 (Wollongong: University of Wollongong, 2001).
6. Corn, "Ngukurr."
7. Aaron Corn and Neparrŋa Gumbula, "Nurturing the Sacred through Yolŋu Popular Song," *Cultural Survival Quarterly* 26, no. 2 (2002): 40–42. Aaron Corn and Neparrŋa Gumbula, "*Djiliwirri Ganha Dhärranhana, Wäŋa Limurruŋgu:* The Creative Foundations of a Yolŋu Popular Song," *Australian Music Research,* 7 (2003): 64–65. Aaron Corn and Neparrŋa Gumbula "Now Balanda Say We Lost Our Land in 1788: Challenges to the Recognition of Yolŋu Law in Contemporary Australia," in *Honour Among Nations? Treaties and Agreements with Indigenous Peoples,* ed. Marcia Langton et al. (Melbourne: Melbourne University Publishing, 2004), 101–114. Aaron Corn and Neparrŋa Gumbula, "Ancestral Precedent as Creative Inspiration: The Influence of Soft Sands on Popular Song Composition in Arnhem Land," in *The Power of Knowledge, The Resonance of Tradition: Indigenous Studies* (Canberra: Aboriginal Studies Press, 2005): 31–68. Aaron Corn and Neparrŋa Gumbula, "*Rom* and the Academy Re-Positioned: Binary Models

in Yolŋu Intellectual Traditions and their Application to Wider Intercultural Dialogues," in *Boundary Writing: An Exploration of Race, Culture and Gender Binaries in Contemporary Australia,* ed. Lynette Russell (Honolulu: University of Hawai'i Press, 2006): 231–265.

8. Allan Marett et al., "The National Recording Project for Indigenous Performance in Australia: Year One in Review," in *Backing Our Creativity—Research, Policy, Practice: National Education and the Arts Symposium Proceedings 2005.* (Melbourne: Australia Council for the Arts, 2006), 84–90.

9. Nancy Williams, *The Yolŋu and Their Land: A System of Land Tenure and the Fight for its Recognition* (Canberra: Australian Institute of Aboriginal Studies, 1986), 42.

10. David Horton, ed., *The Encyclopaedia of Aboriginal Australia* (Canberra: Aboriginal Studies Press, 1994), 201. Yumbulul Yunupiŋu and Djiniyini Dhamarraṉdji, "My Island Home: A Marine Protection Strategy for Manbuyŋa ga Rulyapa (Arafura Sea)," in *Our Land is Our Life: Land Rights—Past, Present and Future,* ed. Yumbulul Yunupiŋu (1997), 181–187. Buku-Larrŋgay Mulka Centre, *Saltwater: Yirrkala Bark Paintings of Sea Country* (Sydney: Isaacs, 1999).

11. C. C. Macknight, *The Voyage to Marege': Macassan Trepangers in Northern Australia* (Melbourne: Melbourne University Publishing, 1976).

12. Charles P. Mountford records Yolŋu descriptions of the Bayini as being seafarers who visited northeast Arnhem Land long before the Maŋgatharra. They are described as being a lighter-skinned people who, unlike the Maŋgatharra, brought with them their wives and children, and built houses during their stay from local timber and imported bamboo. Charles P. Mountford, *Art, Myth and Symbolism,* Records of the American–Australian Scientific Expedition to Arnhem Land, 1 (Melbourne: Melbourne University Publishing, 1956), 333. New evidence presented by Gavin Menzies draws on historical Chinese and European records substantiating these claims, and suggests that the term Bayini could be derived from the Hokkien word for "boat," *joon,* and mean "boat people." Gavin Menzies, *1421: The Year China Discovered the World* (London: Bantam Books, 2002), 197–214. See also http://www.1421.tv.

13. Michael Cooke, ed., *Aboriginal Languages in Contemporary Contexts: Yolŋu-Matha at Galiwin'ku* (Batchelor: Batchelor College, 1996), 1–20.

14. The historical integration of Maŋgatharra themes to hereditary canons of Yolŋu knowledge is discussed and analysed extensively in the following texts: Ronald M. Berndt and Catherine H. Berndt, *Arnhem Land: Its History and its People* (Melbourne: Cheshire, 1954), 22; Peter M. Worsley, "Early Asian Contacts with Australia," *Past and Present* 7 (1955): 1–11 (3–4); Donald Thomson "Early Makassan Visitors to Arnhem Land and their Influence on its People," *Walkabout,* 23 (1957): 29–31; W. L. Warner, *A Black Civilisation: A Social Study of an Australian Tribe,* rev. ed. (New York: Harper, 1969), 455–458; John Rudder, "Yolŋu Cosmology: An Unchanging Cosmos Incorporating a Rapidly Changing World" (D.Phil. diss., Australian National University, 1993), 336–337; Ian S. McIntosh, "The Dog and the Myth Maker: Makassans and Aborigines in northeast Arnhem Land," *Australian Folklore,* 9 (1994): 77–81; Peter G. Toner, "Ideology, Influence and Innovation:

The Impact of Makassan Contact on Yolŋu Music," *Perfect Beat* 5 (2000): 1, 22–41; Corn "*Dreamtime,*" 152–176; and Corn and Gumbula, "*Djiliwirri,*" 64–65.

15. Further discussion and analysis of the contemporary Yolŋu struggle for international recognition of their continuing sovereignty in northeast Arnhem Land is presented in Williams, *Yolŋu;* see also Galarrwuy Yunupiŋu, Djiniyini Gondarra, and Corn and Gumbula, *Honour.* Galarrwuy Yunupiŋu, ed., *Our Land is Our Life: Land Rights—Past, Present and Future* (Brisbane: University of Queensland Press, 1997), 1–17, 210–227. Djiniyini Gondarra, "Customary Law," *Garma Festival, 2001: Ŋärra' Legal Forum,* session 7, http://www.garma.telstra.com/pdfs/ngaarra/Ngaarra_session07.pdf, 15–20.

16. Traditional female singing is limited to the performance of *ŋäthi* (crying) songs which share the same subjects, melodies, rhythmic modes, and lyrics as *manikay* items sung by males. Fiona Magowan, "Melodies of Mourning: A Study of Form and Meaning in Yolŋu Women's Music and Dance in Traditional and Christian Ritual Contexts," D.Phil. diss., Oxford University, 1994. Fiona Magowan, "Shadows of Song: Exploring Research and Performance Strategies in the Yolŋu Women's Crying Songs," *Oceania* 72 (2001): 89–104.

17. Ian Keen, *Knowledge and Secrecy in an Aboriginal Religion* (Oxford: Clarendon Press, 1994), 139–140.

18. Franca Tamisari, "Body, Vision and Movement in the Footprints of the Ancestors," *Oceania* 68 (1998): 249–270 (250–251). Corn and Gumbula, *Honour,* 106.

19. Djiniyini Gondarra, "Customary Law," *Garma Festival, 2001: Ŋärra' Legal Forum* (2001, session 7): 19.

20. Gondarra, "Customary," 15–20, http://www.garma.telstra.com/pdfs/ngaarra/Ngaarra_session07.pdf, 19.

21. Gondarra, "Customary," 16–19.

22. Keen, *Knowledge,* 94–95, 201–239, 309–310.

23. "Track 1" and "Track 14," *Tribal Voice* ext. ed. (Mushroom TVD91017), 1992. "Track 14," *Birrkuda: Wild Honey* (Mushroom TVD93461), 1996.

24. "Track 2" and "Track 15," *Tribal Voice.* "Track 16," *Freedom* (Mushroom TVD93380), 1993. "Track 6," *Birrkuda.* "Track 19," *One Blood* (Mushroom MUSH33229 2).

25. Djirrimbilpilwuy Garawirrtja, telephone interviews with author, Galiwin'ku, Melbourne, February 2, 2001; February 19, 2001; February 27, 2001; and March 6, 2001.

26. Djirrimbilpilwuy Garawirrtja, taped interview with author, Miliŋinbi, November 16, 1997.

27. Ibid.

28. Ibid.

29. Ibid.

30. Soft Sands, *Soft Sands* (Imparja), 1985.

31. "Track 5," *Homeland Movement* (Mushroom D19520), 1989.

32. Djati and Mandawuy had previously performed together in a covers band from Yirrkala called the Diamond Dogs.

33. Mandawuy Yunupiŋu, taped interview with author, Melbourne, March 8, 2001.

34. Yunupiŋu, taped interview, 2001.
35. Neparrŋa Gumbula, taped interviews with author, Galiwin'ku, November 12–13, 1997.
36. Neparrŋa Gumbula and Ŋanganharralil Dhamarraṉdji, "Djiliwirri," perf. Soft Sands, 1997.
37. Corn and Gumbula, "Nurturing." Corn and Gumbula, "*Djiliwirri*." Corn and Gumbula, *Power*, 56–62.
38. Gumbula, taped interviews, 1997.
39. Williams, *Yolŋu*, 85. Tamisari, "Body," 256, 257.
40. Keen, *Knowledge*, 149.
41. Williams, *Yolŋu*, 23–24. Keen, *Knowledge*, 105–106. Rudder, "Yolŋu," 48–50.
42. Ronald M. Berndt and Catherine H. Berndt, *The World of the First Australians: Aboriginal Traditional Life Past and Present*, 5th ed. (Canberra: Aboriginal Studies Press, 1988), 213. Keen, *Knowledge*, 36. Howard Morphy, *Aboriginal Art, Arts and Ideas* (London: Phaidon, 1998), 206.
43. Yothu Yindi, "Track 6," *Garma*.
44. Yothu Yindi, "Mainstream," *Homeland Movement* (Mushroom D19520), 1989.
45. Mandawuy Yunupiŋu, "Yothu Yindi: Finding Balance," *Race and Class*, 35 (1995: 4): 114–120 (116). Helen Verran, response to lecture by Mandawuy Yunupiŋu and Aaron Corn at the Garma Festival of Traditional Culture, Guḻkuḻa, August 24, 2001.
46. Mandawuy Yunupiŋu, taped interview with author, Melbourne, March 8, 2001.
47. Further discussion of *gaṉma* and the creative applications of this concept by Yothu Yindi is provided by Patrick McConvell, Karl Neuenfeldt, and Fiona Magowan. Patrick McConvell, "Cultural Domain Separation: Two-Way Street or Blind Alley? Stephen Harris and the Neo-Whorfians on Aboriginal Education," *Australian Aboriginal Studies* 9, no. 1 (1991): 13–24. Karl Neuenfeldt, "Yothu Yindi and *Gaṉma*: The Cultural Transposition of Aboriginal Agenda Through Metaphor and Music," *Journal of Australian Studies* 38 (1993): 1–11. Fiona Magowan, "Traditions of the Mind or the Music-Video: Imagining the Imagination in Yothu Yindi's "Tribal Voice"," *Arena Journal* 7 (1996): 99–110.
48. Further analysis of "Mainstream" is provided by Corn, "Dreamtime," 77–82.
49. Yirrkala Community School Action Group, *Towards a Gaṉma Curriculum in Yolŋu Schools* (Yirrkala: Yirrkala Community School, 1998). Michael J. Christie, "Literacy, Genocide and the Media," *Aboriginal Child at School* 17, no. 5 (1989): 27–32. Stephen Harris, *Two Way Aboriginal Schooling: Education and Cultural Survival* (Canberra: Aboriginal Studies Press, 1990). Ray-mattja Marika, Ḏayŋawa Ŋurruwutthun and Leon White, "Always Together, *Yaka Gäna*: Participatory Research at Yirrkala as Part of the Development of a Yolŋu Education," *Convergence* 25, no. 1 (1989): 23–39. McConvell, "Cultural." Mandawuy Yunupiŋu, interview, *Sing Loud Play Strong! First Festival of Aboriginal Rock Music*, prod. Jo O'Sullivan (CAAMA Productions, CAAMA V299), 1988. Yunupiŋu, "Yothu."

50. Yothu Yindi Foundation, *Garma Festival,* http://www.garma.telstra.com.
51. Yothu Yindi's albums feature traditional *manikay* settings of "Lorrpu," *Birrkuda* and "Milika," *Freedom* (Mushroom TVD93380), 1993, and a balladic popular resetting of "Maralitja: Crocodile Man," *Tribal Voice.*

Boys Don't Cry: Troubled/ Troubling Masculinity

5

Mum's the Word

Men's Singing and Maternal Law

RICHARD MIDDLETON

"He's got such an extraordinary voice—it could be black, white, male or female."[1] This was Simon Frith's comment on singer Antony Hegarty, of the band Antony and the Johnsons, on the occasion of their success in the 2005 Mercury Music Prize. The biggest surprise is that this vocal ambivalence should be thought surprising: pop music has always offered privileged space for gender and race play, and since records removed the body from sight, radical imaginings of the vocal body have been free to run riot within listening practices. It is tempting to follow, analytically, the particularly transgressive route taken by an Antony; it would, no doubt about it, throw light on the vocal variables of masculinity. But in a sense this is too easy. I want instead to focus on examples of "gender trouble" arising within what seems to be the more mainstream lineage of male singing—the "dark center" without which Antony's provocative sounds, with their transgendering implications, would lose their power (but which is itself defined only in relation to its exclusions and disavowals). I will note in passing, however, the potential importance of the generic territory that Antony occupies: as some critics have remarked, his exquisitely melancholic, even masochistic explorations of loss, hopeless love and death carry his Mercury-winning album, *I Am a Bird Now*,[2] towards the thematics of torch song, in origin and by tradition a female genre. Although there are precedents for this appropriation, in the work of gay singers such as Marc Almond and Boy George, playing provocatively with vocal register and timbre in the context of this specific generic choice remains unusual, and I will return to this point.

My strategy might seem to run counter to an argument persuasively made within queer theory (and presented with clarity by Judith Halberstam, among others[3]) that, because normative (male) masculinity can appear as such only through its positioning within a broader, highly variable range of masculinities (including female masculinity), it is best deconstructed by attending to the latter. There is both a theoretical and a political strength to this argument. However, it ignores the extent to which the specific conventions of vocal performance exist in cultural territory where masculine norms are always already troubled, indeed sometimes self-deconstructing; for men even to perform music—especially to sing—is itself already to query these norms, to "feminize" themselves, at least incipiently.[4] At the same time, patriarchal authority is of course stereotypically asserted by male voices of command—but the shaky foundations of this power make its mechanisms all the more inviting to theory. For this reason, might we even find—to carry the argument to even more provocative lengths—that, if normative masculinity is only defined in a context created by alternative forms, it will sometimes be female masculinities performed by *men* that have especially strong effects?[5]

Singing (to) Mum

Notoriously, the psychoanalytic traditions on which I shall be drawing tend to normalize, or even naturalize, the mapping of sexual difference to the standard gender binary, and, moreover, to embed this map within the hierarchical structure of discursive power. While rejecting this as an a priori, on epistemological (as well as political) grounds, I *am* impressed by the power of psychoanalytic realism; that is to say, if we fail to recognize the historically constituted strength of phallogocentrism, as it has been called, within the performative mechanisms of the Symbolic order, then our grasp both of these mechanisms and of their shaky foundations will fall short. In singing, possession of the symbolic phallus, through which the Law-of-the-Father circulates, typically follows the contours of linguistic authority but also clings to the modes of expression of male desire: narrative and emotional command, and normative masculine imagery, are married together. My interest here lies in those moments when the mask of self-confidence slips and signifying structures threaten to rupture—moments when, perhaps, Mum has the word (that is, one might say, when what had been secret—"mum's the word!"—is brought into the light). For in the delineations of what is clearly an Oedipal drama, the location of the vocal phallus is key; and, if the purpose of this drama is to locate young males and females in their "proper" places in the symbolic as well as sexual order, then any "misfire" may well summon up the figure of the Oedipal or Phallic Mother, holder of the Law in that "other time" before paternal "castration" barred access to the pleasures and tensions of the "preoedipal triangle" (mother-child-imaginary phallus) in which the circulation of vocal energies by the acoustic mirror (babbling, cooing, demanding, crying) played a central role.[6]

It would hardly be possible to imagine a rock singer who, in most of his best known work at any rate, adhered more closely to macho conventions than John Lennon. And those vocal qualities—the driving, sneering, stage-centered cockiness—run parallel to similar traits in the behavioral persona he constructed for himself. (Not that I want to naively align life and music—but there is room to consider the scope of interpenetrating author-functions at work in a subject's diverse textual and quasi-textual projects.) At the same time, however, Lennon notoriously had a mother-problem. This was probably linked—so popular biography suggests—with his sense of early abandonment by his natural mother, Julia, and her cruelly early death; but it also, I suggest, had much deeper roots, roots that lay in the tangled web of sexual possibilities offered by rock 'n' roll, and indeed by twentieth-century popular music generally. The 1970 *Plastic Ono Band* album[7] can be regarded as a crucial "hinge" in this aspect of his psycho-creative biography (as in so many others): before it lay the fraternal dynamic of the Beatles period—a band of rebellious (but also frustrated) brothers; afterwards came the New York period of (sometimes fractious) domesticity with Yoko Ono, who quite clearly assumed a quasi-maternal role for Lennon, within which, however, she was capable of cracking a whip that could subdue the most wayward child. The album is popularly supposed to document the effects of the "primal scream" therapy that Lennon had just gone through with the California psychologist Arthur Janov, although this may have been symptom rather than cause. At any rate, among the treasures that primal digging uncovered were two mother-songs: "Mother" and "My Mummy's Dead."

"Mother" is introduced by the pealing of church bells. A funeral? Who has died?—mother, obviously, but perhaps also Lennon himself—the old Lennon.[8] This ushers us then into the world of ballad—a soul-tinged ballad, sung in his most gorgeously mellifluous tenor, pushing into an incredibly high register, and with even higher excursions into a head voice. (Is this voice male, female, white, black?) In three rigidly repeating verses, Lennon laments the loss of mother, father, childhood. So far, then, in terms both of musical structure and of family relations, we seem to be on an even keel. Yet even here, there are occasional strange "lurches" in the vocal, both rhythmic and in pitch inflection, as if he is discomfited by but at the same time struggling to stick with the insistent tread of the slow-paced, unrelenting metrical-harmonic framework. Increasingly, the underlying instrumental movement has the feel of a bodily machine, summoning images of childlike, quasi-autistic rocking—a figure that is intensified in the lengthy coda, where, over a rigid V-IV-I riff, hammered out by Lennon's own piano chording, his vocal phrases—entreating mother and father to "come home"—evolve into throat-tearing, discordant howls. As the repetitions take root and the vocal cries—tears of rage as well as tears in the fabric of meaning—dominate the sound-space, language retreats from our attention. This is, one might say, a Freudian *fort-da* with a vengeance. And whose is this voice, so multitextured, so rich yet constantly cut open with a rapacious edge (a phallus in the throat)?—Nina Simone's? (Lennon's performance, vocally and, so to speak, theologically, reminds me of nothing so much as Simone's recording of "Sinnerman.")But if this phallus is an offering to mother, it is—like Simone's—double-edged.

The "autistic" motion in "Mother" takes on additional resonance later in the album when we hear the fragment, "My Mummy's Dead." Lasting less than a minute, with Lennon's vocal recorded relatively dead over clanging, metallic guitar (almost like a folk banjo: from hillbilly via "Mr. Tambourine Man," taking the children away?), this song has the feel of a nursery rhyme, its opening phrase mimicking the shape of "Three Blind Mice." It is a nursery rhyme recovered through a haze of memory, though: Lennon's "lifeless" singing over (or rather, behind) the robotic guitar strum forced to be its own mirror, the singer lulling himself.

These two songs have particular import for my purpose here because of their explicit subject matter. But they do not stand alone musically, and indeed take on wider significance in the context of Lennon's overall trajectory. The ripped voice can often be heard in recordings of this period—in "Cold Turkey" and "Well, Well, Well," for example—but also can perhaps be traced back, paradoxical though it may seem, to Lennon's earlier hard-rock voice: as if the "cock-rock" extreme, mutating towards object status, betrays its own authority, revealing the gender-transgressive potential of the male singing-act itself. On the other side, as it were, lie Lennon's surrealistic songs—"I Am the Walrus," "Glass Onion," and again an earlier lineage including "Lucy in the Sky with Diamonds" and "Strawberry Fields Forever"—where, in a parallel mechanism, language subverts itself, this time in child-like word-play. At the same time, there is a sequence of ballads—from "If I Fell" and "In My Life" to "Because" and "Julia"—whose "feminized" orientation comes to full fruition in the "girly" ballads he addressed to Yoko in the 1970s. Overall, the question that comes through is how gender comes to be, and how vocal articulation, which seems as a rule to pin it in place, can also open it up to doubt.

My suspicion—though it would require detailed investigation to document this—is that Lennon's articulation of this question stands in a lengthy twentieth-century tradition. Not that the subject matter would always be overtly "maternal." However, in the work of an equally celebrated early-century singer, Al Jolson, this aspect does loom large—indeed, even larger than in Lennon. The classic example, first recorded for the movie *The Jazz Singer* (dir. Crosland, 1927), where it closed out this, the first sound-film, assuming a key historical status, is Jolson's "My Mammy" (he had been performing it since 1918).[10] As with Lennon, there is an intriguing biographical link. The film story, in which the Jewish hero refuses the role of rabbi laid out for him in favor of a career in show business and cuts himself off from his father in the process, loosely parallels Jolson's own history. In the movie, however, there is a final reconciliation, in which the hero, Jack Robin, forced to choose between a longed-for Broadway opening and standing in for his ailing father to sing the traditional "Kol Nidre" at the Day of Atonement service, opts for the latter. (During his performance, his father—in proper Oedipal fashion—dies.) But, although this might seem to settle for family norms rather than "prostituting" his vocal talent in the theatre, Jack's showbiz career in fact resumes in due course, and the next (and final) scene—which follows so quickly as to make comparison of the two contexts and their music unavoidable—relocates the family romance on to a stage organized around his performance of, and to, "Mammy."

Jolson's rendition made world-famous the hyperemotional gestures he had been working up for years: down on one knee, his arms stretched pleadingly wide, he sobs his appeal in a keening high tenor full of "cantorial" rubatos, passages of heightened, chanted parlando, mordents, glides and other ornaments, and "counterrepresentational" diction (strangled vowels, exaggerated consonants, accents in the "wrong" place). The camera positions us alternately with him, addressing his mother in the front row of the stalls, and with her, lovingly listening, its dialogic gaze-structure supplementing the vocal flow, filling in for her missing voice (we see her lips move but cannot hear her) and completing the mirror-relay. Jolson, like Lennon, pushes the qualities of a "masculine" vocal style—here an emotion-wringing operatic-cantorial tenor—to such an extreme that in effect they undo themselves, resulting in singing that is at one and the same time "feminized" and (not untypically for female vocalities as they are often imagined) out of control: the voice seems to be, as it were, operating itself, and Jolson's body, jerking this way and that, follows. But if Lennon situates the Mother-relation in a context of *loss,* Jolson focuses it on a trajectory of *return:* "I'm coming," he repeatedly exclaims, hoping fervently that he won't be too late.

As I suggested, we cannot but compare this performance with that of the "Kol Nidre." Not only are the vocal qualities and bodily gestures similar, but in both cases Jolson's "queering" of normative masculine vocality is enabled by the device of a *mask,* on the one hand the accoutrements of "blackface" (Jolson's standard performing persona since 1905, but widely used, still, in the 1920s, by some blacks as well as by whites), on the other the vestments of priesthood. In the synagogue, we might say, he stands in for and at the same time supplants his father—but in the shape of an "orientalized" feminine, who stands to the patriarchal God as bride (and to Mammy, therefore, when he subsequently sings to her, as child-bride?). The religious motif implicit but atrophied in Lennon (his "Imagine" is the song of an atheism for which the authority of a murdered god has been reinscribed in the emotional injunctions of celebrity-humanism) is explicit here: it is the "Kol Nidre," sung, significantly, on the Day of Atonement, that makes Jolson's secular success with "Mammy" possible, that legitimates its "feminine" sentimentality; if God is not in his voice, his mother says, his father will know. (For Lennon, the relations are inverted: vocalizing the guilt adhering to his fractured maternal bond is what authorizes his attempted murder of the father in himself, most clearly enunciated in the song "God."[11])

"My Mammy" is only the best known in a rich corpus of "Mammy songs" for which Jolson had long been famous, including "Coal Black Mammy" (1921), "Give Me My Mammy" (1921), "Chloe" (1923) and "Mother of Mine, I Still Have You" (1927). In turn, these songs fit into a broader repertoire of "Southern Plantation" material, indebted to nineteenth-century minstrelsy and the turn-of-the-century coon song; "My Mammy," for example, was one of three Jolson interpolations in the 1918 show *Sinbad,* the others being "Rock-a-Bye Your Baby to a Dixie Melody" and George Gershwin's "Swanee." Within this tradition, the "Southern Mammy" stereotype was a key trope. For Lennon, the favored African-American influences were blues and soul rather than coon song and ragtime, and there were contemporaries of his—Elvis Presley, Mick Jagger, Jimi Hendrix—and later artists, too—Michael Jackson, Eminem—whose debt to the legacy of blackface performance conventions was far more obvious. Nevertheless, placed in this context, Lennon's singing can hardly help but remind us of the importance of this lineage in twentieth-century popular music as a whole, in terms both of musical features and of the psychoracial dynamic that has accompanied them. And we are reminded then that a key strand within this lineage is its matriarchal twist. The familiar stereotypes—the "strong black woman," the haven of the maternal arms, the voice as enveloping as the bosom, set against the complementary clichés of male emasculation—are of course ideologically distorted tools in that psychoracial conflict; yet they are grounded in lived-out black identities with, certainly on the female side, a power that cannot be denied. In a similar way, the misogynistic cast of many of the "Phallic Mother" myths should not be allowed to disqualify the psychoanalytic significance of the figure of maternal law, nor its possible potency as a cultural resource. From blues pioneer Gertrude "Ma" Rainey to Nina Simone, "high priestess of soul" with a voice of "warrior energy," and beyond, there is a tradition here that offers a powerful inverse trajectory to the equally familiar lineage of black male raunch (from the down-home bluesmen through Muddy Waters to Ice Cube and 50 Cent).[12] Add to this the parallel case of the Jewish "matriarchate"—where again a controlling maternal presence goes along with figures of male emasculation, this time the product of a feminizing orientalism[13]—and register in its full importance (as is not often done) the centrality of the intertwining traditions of African-American and Jewish-diasporic vocalities to the development of American popular music as a whole, and one cannot help wondering if Al Jolson's mediation of the two—like George Gershwin, he was a Jew clothing his marginality in blackface—is not a symptom of a cultural mechanism of historic significance, in which the patriarchal cast of Western traditions is given a decidedly matriarchal twist.

Although I want to suggest that this mechanism has a deeply embedded continuity and that careful analysis might unpick symptoms, albeit often less clear-cut ones, at many points along its path of development, it is clear that some particularly revealing nodes do stick out. An obvious case is Elvis Presley, an acknowledged model for the young John Lennon and, although less directly connected to Jolson, a performer who in his early work can in many respects be situated in the wake of Jolson's passage: his voice moves enigmatically through a wide range of registers, including into falsetto; it pops, hiccups, strangles words and plays rhythmically with their dismantled components (vowels, consonants) in a way that, as it were, reembodies itself in the image of a dancing machine;[14] he caresses lyrical phrases like a cooing mother stroking her baby's skin; above all, perhaps, he sings "as if" black (an effect that, as is well known, led to widespread racial misidentification when his records were first broadcast). The young Elvis's education in black music is well documented, and this must have included an assimilation, if only unwitting, of blackface performance codes: the success of Jolson's late movies, *The Jolson Story* (dir. Green, 1946) and *Jolson Sings Again* (dir. Levin, 1949), revived his faltering career, and this is the period, too, when African-American performers with a penchant for "clowning"—Louis Armstrong, Dizzy Gillespie, Louis Jordan—began to be criticized for what modernizing opinion saw increasingly as variants (albeit less old-fashioned variants) of these codes. In the rural and small-town hinterland of Memphis, the legacy of a minstrelized racial dynamic was all around. Robert Fink has described how Presley's version of "Hound Dog" started its life as blackface comedy—"a witty multiracial piece of signifyin' humor, troping off white overreactions to black sexual innuendo"[15]; if his recording ended up being sung, furiously, *at* the media establishment who criticized his indulgence in such innuendo—which is Fink's argument—it may not be too fanciful to think that it was also sung, in tribute and gratitude, *to* the song's first proponent, Willie Mae "Big Mama" Thornton.

The histrionic qualities of Presley's early style—the title of "All Shook Up" can stand as its key trope—was matched by the hysterical character of its reception, particularly in the context of live performance.[16] As with Jolson, who blazed a trail for Presley in this respect, the symptoms of this mass hysteria were largely associated with girls, and their frenzied adulation reached new levels: according to Hollywood director, Hal Kanter, who watched a 1956 show, "I'm a man who saw Al Jolson on the stage, and I never saw anything like the reception that Al Jolson got until Elvis Presley—and he made Al Jolson seem like a passing fancy."[17] Presley did not have a repertoire of Mammy songs, but the biographical Elvis was very much a mammy's boy[18] and it is not difficult to imagine that both the female lovers he would address in his songs and the young women he addressed in his hysterical audiences functioned as displacement objects of desire, mediating his mammy-love. In this feminized emotional economy, an intricate triangular trade of identity and desire seems to be set up, in which—we might think—Elvis assumes a position of "phallic mediator" between his female fans on the one hand, the mothers they have lost and those they believe they must become (as in imagination they mother him), on the other. The "shook up" quality of his singing—fracturing sense, jerking the body uncontrollably, cooing like a baby, emoting like a woman—marks out a troubled territory that all gestures of "manliness" (even GI service) could not completely settle.[19]

Arguably, the nearest Presley comes to a Mammy song is his early classic, "That's All Right Mama." But isn't this song addressed not to mother but to a lover? Yes and no (perhaps).[20] Barbara Bradby and Brian Torode, in their analysis of Buddy Holly's "Peggy Sue," argue that metaphorical "baby" discourse in rock 'n' roll should be taken seriously.[21] For them, Holly's vocal performance—with register shifts, hiccups, and linguistic fractures that bear comparison with the young Presley's—is about his growing from boy to man, a process he achieves through addressing "Peggy" as a baby (addressing her in babyish language) and eventually "disciplining" her wayward rhythms, bringing musical and verbal "sense" into line with his masculine authority. But this relationship works like that between mother and child: "the crying of a baby is silenced not by words, but by the union of the bodies of mother and baby in a rhythmic rocking motion. 'Rock 'n' roll' songs take this bodily relation between mother and baby as a metaphor for the sexual relation between man and woman, in which the man rocks his 'baby,' the woman . . . 'man' stands in for 'mother' and 'woman' for 'baby' in the 'rocking' relationship."[22] Because Holly finally reaches a position of control, of fatherhood to come indeed, Bradby and Torode conclude that the performance in the end confirms a conventional model of male socialization. But where has "mother" gone? Holly not only speaks to his "baby"; like Presley in "That's All Right Mama" (where again words are scrambled, producing almost a babbling effect, and ending with a whole chorus sung to meaningless, "infantile" vocables—"Dee dah dee dee"), Holly sings *like* a baby. The trade is triangular (actually it is a four-some: the absence of the real father, positioned surely just off-mike, looms over the whole scenario); and the shifting relations encapsulated in the vicissitudes of the whole baby/mama discourse (which is not specific to rock 'n' roll but goes back at least to early twentieth-century song) identi-fies popular music as a scene of unstable family romance with much to play for.

If, in the context of the lineage I am reconstructing, rock 'n' roll mediates between Jolsonian minstrelsy and Lennonesque rock, we would expect to find similar historical mechanisms subsequently. Perhaps in rap music—certainly a field of tension implicating both racially and gender-defined protagonists: but here violently transmuted, with a decidedly negative twist, so that mammy-and-baby is rewritten as bitch/whore and—*mother-fucker.* (Not that this term is exclusive to rap. Indeed, from its early-twenti-eth-century origins, as the most extreme insult, its meanings expanded so that by the 1950s it could have positive as well as negative connotations—a history similar to that of "bad" and "wicked." Nevertheless, it assumes an unprecedented centrality in rap discourse, and a background of Oedipal frisson surely remains.[23]) What is placed before us, at least at first hearing, is a family of *orphans,* but one where the presence of the missing mother is all the more palpable because the rappers' continuing entanglement with her—typically displaced on to their "bitches"—takes such a venge-ful form.[24] The maternal voice imagined here is not the comforting one of Julia Kristeva's "choric fantasy," which she associates with a develop-mental stage before the "castrating" force of paternal law arrives, but that of the phallic mother, source of law (and often terrifyingly so). It is from this relation that the "perversion" of sadism/masochism arises—for where might we locate the first signifiers of deprivation and punishment but in the mother's acts and words of admonishment?—and the often noticed sadomasochistic cast of rap lyrics reminds us that, for Lacan, this complex is associated with one of the "partial drives" in particular, the invocatory drive: the maternal sounds that at one and the same time convey discipline and, as object-voice, immediately cut off from its body of origin, offer the lure of a quite specific *jouissance.*[25]

But surely, it might be objected, rap is the genre par excellence where, not maternal, but paternal law is asserted; where masculine authority is imposed through, precisely, words—mastery of rhymes, aggressively delivered. Yet once again (indeed in particularly spectacular fashion) the signifiers of masculine control—speed of verbal articulation, dexterity of rhyming, percussively injunctive diction—are, often, pushed to such excessive lengths that they undercut their own ostensible goal, hysterical gabble matching grotesque bodily gestures and turning language into, not so much a tool of meaning, as an object of play that at the same time acts, by its own force as it were, on the surface of the body itself. This tendency reaches a peak, and rap its crisis point, in the 1990s. To listen, for example, to the Wu-Tang Clan's trend-setting first album from 1993[26] is to hear a surreal mix of "meaningless" repetitions, arbitrary jump cuts, and bizarre overlays of voices, often with grotesque timbres, sometimes "inhuman," sometimes in sequences of "childlike" rhyming. The backgrounds combine abstract, near-atonal riffs and nostalgic, even "cheesy" samples. The range of rap styles deployed here perhaps finds its most telling voice in the weirdly shifting, half-bark, half-singsong persona offered by Ol' Dirty Bastard (a.k.a. Russell Jones: has his father gone missing, in a pathology dating back to slavery?). Even allowing for the effects of cultural distance, explicit verbal meaning seems to me way below the listening horizon. Although rapping is conventionally read as a transplantation of the soundscape of the ghetto street (sometimes seen as a metonym of the "cut-up" culture of a postmodern globalopolis), I hear this music just as much as referencing a phantasmatic aural interior; perhaps that originary "umbilical web" of which Michel Chion writes, a maternal vocalized web that for him marks, all at the same time, desire for an object (a c(h)ord) that is lost, the cut that severed it, and the tentacular grip that it nevertheless retains.[27] The same inside-outside tension, at a different level, animates the characteristic interplay in rap between its claim to authenticity—rap reflects real life—and its status as high spectacle, a knowing performativity reflected in the masquerade of stage-names and doubles.[28] Indeed, too often "real life" has *become* a performance, verbal bullets confused with real ones, both (phallic) object-types marking, machining and dismembering the body. This foot-stamping tantrum is most memorably encapsulated by the Clan: "Bring the motherfucking ruckus!"[29]

From minstrelsy to hip-hop: a history of the family that at the same time documents a continuing if mutating crisis of masculinity. Three overarching points are worth emphasizing:

- Not surprisingly perhaps, the moments I have picked out with my examples map easily to points of masculine crisis in the social history, and each is accompanied by a "feminizing" partner: Jolson (first-wave feminism; the threat of emasculation heard in crooning); rock 'n' roll (Cold War domestication and its anxieties; the camp of such performers as Little Richard); Lennon (second-wave feminism; the feminization heard in progressive and glam rock); rap (late-century "post-feminism"; post-disco dance music, and its gay elements).

- The "involuntary voice" in play in all the examples—the voice seemingly writing itself, outside conscious control, and in the process both separating itself from the body and gesturing it into a particular shape—can be regarded as one aspect of the Lacanian "object-voice," that impossible voice, inaudible as such, which is left over when all signifying processes have been accounted for, the voice which, in one form or another, is ultimately the voice of the Other. Although this voice, typically, stands alteritously to logos—and therefore, in the conventional psychoanalytic scheme, marks the place of a "feminine" *jouissance*—for the later Lacan, it is also what "sticks" to logos, what makes logos work, gives it its god-like authority; in this latter guise, voice is that senseless cry which gives law its force, which therefore summons its own ecstasy—*le-père-la-jouissance*. "There are not two voices, but only one object voice, which cleaves and bars the Other in an ineradicable 'extimacy'"; and, as Lacan himself put it, "why not interpret one face of the Other, the God face, as *supported* by feminine *jouissance*. . . . And since it is there too that the function of the father is inscribed in so far as this is the function to which castration refers, one can see that while this may not make for two Gods, nor does it make for one alone."[30] But to limit this structure to "support" is too grudging: surely it opens the way for the possibility of a reconfiguration of "castration" itself, based on recognition of the role of the phallic mother in weaving the "web" of the symbolic—a possibility that Lacan does not pursue.

- The symptoms we might expect of such a radical, indeed dangerous move—loss of vocal control, automatism, dismemberment or imaginary reconstruction of the body, confusion of gender signifiers, defensive reinforcement of patriarchal markers accompanying their simultaneous fracturing—are all over the examples I have introduced. They bring inescapably to mind a condition that was at the core of the psychoanalytic project from its beginnings, but that Lacan subsequently broadened into one of the modes in his typology of discourse—*hysteria*.

What Is it to Be a Man?

Psychoanalysis offers no bar to the traditional assumption that hysteria is, typically, a female condition. Lacan, extrapolating from Freud, describes hysteria as structured by a question: "Who am I? a man or a woman?" or rather "What is it to be a woman?"[31] And the dissymmetrical form this question is given applies to male as well as female hysterics, because the skewed shape attributed to sexual differentiation—Man is normative, Woman is his symptom—makes the "problem" of femininity the key issue for both genders. But if "castration" were to be reconfigured, the mobility of the phallus fully recognized, then the question for hysterical masculinity would shift: What is it to be a man?

Freud made clear that the root of hysteria lies in sexual fantasy[32]—but the fantasy stands for a situation in which something has "gone wrong," the "normal" course of desire has been blocked or refused. Bodily symptoms "convert" this structure of repressed trauma into an "imaginary anatomy"[33] within which disorders, often interlinked, of the genitalia, digestion, lungs, throat and voice have a prominence that is, for my purposes here, particularly striking. What is more, the intertwining economies of sexuality and of the alimentary and vocalimentary canals often throw up tropes of *procreation:* in Freud's classic case study of "Dora," for instance, a bundle of symptoms hinging on mysterious abdominal pain is interpreted as a fantasy of childbirth; and in Lacan's reading of this study he describes how a particular male hysteric suffers a fantasy of pregnancy.[34] The hysteric's question can thus also be written as, "Am I capable of procreating?"[35] But in the case of male singers, what imaginary anatomy is involved in this? Rather than disablement or movement of a womb (the classical understanding of the female complaint), perhaps we should think of the movement of an imaginary phallus, from its "normal" place up into the throat. Here, suggests Lacan, the hysteric probes at the heart of things, for "In the symbolic nothing explains creation" and in the failure of the signifiers, his voice, exposing the object at the core of the subject, opens on to the Real.[36]

Of course, the singer is "only performing." But so, too, is the hysteric. His attacks "are nothing else but phantasies translated into the motor sphere, projected on to motility and portrayed in pantomime"; for him, "the technical term 'acting out' takes on its literal meaning since he is acting outside himself."[37] Freud's interpretative technique here is similar to his approach to "dream-work" (indeed, dreams often figure in hysterical case histories), and in a similar way our singers might be thought to offer examples of "song-work."[38] In both cases, what is performed is conflictual—the staging of a lack, of ambivalence, of "multiple identifications"; paradoxically, it is a "desire for unsatisfaction" that is presented to our gaze, an insistence on failure through which "the subject 'gives body' to his deadlock."[39] Lacan's rereading of "Dora" clarifies the structure of identification and desire typically entailed in hysterical performances. Her ultimate object of desire, he argues, is not Herr K., as Freud initially suggests, but Frau K., her father's mistress; she situates her ego, in effect, with Herr K., identifies with him as her ego-ideal, and uses him to mediate her (illicit, same-sex) desire.[40] For the hysterical subject, Lacan explains, "his ego is in the third party by whose mediation the subject enjoys that object in which his question is embodied."[41] And, picking up what Freud had already spotted ("the entire structure of the hysteric, with his fundamental identification with the individual of the sex opposite to his own by which his own [hetero-]sex is questioned . . ."[42]), Lacan also exposes the homosexual element which typically arises. One can hardly help remarking that, like "Dora," all the singers I have discussed—Jolson, Presley, Lennon, stereotypical male rappers—have a "father-problem" (he is absent, dysfunctional or rejected); nor that there are grounds for identifying a homoerotic charge to their performances, complementing the "feminizing" musical trends that accompanied their work, identified earlier. But if these singers situate their ego with Mother, what is their object of desire? Although the homosexual implication is important, surely their loving but fraught negotiations with the vocal object point us toward the centrality of—the *phallus:* that ambivalent object, circulating narcissistically (do they want to have it or to be it?) between mother and pregendered infant.[43]

Needless to say, there is no reason to think that any of the singers I have discussed could be diagnosed as clinically hysterical. Yet, just as for Freud "normality" is always a bit neurotic, so the later Lacan, thinking through a general model of discourse, included in it an important role for the "discourse of the hysteric." In this discursive mode, represented thus:

$$\frac{\$}{a} \rightarrow \frac{S_1}{S_2}$$

the key part (the function of agency, top left) is played by the always-already split subject ($\$$), whose refusal of "normal" interpellations, and insistence on his transgressive desire, has as its consequence and condition whatever object (*objet petit a*) can function to cover over his self-constitutive lack. This structure, performed out symptomatically, is addressed to, is routed via an identification with, a Master-signifier (S_1), which in turn posits a new value-system (S_2). Mark Bracher's explication—"The hysterical structure is in force whenever a discourse is dominated by the speaker's symptom— that is his or her unique mode of experiencing *jouissance*"[44]—helpfully adds that the function of object *a* can be filled by a range of sexualized body-parts, by another subject (a baby for example) but also by gaze and voice (especially mother's). When mum's the word, we might add, it is the "vocal phallus" that is a key rhetorical figure—a specific case of a general condition whose ubiquity is well caught in Žižek's Hegelian gloss: "the 'figure of consciousness' stages ('figures') the concealed truth of a position [its unspoken surplus or object *a*]—in this sense, every 'figure of consciousness' implies a kind of hysterical theatre."[45] Without placing music in the consulting room, then; without blurring the differences between everyday gender performativity and that specific to musical representations, we can note the contiguities and overlaps of spheres; and if then the twentieth century as a whole starts to appear as hysterically overdetermined—psychoanalysis starts there in the 1890s, heterosexual norms slide and shift hysterically throughout the period, singing acts out symptoms of trauma, desire and impossibility, conditions of mass cultural consumption hystericize star/fan relations (a pattern followed in general politics, from fascism through "1968" (Che?) to Thatcher, Milosevich and Bin Laden)—perhaps this is pointing where our understanding of the history needs to go.

Flaming Desire

In the context of the trajectory I have been outlining, even genres associated with conventional gender politics may come to seem "suspect." In country music, for example, the apparently rigid heteronormative conventions are so strong as positively to invite camp parody (this is the "I'm a lumberjack" factor, to cite the Monty Python song), a pattern that lays the ground for k.d. lang's lesbian appropriation. But in lang's *Absolute Torch and Twang* album, her subject position is particularly complex: here is some form of female masculinity (lang was not yet publicly "out" but her sexuality was well known), applied to country (including covers of songs "belonging" to men), yet also performing torch songs (a genre traditionally associated with submissive, suffering femininity—including in the country lineage, in the work for instance of Patsy Cline, a strong influence on lang).[46] Her bluesy articulations come from torch song, but are smoothly integrated into a full range of country vocal conventions (growl, falsetto, catch in the throat) so that the overall impression, particularly in light of her powerful, gleaming timbres produced through a wide range of registers, is one of (phallic?) control; "torch" is mitigated by "twang" ("pullin' back the reins," she rides "tall in the saddle"). If the identification is with a maternal phallicism, what lost object does she cling to? Her lament is for childhood—"memories of children . . . buried . . . deep down inside" which, however, "won't be denied."[47] This position assumes a special force if we listen with a knowledge of traditions of hysterical male and submissive female singing. In that perspective, lang so to speak dehystericizes the schematic female (same sex) hysterical relation; in following the male hysteric's path, she *normalizes* it.

In which case, the transvestite, transgendering Antony—also covering a repertoire that can broadly be described as torch song, but from within performing traditions more obviously amenable to transgressive gesture (performance art, cabaret)—may be said to rehystericize it. Ranging through the registers from chesty countertenor to powerful falsetto, his fast rhythm vibrato sometimes tremulous (read: torch song), sometimes strong and edgy (read: soul; Nina Simone?), Antony's unpredictable surges of phrasing and dynamics, and often jerky, disjointed rhythms connect him back to Jolson, Presley and Lennon, but position him, too, in complex generic territory where torch and soul meet crooning (read: sensitive, even "effeminate" male). Many of the songs thematize childhood or sisterhood, and empathize with women. Striving, perhaps, for a phallic mother identification (most clearly in the soul-shout, "Fistful of Love"), this quest seems confused by body dysmorphia—a misfire between imagined body and its appearance (or "clothing"). Frequent references to birds and flight suggest a desire for the spirit to flee this body, to cast off its burden—the burden of the phallus perhaps (is he a *castrato*?[48]).

Compared to lang's twanging authority, Antony's melodies circle naggingly around themselves; his lyrics return obsessively to themes of hopelessness and death. Obsessional neurosis—the condition towards which classic torch song points—was considered by Freud to be a "dialect" of hysteria. The formative question flips: from sexual identity, hence procreation, to existence as such, hence death; "why is he here?," the subject asks, and "why is he going to disappear?," his rituals designed to ward off the threat of death. Indeed, the obsessive refuses the question of sexual difference: "The obsessional is precisely neither one [sex] nor the other—one may also say that he is both at once."[49] Yet, as the Freud of *Beyond the Pleasure Principle* insisted, life and death create each other. Perhaps it is to this "beyond" that torch song, at the end of the twentieth century and the beginning of the twenty-first, building on all the vocal transgressions of previous decades, has the power to point, offering possibilities of new economies of desire, fueled by multitudinous routes and identifications of love. Fire consumes, but also clears the ground and lights the way. A bonfire of vanities—those vanities that sustain patriarchal norms—may turn out, too, to be a bonfire of profanity: that obscene "Thou shalt not" which brought Law into existence in the first place. And if, then, the word returns to mum,[50] perhaps it will reveal its originary surplus, at the level of the drives, as that act of creation which men either stole or dared not face.

Notes

Thanks to Freya Jarman-Ivens and Ian Biddle for comments on an earlier draft of this chapter.

1. Simon Frith, quoted, http://www.timesonline.co.uk/article/0,,2-1769107,00. html.
2. Antony and the Johnsons, *I Am a Bird Now* (Rough Trade RTRADCD223), 2005.
3. Judith Halberstam, *Female Masculinity* (Durham, NC: Duke University Press, 1998).
4. For an example from what might appear the very heart of musical patriarchalism, heavy metal, see Robert Walser, *Running with the Devil: Power, Gender, and Madness in Heavy Metal Music* (Hanover, NH: University Press of New England, 1993), Chapter 4. As Walser observes, "Spectacles are problematic in the context of a patriarchal order that is invested in the stability of signs and that seeks to maintain women in the position of objects of the male gaze" (108).

    Halberstam argues that normative masculinity presents itself as "non-performative": it does not need performance, it tells us, because it is taken to be natural; thus in the very few places where such performance does reveal itself, the masquerade can turn out to be very fragile (*Female*, 234–235). She hardly mentions music, but in fact her discussion of female Elvis impersonators (257–259) supports my point since, as she explains, their technique—which is one of hyperbole—can only work by exposing through exaggeration the outrageously constructed nature of their source (e.g., the performativity of the "real" Elvis, seen as already an impersonation of itself).
5. This suggestion may seem outrageous; at the least, it risks dismissal as just another male appropriation. Yet any antiessentialist theory of gender must surely allow the possibility of such multiphase (de-)constructions. How far could they go? Could a woman reappropriate such a male appropriation? Of course (cf. my discussion of k. d. lang later).
6. For a clear summary of Lacan's rewriting of the Freudian Oedipus Complex, in which a "first time" (the "preoedipal triangle") is succeeded by second and third times marked by paternal "castration," first of the mother, then of the child, see Dylan Evans, *An Introductory Dictionary of Lacanian Pyschoanalysis* (London and New York: Routledge, 1996), 127–130. The idea that the voice might have a privileged role in the phallic function of the first time is implicit in many neo-Lacanian feminist accounts, but the speculation that this role might have a symbolic (that is, law-making) as well as imaginary dimension is most incisively put forward in Kaja Silverman, *The Acoustic Mirror: The Female Voice in Psychoanalysis and Cinema* (Bloomington, IN: Indiana University Press, 1988), 72–100. In effect, the status of the maternal-infantile voice-nexus as part-object (*objet petit a*) arises at this time out of its "substitution" (as it might seem subsequently) for what has yet to rear its ugly head.
7. *John Lennon/Plastic Ono Band,* EMI 7243 5 28740 2 6 (2000 [1970]).

8. Lennon's own commentary suggests, intriguingly, that the bells are meant to convey "the death knell of the mother/father, Freudian trip"; this is, then, an anti-Oedipus. (Lennon, quoted in Anthony Elliott, *The Mourning of John Lennon* [Berkeley, Los Angeles and London: University of California Press, 1999], 49. Elliott's interpretation of the song [49–53] is powerful.)

9. I discuss Nina Simone, including "Sinnerman" specifically, in the context of a theory of "phallic motherhood," in my *Voicing the Popular: On the Subjects of Popular Music* (London and New York: Routledge, 2006), 121-123.

10. *The Jazz Singer* (Warner PES 99321), 1988 [1927]. Jolson's 1928 audio recording of "My Mammy" (reissued on *Al Jolson: Great Original Performances 1926–1932* [CDS RPCD 300], 1992) is vocally even more extravagant than his film performance. W. T. Lhamon is characteristically brilliant on Jolson's performance style in *Raising Cain: Blackface Performance from Jim Crow to Hip Hop* (Cambridge, MA: Harvard University Press, 1998), 102–115. Stephen Banfield is good on his vocal technique in "Stage and Screen Entertainers in the Twentieth Century," in *The Cambridge Companion to Singing,* ed. John Potter (Cambridge: Cambridge University Press, 2000), 63–82.

11. "God" was included on the same album as "Mother" and "My Mummy's Dead"; "Imagine" followed closely afterwards, on the album *Imagine* (Parlophone 7243 5 24858 2 6), 2000 [1971].

12. According to jazz musician Danny Barker, "When you said 'Ma,' that means mother. 'Ma,' that means the tops. That's the boss, the shack bully of the house, Ma Rainey. She'd take charge." Quoted in Angela Y. Davis, *Blues Legacies and Black Feminism* (New York: Pantheon, 1998), 121. The "warrior energy" reference comes from singer Bernice Johnson Reagon, quoted in Brian Ward, *Just My Soul Responding: Rhythm and Blues, Black Consciousness and Race Relations* (London: UCL Press, 1998), 302. The lineage of such female black singers has continued to be productive, as may be heard in the work of, for example, Queen Latifah and Mary J. Blige.

    It is important to view the distorting myths of the "black matriarchy" through the lens of revisionist African-American scholarship, which has rescued its progressive political potential; Angela Davis, bell hooks, and Hortense Spillers are the key authors. I discuss their work, in the context of the "phallic mother" argument, in *Voicing the Popular,* Chapter 3.

    See also Judith Halberstam's chapter in this collection, on "Big Mama" Thornton.

13. For the nineteenth- and early-twentieth-century gentile mind, this emasculation was marked by the "perversion" of circumcision, while maternal control was confirmed by the matrilineal descent of Jewish racial identity.

14. Elsewhere I call this "boogification," the voice acting rhythmically as if it were a boogie-woogie pianist's right hand; see Richard Middleton, "All Shook Up? Innovation and Continuity in Elvis Presley's Vocal Style," in *Elvis: Images and Fancies,* ed. Jac Tharpe (London: W. H. Allen, 1983), 155–166.

15. Robert Fink, "Elvis Everywhere: Musicology and Popular Music Studies at the Twilight of the Canon," *American Music*, 16 (1998), 135–179 (169). In a further interesting connection, "Hound Dog"—along with many other rock 'n' roll songs—was composed by two Jewish writers, Jerry Lieber and Mike Stoller. As far as the Tin Pan Alley period is concerned, the importance of the African-American/Jewish alliance has often been noted; even at the time, Isaac Goldberg, in his 1930 book on Tin Pan Alley, had suggested that both groups shared "the sad, the hysterical psychology of the oppressed race," a comment whose terms will become intensely relevant to my argument later. Michael Billig, who quotes this comment (*Rock 'n' Roll Jews* [Nottingham: Five Leaves Publications, 2000], 77–78), has documented the continuation of the alliance in rock 'n' roll and rock music, where it has attracted less attention. Billig argues that Jews mediated black culture to WASPs, but the story he tells—that in this role they gradually retreated from the stage (Jolson, Eddie Cantor, Irving Berlin, Sophie Tucker, Fanny Brice, et al.) into song-writing and record production and then, by the 1960s, more or less disappeared from view—locates them as what Slavoj Žižek has termed a "vanishing mediator": they do their work then vanish from sight (see Žižek, *For They Know Not What They Do: Enjoyment as a Political Factor*, 2nd ed. [London: Verso, 2002], 182–197). Still, it would be worth asking whether Jews, as Billig argues, not only played a key role in "feminizing" rock 'n' roll (*Rock 'n' Roll Jews*, 90) but also contributed to African-American and thence rock singing an emotive, even histrionic approach, especially in ballads, that could even now be restored to critical view.

    On the blackface Elvis, see also Greil Marcus, *Mystery Train: Images of America in Rock 'n' Roll Music*, 4th ed. (London: Penguin, 1991), 152: "At the start, Elvis sounded black to those who heard him; when they called him the Hillbilly Cat, they meant the White Negro. Or as Elvis put it, years later: ' . . . made a record and when the record came out a lot of people liked it and you could hear folks around town saying, "Is he, is he?" and I'm going, "Am I, am I?"'"

16. It seems a pity that there is no etymological connection between "histrionic" (from Latin *histrio*, a stage-player) and "hysterical" (from Greek *hystera*, the womb); although we might note that the conditions of "histrionic paralysis" and "histrionic spasm" (muscular paralysis, or spasm of the face, respectively) were first named at exactly the same time (the late nineteenth century) as hysteria was being first defined as a neurosis by psychiatrists, including the young Freud. Had the two semantic territories intersected each other, perhaps unwittingly (the discursive unconscious at work)?

17. Quoted in Peter Guralnick, *Last Train to Memphis: The Rise of Elvis Presley* (London: Abacus, 1995), 374.

18. See, for example, Elaine Dundy, *Elvis and Gladys* (London: Pimlico, 1995).

19. This view of the feminized Elvis is far from new. The literature starts with Sue Wise's "Sexing Elvis," in *On Record: Rock, Pop and the Written Word*, ed. Simon Frith and Andrew Goodwin (London and New York: Routledge, 1990 [1984]), 390–398, and is expertly drawn on by Freya Jarman-Ivens in "Breaking Voices: Voice, Subjectivity and Fragmentation in Popular Music" (Ph.D. thesis, University of Newcastle, 2006), 226–244. However, this picture of Presley has not, I think, been located in the historical perspective I am attempting here.

It is ironic that joining the army, far from "making a man" of Presley, has been regarded by mainstream (i.e., masculinist) commentary as a key factor in his "emasculation"; afterwards, so it is argued, rebellious erotics gave way to middle-of-the-road crooning. So was Elvis at his "sexiest" when his "masculinity" was at its most ambiguous—when, one might even hazard, most incipiently *female?*

20. The original that Presley is covering was by Arthur "Big Boy" Crudup. The nomenclature of "big boys," while no doubt a response to the diminutive "boy" of white racist discourse, also may function as a challenge to that of "big mamas" (as well as being a variation on the "papas" who were not uncommon in earlier blues; Papa Charlie Jackson, for instance). The discourse of the family romance is perhaps at its most discursively complex in the field of African-American music.

21. Barbara Bradby and Brian Torode, "Pity Peggy Sue," *Popular Music*, 4 (1984): 183–205.

22. Ibid., 201, 202.

23. The "motherfucker" trope sits in a broader African-American tradition of ritual insult that has the opponent's mother as its central object and that finds its most typical form in the street game known as "The Dozens"; see William Labov, *Language in the Inner City: Studies in the Black English Vernacular* (Philadelphia: University of Pennsylvania Press, 1972), 306–353; Lawrence W. Levine, *Black Culture and Black Consciousness: Afro-American Folk Thought from Slavery to Freedom* (New York: Oxford University Press, 1977), 344–358. Levine doubts the force of Oedipal explanations, but I think he is reading too narrowly. Roger D. Abrahams is surely closer to the mark when, in situating the discourse of male, often apparently misogynist African-American ritual boasting in the context of historically contingent black family structure, he emphasizes the *ambivalence* inherent both in the motherfucker trope and in the typical relationship of young male to mother-figure (both actual and displaced) that the trope maps. (Roger D. Abrahams, *Deep Down in the Jungle: Negro Narrative Folklore from the Streets of Philadelphia,* 2nd ed. [Chicago: Aldine Publishing Company, 1970], 20–35.)

In rap the violence implicit in the term is rarely aimed explicitly at the mother herself, but Eminem's obsession with the subject of his allegedly abusive mother represents a rare moment when it is. In his song "Kill You," he fantasizes raping her.

24. Rap's typical grouping into posses, crews, clans, mobs, and tribes immediately suggests the dynamics of dysfunctional family romance—or perhaps recalls Freud's mythic figure (for such it surely is) of the parricidal "primal horde"; but in this case our murderous band of brothers find the Father has already disappeared, victim of a higher authority (the Man; the System), and the Mother—desired but feared—turns out not to offer what might have been hoped. See Sigmund Freud, *Totem and Taboo: Some Points of Agreement between the Mental Lives of Savages and Neurotics,* trans. James Strachey (London: Routledge and Kegan Paul, 1950).

25. For a critique of Kristeva's mother/child theory along the lines outlined here, see Silverman, *Acoustic,* 101–126. On sadism/masochism and the invocatory drive (with voice as its *objet petit a*), see Jacques Lacan, *The Four Fundamental Concepts of Psychoanalysis,* trans. Alan Sheridan (Harmondsworth: Penguin, 1979), 183–186. On sadism/masochism in rap, see Jarman-Ivens, "Breaking," 157–166.

26. Wu-Tang Clan, *Enter the Wu-Tang Clan (36 Chambers)* (BMG 74321203672), 1993.

27. Michel Chion, *The Voice in Cinema,* trans. Claudia Gorbman (New York: Columbia University Press, 1999), 61–62. Kaja Silverman's critique of this passage (*Acoustic,* 72–79) takes Chion to task, rightly I feel, for situating the "web" entirely in a mythical, quasi-uterine, symbolically impotent stage and transferring the baby's discursive helplessness on to the mother. The image can be rescued, however, if this web is seen as, among other things, an early materialization of the symbolic network itself.

28. Again Eminem, with his multiple personae, offers the most clearly worked-out example.

    "Spectacle" is a key trope in Russell A. Potter's *Spectacular Vernaculars: Hip-Hop and the Politics of Postmodernism* (New York: State University of New York Press, 1995). For Potter, this relates primarily to rap's place within, and resistance to, the "society of the spectacle" described by Guy Debord—where mass media signs become the most potent vehicle of commodification. Although rap is undoubtedly, and importantly, located in this place, I see its spectacular performance gestures (both live and recorded) as resonating more broadly: with the specular mechanisms of identity performance theorized by Lacan and Althusser, and, especially, with the specific African-American variant of such mechanisms evident in the extreme theatre (the "hysterical theatre," as I shall shortly want to call it) of blackface.

29. "Bring Da Ruckus," *Enter the Wu-Tang Clan,* track 1.

30. Mladen Dolar, "The Object Voice," in *Gaze and Voice as Love Objects,* ed. Renata Salecl and Slavoj Žižek (Durham, NC: Duke University Press, 1996), 7–31 (27); Lacan, in *Feminine Sexuality: Jacques Lacan and the École freudienne,* ed. Juliet Mitchell and Jacqueline Rose (London: Macmillan, 1982), 147 (my emphasis).

31. Jacques Lacan, *The Psychoses: The Seminar of Jacques Lacan, Book III 1955–1956,* ed. Jacques-Alain Miller, trans. Russell Grigg (London and New York: Routledge, 1993), 171.

32. For example, "at least *one* of the meanings of a [hysterical] symptom is the representation of a sexual phantasy." (Sigmund Freud, "Fragment of an Analysis of a Case of Hysteria," in *The Standard Edition of the Complete Psychological Works of Sigmund Freud,* vol. VII [London: Hogarth Press, 1953 (1905)], 3–122 [47].)

33. See Jacques Lacan, *Écrits: A Selection,* trans. Alan Sheridan (London: Tavistock Publications, 1977), 4–5.

34. See Freud, "Fragment," 101–103; Lacan, *Psychoses,* 168–171, 178–179. "Dora"'s symptoms include nausea, coughing, catarrh, genital discharge and loss of voice, and Freud links them, via processes of displacement, to a fantasy of fellatio. "Vocalimentary canal" is my term for the imaginary anatomy along which vocal energies—of ingestion and ejaculation, dissemination and invagination (to use Derridean terms)—might be felt to flow; see Middleton, *Voicing,* 93.

35. Lacan, *Psychoses,* 171.

36. Ibid., 179. Lacan, as he points out, is here following Freud in moving "beyond the pleasure principle" (179–180).

37. Sigmund Freud, "Some General Remarks on Hysterical Attacks," *The Standard Edition of the Complete Psychological Works of Sigmund Freud,* vol. IX (London: Hogarth Press, 1959 [1909]), 228–234 (229); Lacan, *Écrits,* 90. Freud's "pantomime" reminds us that *silence* (the hysteric's aphonia or muteness) can be seen as the extreme manifestation of the vocal subversion of language—object voice in its purest form.

38. The concept of "song-work," and the analogy with "dream-work," come from Barbara Bradby and Brian Torode, "Song-work: The Musical Inclusion, Exclusion and Representation of Women," unpublished conference paper, British Sociological Association, Manchester, 1982.

39. Freud, "General," 230; Žižek, *For,* 144, 142.

40. Lacan, *Psychoses,* 174–175.

41. Lacan, *Écrits,* 89–90.

42. Lacan, *Psychoses,* 249; Freud had argued that hysterical desire might be split bisexually: "Hysterical symptoms are the expression on the one hand of a masculine unconscious and on the other hand of a feminine one." ("Hysterical Phantasies and their Relation to Bisexuality," *The Standard Edition of the Complete Psychological Works of Sigmund Freud,* vol. IX [London: Hogarth Press, 1959 (1908)], 157–166 (165); and cf. "Fragment," 59–63, where Freud applies this argument to the case of "Dora," adding by the way that in his experience it affects male hysterics more than females.)

43. Why this (rather speculative) structure? Because of the dissymmetry of the Oedipal process to which Lacan, following Freud, persistently drew attention. Where the hysterical female, failing to pursue the "normal" course towards a maternal identification, will get "stuck" on father, or a father-substitute, the male, if his paternal identification is blocked or refused, can readily fall back on an earlier relation with mother. Of course, this assumes—wrongly, I suggest—that the dissymmetry is fixed. If the Oedipal process can be reconfigured, the way would be open for the female hysteric to follow the male path (Silverman, in *Acoustic,* 120–125, argues something similar). Is this part of what is at stake for female masculinity?

44. Mark Bracher, "On the Psychological and Social Functions of Language: Lacan's Theory of the Four Discourses," in *Lacanian Theory of Discourse: Subject, Structure, and Society,* ed. Mark Bracher, Marshall W. Alcorn Jr., Ronald J. Corthell, and François Massardier-Kenney (New York: New York University Press, 1994), 107–128 (122, 114). If hysteria qua clinical condition stands in a metonymical relationship to the "discourse of the hysteric," we might be prompted to widen the social net of hysterical desire beyond the gender question on its own; recalling Elvis Presley's pregnant "Am I, am I?," for instance (note 15 above), we might wonder about the possibility of racial hysteria. Here, however, if "the symbolic is not merely organised by 'phallic power' but by a 'phallicism' that is centrally sustained by racial anxiety" (Judith Butler, *Bodies that Matter: On the Discursive Limits of "Sex"* [London and New York: Routledge, 1993], 184), a specific structure of overdetermination is clearly in play, one that casts light retrospectively on the Jewish/blackface strand of my argument.

45. Žižek, *For,* 143.

46. k.d. lang, *Absolute Torch and Twang* (Sire 7599–25877–2), 1989.

47. These two quotations are from "Pullin' Back the Reins" and "Nowhere to Stand," respectively.

48. Compare his sound to that of Alessandro Moreschi, on *The Last Castrato* (Opal CD 9823), 1987; or that of Dana International, a real castrate (we assume) rather than a virtual one, whom I discuss in *Voicing the Popular,* 131-134.

49. Lacan, *Psychoses,* 179, 249.

50. I intend to leave the exact implications of such a return to "mum's (the) word" hanging somewhat. The etymology is tantalizing, however. "Mum" is baby-talk of course (as we would expect here); but its source ("mamma") not only stems (allegedly) from a baby's "natural" first word but also means, lip-smackingly, "breast" (from Latin, *mamma*). At the same time, "mum" means "silence" too (Hush! Mum's the word)—we recall that the "silent cry" has been considered the purest manifestation of object voice—and from here we find that to "mumm" (to act in a mummer's play or dumb-show) carries us into the territories both of *mime* (including the "pantomime" of hysterical behavior, as Freud described it) and of *masquerade* (including blackface performance). We cannot rule out the possibility that the association of mother and silence marks a patriarchal act of, precisely, silencing; yet perhaps this rich nexus of, equally precisely, word-play also reveals a site of theatre where Law is *in the making,* where word is (also, still) act, and where such malleability opens the social formation of the Symbolic itself to change. Maybe song—"mum" in its final sense (mmm . . . : "an inarticulate sound with closing of the lips" [*OED*])—is the practice in which all these meanings can be stitched together.

6

"The Singsong of Undead Labor"

Gender Nostalgia and the Vocal Fantasy of Intimacy in the "New" Male Singer/Songwriter

IAN BIDDLE

We released Devendra's recordings because we'd never heard any-thing quite like him, ever. His voice—a quivering high-tension wire, sounded like it could have been recorded 70 years ago—these songs could have been sitting in someone's attic, left there since the 1930s.[1]

Introduction: Song, Labor, Masculinity

This chapter sets out some of the ways in which it might be possible to theorize the complex relationship among voice, nostalgia, and masculin-ity, by referencing the work of a number of Anglophone male, white, often straight singer/songwriters (José González, Damien Rice, Sufjan Stevens, Devendra Banhart) working over the last five years. The music of these artists is particularly interesting for its commitment in a highly technolo-gized and distributed world to place and presence. They all seem in some sense to want to represent in their work a kind of openness to vulnerabil-ity, a commitment to social and sexual intimacy, and a tendency to want to avoid the overt spectacularization of masculinity. Commitments such as these bring with them a set of quite complex questions about herme-neutic strategy, subject location, and gender politics, and this chapter is an attempt to work through these by paying particular attention to what

might be termed the "fantasy work" of contemporary popular song: what
demons does that song seek to exercise, what epistemological gaps does it
paper over?

In recent years, a tendency has emerged in some Anglophone popular musics to represent men (including straight men) as *vulnerable*. I
have always been fascinated with the various ways in which these artists
(straight singer/songwriters in particular) have sought to display their
putative vulnerability in public: what better exemplification of a becoming
susceptible to the operation of discourse, a ceding of power, of a handing
of hegemonic culture-work over to the sisters? This display—of a susceptibility to hurt, an openness to (cathartic?) suffering—now so commonplace
in the thematics of the music of bands like REM, Coldplay, and of straight
singer/songwriters like those mentioned earlier, is also about a recasting of
gender norms: the question that is perhaps most difficult to answer here is
the extent to which this new discourse of masculinity might constitute a
radicalizing or a conservative move.

One way to understand this posited discourse is to try to embed the
discursive gestures of these musics in the broader cultural and material
processes at work in the construction, projection, performance, and critique of contemporary masculinities, as a way of testing the flow of cultural materials between media, across gender spaces. Perhaps *the* place
where these processes have been staged, worked through, and contested
with most intensity is the workplace: as we shall see, recent transformations of the workplace (the turn from manufacturing to service industries)
has brought with it a range of challenges to "traditional" (straight, white)
masculine roles that have generated a new symbolic in which masculinity
and labor are more detached from each other than in the so-called guild
(artisan or pre- and early modern) and Fordist (modernist, industrial)
models of labor and production.

In Western popular musics, there are in play a whole range of images of
men and masculine labor that parallel, aestheticize, or otherwise embed,
a range of both socially sanctioned and/or prohibited masculinities. One
useful exemplification is afforded by Bruce Springsteen's "Born in the
U.S.A.," the video which presents the singer adorned with the accoutrements of both Fordist and workshop male labor: machinery, automobiles,
oil, a casual muscularity, a set of gender codes paralleled in the throaty
strained articulations of his voice (a "throat voice"). In this work, then, the
musical materials and the imagery that attends them are presented in a
coherent semiotic scheme (committed vocal delivery, working-class attire,
rock aesthetic). Of course, the imagery of the album cover is available also
for a different reading in which the codes of gay subcultural identification can be surreptitiously recuperated here: certainly, the hanky (of the

gay "hanky codes") has been replaced by a cap, and yet the fixation on the back pocket and the perfectly curved male arse would seem to suggest that the potentiality of a queer reading has not been fully eschewed; the figure's casual muscularity and his white sleeveless T-shirt, drawing the gaze also to the hairy arms (traditional symbols of male power but also fetishes of masculinity in consumer culture for both straight and gay audiences) would also seem to support this counterhegemonic reading since it is precisely these modalities of presentation (metonymic parts-fixation) that have characterized the consumption of male bodies by gay subcultures in the West. As we shall see, it is the terms and operational opacity of this complexity in representations of masculinity (gay or straight, self-assured or vulnerable) in the post-Fordist era that is dealt with in the work of a number of male white artists from the late 90s. The nostalgia for Fordist imageries of masculinity is thus a nostalgia available to both straight and gay male audiences. What is striking even in this fairly straightforward example is the ambiguity of its ideological commitment: putting the "gay" reading aside for one moment, how are we supposed to understand Springsteen's "naive" working-class masculinity here? Should we read it as some kind of positive recuperation of working class masculinity, or is this imagery somehow nostalgic for masculine codes of labor that have already died? Are we to understand the aggressive articulation of the voice simply as that, as gender aggression, or might it represent something of the intensity of debates in Reagan's America about the right to work, the connection of masculinity to economic autonomy, the mythology of the frontier, venturism, and so on? Clearly, even when the question of its queer reading is put to one side, the relationship between imagery, musical materials, and other more explicit gender discourses here is quite complex and rather unstable: an apparently straightforward masculine imagery shows itself impermeable to a coherent political hermeneutics.

Recent modalities of labor (from the last 30 years or so) have been dealt with thoroughly by sociologists of work,[2] and most agree that these modalities seem to be somewhat less densely gendered than "traditional" forms of labor associated with men and hegemonic masculinity (in the manufacturing sector, skilled and unskilled heavy physical labor, labor that foregrounds the physical, competition, venturism). The "newer" forms, so we are led to believe, are more likely than their older counterparts to emphasize the need for good interpersonal skills, to foreground human micro-exchange and to require engagement in so-called emotional labor. Rebecca J. Erickson and Christian Ritter, for example, have drawn attention to the new visibility of the feminine in the Western workplace:

> Two fundamental and overlapping trends underlie twentieth-century changes in the American workplace: the rise in women's rates of

employment and the shift from an industrial economy rooted in the performance of physical labor to a postindustrial economy grounded in the skilled performance of emotional labor.[3]

The so-called Fordist projection of masculinity, which linked collective labor and fraternal working patterns with "being a man," and that, in turn, caused an inevitable decline in the value placed on skilled masculine work had to respond productively to the demands for a new model of working-class masculinities. This was a particularly acute problem since the decline of the older "workshop" or "guild" model of masculine labor— where autonomous work and "skill" helped define masculinity—in the face of the new technologies of the production line brought with it a consequent infantilization of masculine labor.[4] Strangely, it is precisely *this* model of masculinity (forged in the heat of new Fordist technologies at the beginning of the twentieth century) that feeds the imagery of postmodern (nostalgic) masculinity and that feeds the visual aesthetic that frames men as sexual objects (especially for gay men's, but also straight women's, consumption). It is intriguing, therefore, that, as the Fordist model of labor fades into a distant, ever more exotic, past, its masculine aesthetic, "detached" from its labor origins, seems ever more ubiquitous. Perhaps part of why this imagery has retained its symbolic power is because it represents a carefully managed "casuality" of masculinity—a performance of straight masculinity that must always be on its guard against slippage from the merely homosocial to the homosexual. Its casualness is thus a crucial part of the "naturalization" that mode of masculinity seeks to affect—in order to work, it must appear as nothing if not "easy." We might thus make an observation here—that there are certain modalities of masculine labor that have become "aestheticized" and, consequently, discourses about white Anglophone masculine "authenticity" have had to look outside traditionally male-held territories of work for the cultural materials to fill in their symbolic economy.

Singer/Writer: Song/Script

In a sense, then, the complex nature of what the "visibility" of men in academic discourse might mean is the core problematic here: the filling in of the masculine symbolic with "new" male images, as kind of a nostalgia for Fordist masculinities, but also from other places (images of men today are awash with references to street hustlers, urchins, skater boys, preppies, jocks, strong fathers, professional men, service workers, and so on) is also about placing men in new contexts where vulnerability can be represented. It seems as if, for men to become *gendered* (that is to become marked by the operation of discourse), they must now also entertain danger, an openness to hurt, for without entertaining that danger, the figure of masculinity operates without boundaries, as if it were always already the only position from which to wield discourse (a "no-gender").

In short, this regendering of men operates here significantly as a shrinking of the operative male cultural field: as Elaine Scarry has suggested, "those without power" will invariably have a "body made emphatic by being continually altered through various forms of creation, instruction and *wounding*" (my emphasis), and, furthermore, this body marks a territory that contracts one's sphere of existence, "down to the small circle of one's immediate presence."[5] For the male singer/songwriters I want to talk about in this chapter, the *limiting* or *enclosing* of their cultural field onto the body, intimate small spaces, is felt precisely as a *loss*. Another way of saying this (in a more overtly materialist manner, perhaps) is to note that the efficacy of the figure of masculine labor as a "filling in" of the masculine symbolic economy is now radically curtailed and men have to work harder to find the cultural materials that adequately represent their gender. The emphasis on a new kind of intimacy or, at least, a turn to what in German would be rendered (without much embarrassment) as a *neue Innerlichkeit*[6] in recent male singer/songwriters might thus be understood as an analogue of this curtailment of the cultural sphere.

The title "singer/songwriter" suggests that there is, for this idiom, in this very naming of itself, the marking out of a broken continuum between labor and authoriality: agency is inferred in two actions—in singing and in writing. The relationship between the two is also related closely to, but not strictly synonymous with, a division of the cultural field into the public and the private: the image of someone singing, at least in Western popular and vernacular musics, sometimes invokes the notion of a performance *in public*, often linked to "open" social spaces, spaces where humanity operates in the plural (although this is by no means ubiquitous since singing can also invoke a kind of private—domestic—introspection, often linked, as Lucy Green has shown, with the maternal voice[7]); the figure of someone *writing*, on the other hand, is more resolutely invocative of *private* activity, distanced in some way from the public "outside," even when that labor ideally results in a text destined for the public domain. What both actions share, however, is some sense of a close relationship to the materials, to the missing third term in the singing/writing binarism: *song*.

Song is pointedly to be both performed and "written," and, in a sense, it is, for the singer/SONG/writer, this central substantive that binds the two outer actions together, binding the public- and private-performative into each other. The broken continuum between public and private is "fixed" by his substantive: "song" works here as a suture that binds over the space between public and private fields. Devendra Banhart's "At the Hop",[8] for example, thematizes the need for intimacy at the very moment when a lover is leaving. The "Hop" of the title refers to Central Texas's Regional Public Transit System operated by Hill Country Transit District through offices in Killeen, Temple, and San Saba, Texas, and constitutes here the incursion of the public into the private. The pain of loss is worked through here over picked guitar accompaniment with an effective simple harmonic structure (I-IV-I-vi-IV-I); the melodic line hovers around the 5th and 6th degrees of the scale. Hence the semantic space of the song is delicately ranged between intense intimacy ("Wrap me in your marrow / Stuff me in your bones") and the public site of leaving and arriving, the "Hop" of the title. This kind of structuring generates the epistemological and aesthetic space in which the staging of intimacy flourishes—in the liminal space between putatively "authentic" subjectivities of the private and the "staged" or performed signification of that into the public space. This structuring also inevitably involves a certain amount of danger: expansion of the intimate into the public here is also that site at which the couple becomes vulnerable. Song works here then as a way of grounding a certain kind of *fantasy*: that there might after all be an articulable relationship between the inner and outer worlds, that the continuum of public and private is not, after all, broken.

So, singer/songwriters like Banhart who do not engage the explicitly political (although for many there is a strong sense of the personal-political at work in their materials) tend to examine the close-up, the small, the particular, and are often figured as "close by," near, even "in the same room" by those who write about them and enjoy them. This putative micro-expressivity is part of a larger vocality matrix centered on the dichotomous functionality of the small-yet-spectacular: the intimate becomes "spectacular" by virtue of its departure from more commonplace expansive realizations of spectacle in late capitalism; it draws attention to itself by virtue of its departure from those norms. This matrix, furthermore, works towards representing the process of cultural production as somehow immediate, free, infinitely open-ended and yet, paradoxically, carefully managed, honed in, kept within the small space of this new disciplined intimacy. In short, the "production" element in "cultural production" is effaced here; labor is written out of the performative moment and replaced by a free-floating immediacy.

Often, in response to this kind of music, critics have tended to embrace its putative intimacy as the primary mechanism of its *Affekt,* by stressing the pared-down and understated quality of the vocal production and the gentle rustling of the guitar, bass, piano, or other limited (usually "acoustic") means. In reviews of José González's first album *Veneer,*[9] for example, the pared-down means seem to occasion a bewildering array of super-charged images, as if compensating, perhaps, for the putative "absences" or lacks in his work. This publicity copy from Dog Day Press, promoters for his London tour in 2005, is a good example:

> With just his own dextrously picked classical guitar and a captivating, ineffably familiar voice, he ushers the listener into a hushed, spell-like intimacy; stealing the heart with aching, timeless melodies and filling the head with confessional, life-affirming and gently provoca-tive lyrical intrigues. Recorded with the minimum of fuss at home on basic equipment, "Crosses" seems to encapsulate José's eclectic influ-ences—flamenco, Joy Division, bossa nova . . . along with undeniable flourishes of John Martyn, Will Oldham, Tim Buckley and Arthur Russell's *World of Echo* (and even a hint of Paul Simon). Yet, José's achievement is to nod to these antecedents while crafting a sublimely emotional signature that is undeniably all his own—a unique and compelling new addition to the singer-songwriter firmament.[10]

See also this fragment from a review by David Peacock in *The Guardian* of a performance during that same tour:

> Floating in a stark, beatless vacuum, the nearest these songs get to percussive is the occasional soft, woody knocking of the ball of Gon-zalez's [*sic*] hand against his classical guitar; rhythm deriving princi-pally from the repetitions of prickly, spooked figures that draw on the sinuous metre and chromatic inflections of bossa nova and folk, free of the oppressive march of anything connected with rock. . . . That is Gonzalez's [*sic*] other talent: fractured missives from a place of numb reflection that are anything but numb. Memories of emotional cri-sis delivered in shards, like looking into a mirror reconstituted from fragments. In this sweltering room, the billowing of icy air.[11]

These observations seem to reference an element of *enchantment* in González's work, as "spooked," "spell-like," and as something akin to the uncanny, "prickly," "sinuous," "fractured," articulating "intrigues." In this supernatural "firmament," González seems to represent for both com-mentators *the* foundational fantasy of the male singer/songwriter: through small means, he can captivate, spook, mesmerize and beguile whilst pick-ing his way through the detritus of our own darkest inner desires. The hyperbole here, then, is not just a matter of simple rhetorical bluster but works rather in the manner of a cultural hysteria: Lacan, after Freud, for example, articulated the question of the hysteric as a question about his or her gender.[12] Often, overblown rhetorical flourishes draw attention to there being something out of place, something sitting outside a putative norm, even if the explicit intentions of that rhetoric are not to be taken at face value. In this case, it seems to me, if there is a desire, evident in all this hype about González, to present him as voicing a paradoxically spectacularized intimacy, then that desire must surely also find expression in a parallel desire to efface the process of spectacularization: the *raison d'être* of this intimacy-fantasy is that it seeks, like all fantasies, to *suture* an epistemological gap between, on the one hand, the singer/songwriter's commitment to a cogent expressive aesthetic and, on the other, his ensnarement in the "staging" of that expression. (This is an augmentation of the public/private continuum to a more general cultural problem: that of the relationship between "content" and its "expression.") Intimacy is staged here both as a materially specific sonic gesture (gentle vocal tones, the rustle and lilt of a softly picked guitar) and as articulating a certain kind of circumscribed social space (close, small, with little or no resonance) that stands as an ideal other to the incursion of the Real social/public that can never be accounted for or managed within this sonic space. In this sense, the sociocultural dimension is "articulated" (or at least "articulable") in the materials, in their claustrophobic woody dry tones, the strangely detached and yet persuasively "emotional" voice, its quiet unassuming eloquence.[13] As we shall see, this fantasy also works in such a way as to keep hidden the precarious predicament of contemporary constructions of masculinity.

Culture-Work and Labor

The artists I am dealing with here all seem to take the hermeneutic complexity of gender and ideology we recognized in Springsteen's "Born in the U.S.A." to another level. On first encounter, they would all seem to represent a challenge to, or diversion around, what has been termed the "classic" rock masculinity, so well accounted for by, amongst others, Robert Walser (represented here, perhaps, by Springsteen, but exemplified much more overtly and clearly in the 80s' metal scene, the 70s' later [anti-glam] prog rock scene, the 60s' countercultural music scenes).[14] In this sense, the initial response one might make to the work of these artists is to celebrate the extent to which they seem to be unseating the more overtly exhibitionist, apparently self-assured, phallocentrism of the (cock-)rock persona from previous decades.

Damien Rice's "Eskimo" from his album *O*,[15] for example, raises several interesting questions about the nature of male vulnerability: the "Eskimo" friend referenced in the track (a symptom, or figure, of the exotic, perhaps) works in this song as an ideal other, a figure of naivety, and, as with many exoticized others, a figure of infantilization. The simple harmonic structure of the chorus with its falling triadic melody (I-V-vi-IV) adds to this effect of naivety or infantile simplicity. This encounter between self and Ideal (naive) Other works as a prelude to a sudden expansion of the sonic frame: a classically trained singer repeats the chorus "I look to my Eskimo friend" over and over in the last third of the track, thus expanding the frame well beyond singer/SONG/writer micro-expressivity. The track thereby throws both the vocalization of the singer/songwriter and that "operatic" vocalization into question: the last third of the song draws on vocal codes which sit awkwardly within the frame as set up at the beginning. This unusual gesture points up the cultural incommensurateness of different vocalizations, especially in this kind of music. (One can compare this for example, with Freddy Mercury and Monserrat Caballé in "Barcelona" in which both vocalizations in some sense "match" or dovetail into each other.) The incommensurateness here makes it clear that this new vocality matrix is able to deal with expansive vocalization only rather clumsily or ironically. This music, is seems, must always be smallscale.

Musics like this, then, would seem to share a common concern for avoiding the *overt* display of hegemonic masculinity, or the "spectacular" at its most generalized, by concentrating on the staging of intimacy in their work, as if, to echo one recent review of José González, the singers could be imagined "sitting right on the end of your bed singing just for you"[16]; this is an idiom in which a putative vocal "naturalism" is carefully framed by a highly delicate and unobtrusive employment of recording technology and in which the masculinity-technology matrix is problematized, as if the machinic industrial masculinities of, for example, 80s rock, had once and for all been banished to the rubbish heap of history. González is particularly interesting in this regard: his music seems, perhaps more than any of the others, to want to efface technology altogether and to produce a sonic image of presence or immediacy, an "aura" of authenticity, so to speak, which allows for himself a patent susceptibility to emotion, a softness, even a weakness perhaps, that would seem to unsettle the normative constructions of straight masculinity.

Yet this putative inversion is also usefully understood, it seems to me, not simply as a critical moment but also as part of a process of *enchantment* (a term we have already encountered in hyperbolic reviews of González), a making "supernatural" or "mystical" of that which is constructed to quite specific ideological ends. Indeed, in the terms of the much trumpeted "crisis of masculinity," this music might also be understood not simply as articulating a new critical masculinity, but as a restaging of traditional forms of masculinity by seeming to be something else: this gender nostalgia, hinted at in the quotation that opens this chapter, is politically ambivalent but strikingly committed to images of vulnerability.[17] In the context of the detachment of masculinity from labor (the rupture of male identity formation from physical work), the enchantments enacted by the music of these artists might be understood, furthermore, as both a nostalgic recuperation of a masculinity "under siege" and yet also as an attempt to fashion spectacle out of that recuperation, whilst also refuting the traditional expansiveness of that spectacle. This is the double-edgedness of this new male expressivity: its apparent commitment, on the one hand, to an "authentic" expressive aesthetic and, on the other, its ensnarement in the "staging" of that expression.

Labor Fetish, Commodity Kink, Fantasy Work

Perhaps the most interesting feature of this new situation, then, is the sense in which it appears to recast traditionally held imaginations of agency and its connection to authorship, expressivity, and the so-called inner world of the artist: what is at work here, it seems to me, is a quite radical reworking of creative labor and, more specifically, its relationship with its commodity. A materialist analysis of this situation uncovers some of the ways in which this shift in the relationship between creative labor and its commodity can be identified as a symptom of a change in the relations of production: the shift also constitutes, that is, a recasting of the very nature of the relationship between what Marx termed "use value" (the value something has for its use—a horse shoe or a tool of some kind) and "exchange value" (the value given to it within an exchange economy, usually now in cash terms). In *Kapital,* Marx identifies the separation of these two values under capitalism (their abstraction out from each other) as a kind of commodity "fetishism."[18] The fetishism at work in the work of our singer/ songwriters is characteristically *hidden*: song works as a kind of mesmerism (a ritual mystification) of the structuring together of creative labor (which circulates rather in the manner of use value) and the closed object-oriented nature of the product of songcraft, the self-possessed universe of the song, its very "thing-ness." Hence, for a critical materialist, the work being undertaken here is a kind of fantasy work—song posits itself as in some sense complete, thus seeking to hide the radical *continuity* between creative labor (and all its synonyms—authenticity, expressivity, committedness, and so on) and artifice (performance, constructedness, pretense, staging). The structure of song works as an apocryphal "testament" to the "truth" of male expressivity here.

This enchantment enacted in the name of commodity fetishism has also been identified in a somewhat different context by Timothy W. Luke in a recent article on the work of Donna Haraway and human/machine interactions. Indeed, that process described by Marx in *Kapital* whereby a commodity becomes charged with a certain semantic power or with meanings and connotations that reach far beyond its material limits[19]—is characterized by Luke as the "singsong of undead labor."[20] The suggestive and fortuitous invocation of singing and of song here, and their proximity to labor that is "undead," is particularly useful, not just because the image is enticing (for it is undoubtedly that) but because its very recasting of the relationship between "expression" (for want of a less densely resonant word) or authorship in the broadest sense, and labor (no less resonant, but located at a very different register) is both timely and, I suggest, quite disturbing.[21] The nature of this recasting, as we have already seen, is describable in materialist terms as a kind of mesmerism in which the medium of song enacts a pretense at authenticity: song represents a kind of ritualized forgetting of the relations of production and an enchantment of that mundane reality. And yet, the crucial term "undead" here offers a suggestive supplement to this reading: song itself might also constitute that very place in our culture where the death of labor (its transformation into capital exchange value) is ritually refused.[22]

Yet there is another fantasy at work here, a radical consequence of that first fantasy of forgetting: this second fantasy at work in the *symbolic* of the singer/songwriter is a familiar one, focused on the ambiguous status of masculinity in a culture that both objectifies men as sexual objects[23] and yet that nonetheless seeks to hold on to men's status as primary operators of discourse (a predicament that is epistemologically unworkable and therefore inherently unstable). The expulsion of traditional (nostalgic, Fordist) articulations of masculine labor from the masculine microauthorial and their thoroughgoing aestheticization (such as those available in the pin-up) leaves a gap between the gender-giving territory of labor and white masculine expression that the singer/SONG/writer fantasy must also paper over: this has been the classically "Freudian" articulation of the structure of fantasy, to form a kind of suture over an epistemological gap and both fantasies hold true to this articulation here.

One of the complexities to note in this situation, and one that, as we shall see, José González articulates most eloquently, is that relating to the im/possibility of what might be termed cultural exemplification, that is, the need for public figures who can exemplify certain commonly held truths and which nonetheless are never fully able to represent those "truths." This complexity has a long history. In nineteenth-century bourgeois and proletarian literatures, opera, and popular song, for example, masculinity could be dealt with (shown, exemplified) in the public domain through the projection of masculine narrative agents who were able to function as a mediation between two mutually incompatible subject positions: on the one hand such characters could function as exemplars of bourgeois masculinity, as constituted as part of it, its outward signifier; on the other hand, such characters were also thereby necessarily constituted as being somehow *above* the mundane, *above* the petty collective. Recent years have seen the exposure of this kind of exemplification for what it is—a fantasy *that can no longer hold itself together.* In our so-called "post-ideological" world where we are supposed to be cynical about "heroes" such as these, we are often entreated to figure such agents as unhealthy ciphers of the submissive-authoritarian impulse, or to dismiss them as hopelessly flawed, a poor match for the hype: "unglücklich das Land, das Helden nötig hat" [unhappy the land in need of heroes] as that radical and deliciously capricious materialist Bertolt Brecht has his Galilei respond to Andrea's valorization of heroes in his 1938 drama *Das Leben des Galilei.*[24] Yet it is precisely in this mismatch, in this inadequacy of any empirically encountered "hero" to its ideal that the requirement for *fantasy* is generated. And for Jacques Lacan, perhaps the most Hegelian of Freudians, the place of the hero in contemporary discourse is far from exhaustible. Slavoj Žižek ventriloquizes Lacan usefully: "the hero is immoral yet ethical—that is to say he violates (or rather, suspends the validity of) existing explicit moral norms in the name of a higher ethics of life, historical Necessity, and so on."[25] This observation is based on a schematization Žižek makes of the relationship between four types of ethical agent—saint, hero, scoundrel, and superego, (Figure 6.1).[26]

The hero, then, is a paradoxical figure in this schema, one that is ethical and yet immoral (one who "suspends the validity" of moral norms). He is ranged in clear opposition to the superego, "an unethical moral Law, a Law in which an obscene enjoyment sticks to obedience to the moral norms (say, a severe teacher who torments his pupils for the sake of their own good, and is not ready to acknowledge his own sadistic investment in this torment)."[27] In short, the hero as articulated in this schema is both epistemologically unstable and exposed, vulnerable even. One could even say here that the hero's vulnerability is a quality *necessary* for the hero to exist at all. For a hero to emerge, he must have been placed in a certain amount of danger, be exposed to the possibility of his ruin: the hero's "labor," so to speak, is to toil under the burden of vulnerability again and again, to expose himself to such self-unraveling dangers. This adds an interesting dimension to the display of vulnerability in the work of male singer/songwriters: in order for the hegemonic fantasy of invulnerable masculinity to work, it must come under a certain kind of cultural pressure, be placed in danger. The fantasy of the hero as a figure of male hegemony, then, seeks to enable *precisely* this separation of labor from gender formation, and it is precisely here that we encounter something of the *longue durée* of masculinity in the Western imagination: masculinity as a set of culturally maintained codes has been consistently presented as if it were self-evident,

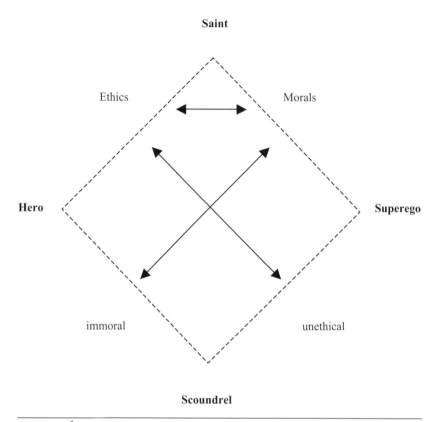

Figure 6.1 Žižek's four types of ethical agent.

autonomously generated, and yet it has relied nonetheless for images of industrial labor to ground its claims to the public space. In this, the putative vulnerability of the new white male singer/SONG/writer begins to look something like a micro-articulation of the same old ideological sleight of hand: feign autonomy by hiding away the material ground of masculinity, feign vulnerability by hiding away the power structures that underpin the operation of male hegemony.

One of the ways in which this sleight of hand has been nurtured over the Western *longue durée* is through a tendency to project discursively a series of epistemological mismatches as if they could be reimagined as *equivalences*. The shaking up of gender stereotyping in the Hollywood movie through such practices as inversion (where the woman plays a tough uncompromising autonomous "hero" whilst the man is placed in a situation in which he must learn to network, be nurturing, embrace social complexity) is a good example of this kind of equivalencing where the carnivalesque inversion is structured around the same logic that put the older power structures in place in the first place. One place to look for these non-subversive inversions is in the kinds of discursive dualisms that seem to have been inverted and which are common to male heterosexual modalities of expression in the singer/songwriter idiom. To this end, I want to turn now to an album that dramatizes precisely this equivalencing.

Veneer: Surface and Depth

Swedish-born José González's debut album *Veneer,* although it has met with considerable critical acclaim, has generated a range of discursively ambiguous responses, which point to something culturally specific about contemporary Western figurations of white masculinity and the im/possibility of white male vulnerability. Hailed variously as beautifully understated, beguiling, eloquent, this extraordinary album is radically pared down, apparently unsentimental, and yet in some sense nonetheless emotionally charged and committed to its small but effective expressive means. His is a music forged of distinctly economical means—voice, guitar, and very little else—and deals variously with the thematics of abstracted social interactions, images of loss and painful renewal, the detritus of failed relationships, missed opportunities for intimacy, darkness, loneliness and the need to need and to be needed. The album demands particularly "close-up" listening and his music deals, apparently through very subtle and understated means, with some of the core problematics of white male subjectivity, white male experience and white male sentiment structured around a number of core elements: dualism, inversion, putative gender morphing. These elements are both crucial to the semantic structure of this album and constitute the core problematic of this chapter. The album contains 11 tracks, each of which deals in various ways with images of covering, of surfaces and, conversely, of hiding. What is striking about the album is its sonoric homogeneity: all of the tracks present the voice in an almost identically mixed manner (somewhere back from the front of the mix, treated subtly with what sounds like reverb and filters) with the guitar always mixed to the front. In this sense, the album as a whole is quite uniform, perhaps too uniform: what distinguishes the tracks from each other is the various guitar articulations González employs, drawn variously from bossa nova, blue grass, country, rock, folk.

The first track, "Slow Moves" sets this tone. Simply constructed over a modal (Aeolian, with a strong pentatonic middleground) ostinato bass figure (oscillating between the tonic and the seventh degree of the mode) in a curtailed bossa nova rhythmic pattern (8 quavers articulated in groups of 3–3–2). The lyrics invoke a rather abstracted sense of disjointedness, playing in particular with the mismatch between representation and that which "is represented." Fragments such as "honesty and lies," "sly disguise," "schemes," "fractions," "mantras" all add to the sense that here is a track that deals with duality (or even duplicity). The dramatization of this binarism in this track points again to the core problematic of the male singer/song-writer idiom: how to efface the distinction between artifice and meaning.

Other tracks partake similarly of this structure: the second track, "Remain" deals with the "washing away" of surfaces by rain, and the leaving behind of some kind of putative "core" reality: "we'll remain. . . ." Again, the vulnerability of that core element is what, in the end, affirms its effectiveness and, paradoxically, its *invulnerability,* its permanence: "We will stand upright as we stand today." The track "Lovestain" also deals with the relationship between surface, permanence and the delible: the lyrics contrast a "lovestain" on the heart, which is indelible and a bloodstain "on the ground," which "comes off." The contrast between external and internal surfaces ("ground" and "heart") foregrounds again the tensions between external and internal realities, a commonplace trope in this kind of music: men suffer silently inside, to externalize that suffering is to question the very ontological claims to being masculine and so the feminine must be delicately invoked in order to hold masculinity together: both the "lovestain" and the "bloodstain" are attributed to an unknown someone invoked by the pronoun "you" in the lyrics of this track. S/he stands as an ideal Other, located in the text as the general addressee. It would make no sense, of course, to assume that the addressee here could be identified "simply" as female. What does make sense, however, is to understand the power relationships at work here as working in favor of a masculine voice in the song—the feminine is one of the many Others that could be poured into this empty object-space, without necessarily mapping this onto a male/female binarism: the crucial structure of this and many other songs on this album is around a highly abstracted encounter between the textual implied author figure in the songs and some unnamed Other. Other tracks on this album abound with similar structurings of encounter and they are also invariably framed by the dualisms false/true.

Sufjan Stevens's work has similarly embarked on this kind of discursivization of micro-social encounter by embracing ambiguity and abstraction. His work has a more overtly "spiritual" tone, but shares many features with the other artists we have already mentioned. His 2004 album *Seven Swans* deals with Christian topics but also with how to address oneself to any Other. The first track on the album "All the Trees of the Field Will Clap their Hands" can be read in its strictly evangelical meaning, that everything one does is for the praise of God, and that praise *is to be shared*: "Will I have arrived in time to share/ . . . /And I am joining all my thoughts to you / And I'm preparing every part for you." "Sharing" here nonetheless works also as a cipher for externalization and is another instance of the topos of spectacularization in an idiom that does not spectacularize. The track is pared down (voice and banjo only at the start) and makes similar claims to the "authenticity" of its sentiment: the voice, recorded in very similar tone to that of González, is a head voice and is deliberately untutored, simple, naive even and its close-mic-ing also ensures that the experience of listening to this is an intimate one. The voice also employs the usual throat articulation at the beginning of lines and some words as a further marker of the singer's intense commitment to the song's message.

The apparent naive simplicity of this work belies a sophisticated structuring through accumulation (a structure that works in marked difference to Damien Rice's "Eskimo" since it does not ironize), a structuring that is repeated over and over throughout the album. In this first track, for example, a simple ostinato pattern (on the banjo) is joined by a group of untutored female voices singing to "da" and eventually percussion and a very quiet bass guitar bottom out the sonic frame. The slow move from intimacy to a larger sonic frame brings to the production a sense of holding off, of discipline, the paradoxical effect of performing spontaneity we have already recognized in other artists' work. Stevens, like Banhart, has been linked to the "freak folk" or New Weird America movements and both reference American folk idioms which gives their work a territorialization missing in González or Rice. Nonetheless, as we have seen, all these artists share a concern for a certain disciplining of representation.

Conclusion: Ideology, Politics, and Male Fantasy

Masculinity in the *longue durée* has been anxious about display for a long time: for the early-nineteenth-century bourgeois, for example, overt display was linked to venality and femininity, and male hegemony has had to work hard to find ways of demonstrating the avowed "masculinity" of the public space without thereby falling foul to accusation of being "demonstrative" or "flamboyant."[28] The disciplining of display we encounter in these musics would seem to contribute to a continued fantasy formation: male vulnerability performed in this music rests on an ideological structure designed to effect some kind of mystification or enchantment of men's real stake in the continued marginalization of the feminine; what stands here for the "feminine" is not the articulation of a mode of expressivity attributable to women, but a disciplined figuration, an effect of masculine discourse which seems on the surface to construe male vulnerability as in some sense partaking of, crossing over into, what Luce Irigaray has termed "feminine culture," whilst, at a deeper more fundamental level, nonetheless shoring up men's claims to a priori ownership of public discourse.

I think that this point is crucial to my reading of these artists' work: any claims to a putative "critical" regendering that this music might make must be tested against the manner in which it deals with the feminine. If the feminine is to function as anything other than a ghostly cipher here, it must be given reign to challenge the very ground on which contemporary masculinity is built. It is crucial here, then, to distinguish between any explicit claims this music might be making (its "political" commitment, if you like) from the ideology work it undertakes. This distinction is quite difficult to maintain, but, put simply, it requires that not just the semantic frame but also the structural proclivities and the historicism of the music be tested thoroughly against both local and more generalizing gender discourses. These musics effect a spellbinding convergence of semantic strategies: the display of apparent intimacy, of an openness to vulnerability, the semantic disengagement of the material ground of masculine identity formation (the refusal of Fordist nostalgia), the enactment of a new nostalgia centered around the abstracted, disembodied feminine "you."

She is addressed, but is all but silenced: zombielike backing vocals, over-spectacularized ("artificial" overtrained) voice or crude anonymous cipher of a "vulnerability" (one's "feminine" side), she is always disciplined into the margins, always held in a tight discursive grip at the service of masculine authenticity. Thus, what seems like a music desperately seeking a post-Fordist masculinity, desperately keen to effect a radical reconfiguration of gender norms, nonetheless falls foul of a quite old and conservative gender ideology. Nostalgia for the kinds of abstracted feminine figurations that haunt romantic fiction is far from an intriguing coincidence, but a core marker of this music's commitment to a very old hegemony.

The thinning of the feminine down to a specter here is also a marker of the ideology at work that seeks to erase the material (contingent) grounds of gender formation. The "enchantments" we have already noted in this music are put in place by erasing altogether the fleshy from the discourse, by placing the voice of authenticity center stage and by allowing that voice to distract and mesmerize. This is the force of the enchantment that this music enacts: to cover over the gap between masculine economic authority (labor) and his symbolic authority; voice is employed as a suture. Lacan recognized in the voice a "partial object," the cause of desire, a forever-lost object that can never be fully recovered. Here, voice clings to some of that meaning, as a site of mourning, as cause of desire, but also as the site of a subjectivity in a constant state of becoming, of *agency-enacting*. The voice of the singer/songwriter idiom works hard to fixate the listener, and to represent the subject-as-presented as subject-as-present. This is a voice which, to use a term I have used elsewhere, is "sticky,"[29] and is particularly effective at ensnaring the listener.

To finish, I want to return to Timothy Luke's engagement of Marx's theory of commodity fetishism. What Luke has put his finger on, in the phrase "singsong of undead labor" it seems to me, is something of the devastating uncanniness we feel in recent representations and engagements of, or discoursing on, gender. In this sense, the nostalgia I have identified in the work of recent singer/songwriters can also be understood as something extraordinarily of the moment: the debilitating disengagement of gender from labor has left both radical and conservative theorists of gender alike with a problem; every invocation of gender seems always already crass, always already exhausted, worn out, ghostly. Without wanting to take away from my analysis of the ideology work of these recent artists, perhaps this spectral quality of gender is at the heart of these men's work. Whatever that truth of the matter, I am spellbound, and it disturbs me.

Notes

1. Michael Gira, "Devendra Banhart," *Young God Records,* http://www.young-godrecords.com/prodtype.asp?PT_ID=71 (2005).
2. The "classic" texts in this area include Daniel Bell, *Work and Its Discontents* (Boston: Beacon Press, 1956) and *The Coming of Post-Industrial Society* (New York: Basic Books, 1973). Other works include Harry Breverman's *Labour and Monopoly Capital* (New York: Monthly Review, 1974), and, of course, Karl Marx's *Kapital* (New York: International Publishers, 1967 [1887]), and Max Weber's *The Protestant Ethic and the Spirit of Capitalism* (New York: Scribner, 1958 [1904]). More recent studies include M. Castells's *The Rise of the Network Society* (Malden, MA: Blackwell, 1996) and his *The Power of Identity* (Malden, MA: Blackwell, 1997). See also: Charles W. Mueller, Munyae Mulinge and Jennifer Glass, "Interactional Processes and Gender Workplace Inequalities," *Social Psychology Quarterly* 65, no. 2 (June 2002): 163–185; Beverly H. Burris "Computerization of the Workplace," *Annual Review of Sociology* 24 (1998): 141–157.
3. Rebecca J. Erickson and Christian Ritter, "Emotional Labour, Burnout, and Inauthenticity: Does Gender Matter?" *Social Psychology Quarterly* 64, no. 2 (2001): 146–163 (146).
4. See a comment made by the Reverend S. S. Marquis, Director, Ford Sociology Department, 1915–1921: "Mr. Ford's business is the making of men, and he manufactures automobiles on the side to defray the expenses of his main business." Quoted in Wayne A. Lewchuk, "Men and Monotony: Fraternalism as a Managerial Strategy at the Ford Motor Company," *The Journal of Economic History* 53, no. 4 (December 1993): 824–856 (824).
5. Elaine Scarry, *The Body in Pain* (Oxford: Oxford University Press, 1985), 207.
6. Literally a "new interiority."
7. Lucy Green, *Music, Gender, Education* (Cambridge: Cambridge University Press, 1997), chap. 2.
8. *Niño Rojo* (Young God Records B0002NRRB0), 2004.

9. *Veneer* (Peacefrog PFG066CD), 2003.

10. Anonymous publicity copy from Dog Day Press, http://www.dogdaypress.com/index.php?page=news&offset=10.

11. David Peacock, "Review of Performance at Old Blue Last, London, 22 February 2005," *The Guardian* (February 25, 2005).

12. Jacques Lacan, *The Seminars. Book III. The Psychoses, 1955–56,* trans. Russell Grigg, with notes by Russell Grigg (London and New York: Routledge, 1993), 170–175.

13. Banhart's voice, for example, is strikingly redolent of that of English-born gay singer Antony Hegarty of Antony and the Johnsons, and uses a floating falsetto voice, with quite rapid vibrato, referred to by Michael Gira as a "quivering high-tension wire" (Gira, "Banhart"). The similarity of the two vocalities might also say something here about the use of "vulnerable" vocalizations in both heterosexual and homosexual musics: it is also worth noting that the singers have served as guest vocalists for each other and are both connected to the New Weird America movement.

14. Robert Walser, *Running With the Devil: Power, Gender, and Madness in Heavy Metal Music* (Hanover, NH: University Press of New England, 1993).

15. Anonymous review from the Web site of the U.S. public broadcasting service radio station PBS, http://www.pbsfm.org.au/Documents.asp?ID=1090&Title=Jose+Gonzalez+-+Veneer.

16. *O* (Vector Recordings 48507-2), 2003.

17. Suzanne R. Stewart has shown how the tendency in men to play as if giving up power, as if ceding their long-held grip on public discourse to others is a strategy that can also be read as a consolidation of power. Her suggestion that the rise of masochism, especially at the *fin de siècle* before this one, represented a strategy for holding on to male power under siege, is useful here. See Suzanne R. Stewart, *Sublime Surrender: Male Masochism at the* Fin-de-siècle (Ithaca, NY: Cornell University Press, 1998).

18. Karl Marx, *Capital: A Critique of Political Economy,* vol. 1, trans. Ben Fowkes (New York: Penguin, 1990), 163.

19. Marx, *Capital,* 170.

20. Timothy W. Luke "Cyborg Enchantments: Commodity Fetishism in Human/Machine Interactions," *Strategies: Journal of Theory, Culture and Politics* 13, no. 1 (May 2000): 39–62 (39).

21. I have suggested elsewhere some of the ways in which the recasting of this relationship might have consequences for our understanding of the cultural meanings of certain types of vocal production and, although I want to draw some of those consequences out in more detail here, I will concentrate my mode of analysis on how the relationship between white male authorship and labor is represented in the staging of intimacy enacted by González and others. See Ian Biddle, "Vox Electronica: Nostalgia, Irony and Cyborgian Vocalities in Kraftwerk's *Radioaktivität* and *Autobahn*," *Twentieth-Century Music* 1, no. 1 (2004): 81–100.

22. As Marx puts it, "Capital is dead labour that, vampire-like, only lives by sucking living labour, and lives the more, the more labour it sucks." *Capital,* 342.

23. A recent calendar of naked French rugby players, for example, shows men in a number of both homoerotic and hypermasculine poses, presented for their consumption by gay men and straight women and yet standing as some kind of exemplars. "Dieux du stade: les joueurs de rugby du stade français Paris: Calendrier 2005" photographed by Carter Smith. For more on the paradoxical status of the male pinup see Richard Dyer, "Don't Look Now: The Male Pin-up," *Screen* 23, no. 134 (1982): 61–73.

24. Bertolt Brecht, *Das Leben des Galilei* in *Ausgewählte Werke in sechs Bänden*, volume 2 (Frankfurt/M: Suhrkamp, 1997), 232.

25. Slavoj Žižek, *Metastases of Enjoyment: Six Essays on Woman and Causality* (London: Verso, 1994), 67.

26. Ibid. See the introduction to this volume for further reading of this diagram.

27. Ibid.

28. Judith Halberstam suggests that the cultural circulations of masculinity and "display" may, in a sense, be mutually exclusive: masculinity, she writes, has a tendency "to define itself as nonperformative." See Judith Halberstam, *Female Masculinity* (Durham, NC: Duke University Press, 1998), 236.

29. "The 'surface noise' on the voice works like a kind of grit in the voice that obliterates any possibility of an (Oedipal) identification with the voice of the father, but creates, in this uncanny monstrous hybrid of the organic and the electronic, the possibility of a new kind of identification, the kind of 'coupling' identified by Deleuze and Guattari in their devastating critique of Freudian psychoanalysis, *Anti-Oedipus: Capitalism and Schizophrenia*. This coupling is an expression of what might be termed the 'stickiness' of this voice, its alluring materiality (and mediality)." Biddle, "Vox," 97.

7

"A Walking Open Wound"

Emo Rock and the "Crisis" of Masculinity in America[1]

SARAH F. WILLIAMS

How could we ever really know or love each other as long as we kept playing those roles that kept us from knowing or being ourselves? Weren't men as well as women still locked in lovely isolation, alienation, no matter how many sexual acrobatics they put their bodies through? Weren't men dying too young, suppressing fears and tears and their own tenderness? It seemed to me that men weren't really the enemy—they were fellow victims, suffering from an outmoded masculine mystique that made them feel unnecessarily inadequate when there were no bears to kill.[2]

In the late 1990s and early 2000s, amid synth-pop- and boy band-saturated airwaves, a band from the suburban beach town of Boca Raton, Florida, began to make waves of their own—first through small crowds generated by Internet communities, and then reaching the masses splashed on the covers of major American music magazines and MTV. Although some would argue their musical style is a far cry from the bands originally saddled with this hardcore punk-derived moniker, Dashboard Confessional brought emo rock to the mainstream. As a musical style and genre, emo, or emotionally oriented rock, has gained credibility and wide acceptance in recent years due to the unparalleled popularity of bands such as Dashboard Confessional, The Get Up Kids, Saves the Day, Brand New, and Thursday as well as the publication of journalist Andy Greenwald's book

Nothing Feels Good: Punk Rock, Teenagers, and Emo.[3] Despite this recent publication and countless journalistic investigations into youth culture's attraction to these artists, there has yet to be an investigation into the actual musical characteristics of emo rock especially with respect to gender studies. Representations of gender stereotypes in popular music have dramatically come to the fore in academic scholarship during the last few years, which discusses everything from 80s New Wave to heavy metal and punk rock, yet little as current or curious as the emo phenomenon.[4] This study will examine the established codes of an extramusical idea such as masculinity as represented in emo rock.

In many ways, current emo rock embodies what journalists and sociologists have referred to as a so-called crisis of masculinity. Men, like women, have been imprisoned by cultural stereotypes not only in the way they reenact social gender codes but also in the subcultures, lyrics, images, and semiotics they choose to represent themselves as popular music artists. Definitions of manhood have shifted over the decades as our culture has moved from one of production, utility, and industry to one of consumption, ornament, and service.[5] This society of industry recognized the essence of masculinity to be stoicism, a backbreaking work ethic, a willingness to shoulder others' burdens, reliability, and unflinching resolve. Our current culture of consumption recognizes manhood, according to Susan Faludi, as "defined by appearance, by youth and attractiveness, by money and aggression, by posture and swagger and 'props,' by the curled lip and petulant sulk and flexed biceps."[6] Expressions of masculinity in popular music must work within these incredibly limited, culturally constructed scenarios as well. As a more contemporary and mainstream expression of underground American punk and hardcore music, emo rock attempts, awkwardly at times, to reconcile the long-established codes of masculinity—musical representations of aggression, pomp, stoicism, misogyny, and determination—with more multifaceted human expressions of heartache, weakness, longing, and loss. For instance, how do emo artists today musically portray the gamut of masculine emotions in an underground genre that has heretofore been characterized by pounding, violent guitar distortion, extreme dynamics, and gritty, hostile vocal timbres? Emo rock, as I will elucidate, is one articulation of the adjustments and redefinitions that masculinity must experience in the face of numerous social shifts from consumer culture to feminist backlash.[7] Perhaps these "crises" and conflicts seemingly arise due to rigid social definitions of gender roles and their inability to adapt to the changing cultural landscape. Perhaps, also, the current state of the male identity is, as sociologist David Morgan notes, not so much in an actual "crisis," but rather "widely disseminated talk about crisis."[8]

"Manhood under Siege": Debate about the "Crisis"

Writers and academics—from sociologist Barbara Ehrenreich to journalist Susan Faludi—have examined the effects of social change on the American masculine identity for decades. They have noted, again, the shifts in cultural values and the rise and subsequent backlash of the feminist movement as contributing factors to what Susan Faludi refers to as "American manhood under siege."[9] Faludi, Michael Kimmel, E. Anthony Rotundo, and others have observed the effects of cultural and economic change on cultural perceptions of manhood in America. Before the Second World War, men's contribution to society, and therefore their worth, was bound up in endeavors that exhibited "social usefulness." The prevailing definition of manhood was those who "carried out their duties to family and community were men to admire."[10] Our culture shifted toward one of celebrity, advertising, technology, consumption, and ornament, and saw the growth of the middle class, suburban sprawl, and service industries perceived as more "feminine" than industry. The movement of labor into office cubicles instead of the factory began to crush the putative individuality and initiative of the working-class male. The "hardness," as author David Riesman wrote about 1950s maleness, understood to be inherent in American masculinity was going "soft" as its spirit was dampened by the collective will of the corporation.[11] This whittling away at the masculine façade as economic provider continued through the 1990s and 2000s despite unemployment, corporate downsizing, and economic highs and lows. Faludi cautions against the viewing of the crisis of masculinity through the lens of these superficial social indicators and suggests, rather, that we consider the fact that:

> we have changed fundamentally from a society that produced a culture to a culture rooted in no real society at all. . . . Where we once lived in a society in which men in particular participated by being useful in public life, we now are surrounded by a culture that encourages people to play almost no functional public roles, only decorative or consumer ones.[12]

The social gender roles became murky—that is, men's roles in society as "breadwinners" and women's as "house makers" evolved beyond these caricature-like stereotypes. For generations of men whose identities were bound up in economy, labor, and wage, this represents a fairly major crisis of self and worth.[13] We can see, in many ways, the parallel between this realignment and renegotiation of the masculine identity in twenty-first-century American culture and the shift in musical aesthetics in hardcore punk and emo genres toward styles more multilayered and expressive.

Because concrete investigations into gender studies and culture began in earnest with the women's movement, feminism as a discipline has been the theoretical basis for the way in which studies of gender, and subsequently masculinities, have been developed. In that respect, theories of male identity and masculinity have been measured against and in relation to feminist methodologies. This influence is less about certain texts or scholarly publications as it is about, as David Morgan asserts, "the influence of a particular social and political movement which had certain consequences for the ways in which some men see their lives."[14] There have been several cultural responses to the feminist movement over the past few decades with direct respect to how men view their own sexuality and their identities within society. This should not be considered a unilateral direction of influence, however. Over time feminist critiques change and modify, as do masculinities, and the response of both men and women to feminism and vice versa evolve as our social environments change. Or, as Morgan again notes:

> "Wimp" can be a term of disapproval amongst feminists as well as amongst groups of men and it is not unknown for some feminists, certainly some women, to be heard saying that they prefer the old men to the new men on the grounds that at least one knew where one was with the old version. Men in their turn are responding to these responses from women and feminists.[15]

Sociologists have cited a "masculine mystique" as responsible for the stereotypes men were working against before, during, and after the feminist movement. The "mystique," or expectations of the male social role, dictated that men be ironclad, impenetrable, stoic breadwinners—roles just as unattainable and unrealistic as the feminine social roles. One publication in the early 1980s in New York attempted to enlighten its readers on these problematic social constraints, especially the masculine façade:

> The American Male—brave, courageous, and bold. . . . He's the provider. He's the bedrock of the American family. He learns to repress emotions like fear, insecurity, compassion which leads to tears, and a certain kind of sensitivity allowed to be felt by women only.[16]

The author goes on to make note of this restrictive definition of masculinity. This unattainable ideal led to what Barbara Ehrenreich describes as "psychic alienation" and the beginnings of the men's liberation movement that, in the popular press, depicted men as "stepping out of [their] armor" and viewing the male role as a "disposable exoskeleton" one sheds to reveal the true man within.[17]

Yet this "softening" of the image of American masculinity came with a price as questions arose as to exactly how malleable the male role truly was:

> The qualities now claimed for the authentic male self—sensitivity, emotional ability, a capacity for self-indulgence, even unpredictability—were still, and despite the feminist campaign to the contrary, recognizably "feminine." How much could a man transform himself, in the name of androgynous progress, without ceasing to be . . . "all male," or visibly heterosexual?[18]

Although the men's liberation movement of the 1970s and 1980s attempted to widen definitions of American masculinity, it was in many ways responsible for the ghettoization and stigmatization of homosexuality and the sharp divide between gay and straight behaviors. This strong identification with one "camp" or the other allowed straight men to adopt or display various traits or behaviors usually reserved for stereotypically "effeminate" lifestyles while remaining firmly entrenched in heterosexuality. So we see again that masculinity has nothing to do, in the end, with the expressions of certain traits. Expressions of sexuality depend more on "the maintenance of certain kinds of relationships, between men and women, and between men."[19] Thus the cultural segregation of the homosexual community and men's continued responses to feminism has contributed to the construction of American masculinity and men's perceptions of their own sexuality in relation to other social groups. The implications of the feminist movement and the general societal shifts in America can be represented, either consciously or unconsciously, in popular music art forms.

Since the inception of the Greek musical modes and their symbolic connections with coded expression, exactly how music communicates meaning has fascinated Western thinkers and composers. Scholars looked for new methodologies and vocabularies to approach popular music—a genre that relies more on aural compositions than written ones—when it became clear that popular and rock musics were eclipsing Western art music in social influence and popularity.[20] The lyrical content, instrumentation, fan base, history of the genre, and the very images of the performers are as important in the construction of meaning in music as are the sounds themselves. As a case in point, we have come to identify fast tempos, declamatory vocal styles, distorted guitars, and loud dynamics with an aggressive, oftentimes rage-filled sentiment in music—a sentiment usually upheld through secondary indicators such as the song lyrics and the constraints of the particular musical genres or subcultures of which the performance or musical ensemble is a part. Because most punk genres were historically male-dominated, as is the rock industry in general, and exhibited these particular musical codes, we consequently uphold these sonic tropes as symbolic of masculine pomp and prowess. Mediated by lyrics, images, performances, and marketing, the musical constructions of problematic concepts like sexuality can be subverted by various layers of representation.[21] Emo is a problematic genre of music in this respect—that is, it situates itself in the lineage of underground punk and hardcore genres, yet its artists strive to venture musically and lyrically beyond the aesthetic effects of nihilism, pessimism, and political frustration.

Emo's Beginnings

The musical representation of rage, anguish, and social defiance were heartily codified in the various punk movements that began in England in the late 1970s and spread west to the United States through New York to the opposite coast in Seattle. The musical roots of emo as a genre distinction lie in America's answer to the British punk invasion. Hardcore, as a genre categorization, has been in use since the mid-1980s when American youth began to rebel against what it saw as the inauthenticity of New Wave and recapture the DIY spirit and raw aggression of punk. Started in Washington, D.C., by bands like Rites of Spring, Jawbreaker, and Minor Threat, with contributions by Southern California bands such as Black Flag and Social Distortion, hardcore retained the aggressive tempos, declamatory vocal styles, and shocking on-stage behavior characteristic of English punk in the late 1970s; however, the lyrical content of hardcore began to shift from outward rage against authority to inner feelings of emotional pain, depression, and loneliness.[22] Seventies punk was, in many ways, about a loss of control in a world of corrupt politics and class wars, whereas hardcore struggles with a loss of emotional grounding and a breakdown of the stoic masculine veneer. It is a movement that strives to retain the musical signifiers of aggressive masculinity while redirecting the focus of the lyrics to more personal and private topics that had heretofore gone unexplored in punk idioms. However, because of its musical and performative allegiance to antiestablishment, antimainstream punk genres, hardcore was destined to remain underground.

Hardcore was, among other things, about disaffected suburban youth raging against the affluence and yuppie greed of the "Gimme Decade" of the 1980s. Unlike the repressed, working-class punk bands in Britain, hardcore appeared in the vast cookie-cutter expanse of Southern California and the sprawling metropolis of Reagan-era Washington, D.C., led by middle-class, complacent youth. Historically, punk scenes emerge out of economic and cultural repression and recession. Not coincidentally, at the apex of the hardcore movement in 1982 the United States was experiencing price increases, record unemployment, and economic recession.[23]

Hardcore as a vibrant scene was short-lived and, in many ways, was not transmittable to the mainstream because of its extreme aesthetic. Popular tastes in America seemed to favor the clean, electronic sounds of New Wave. In fact, in the years following the British punk movement and rise and fall of hardcore, American audiences saw the inception of MTV and the subsequent growth in the record industry due to the massive popularity of New Wave—a far cry from the raw and raucous sounds of punk upon which it was originally founded.[24]

Beyond the violent mosh pits and stage-diving crowd antics, hardcore also dealt with lyrical issues that did not find a ready audience in the 1980s in the midst of apparently superficial, "candy-coated" pop—that is, depression, identity crises, and other personal demons. For instance, the brawny, tattooed leader of the seminal hardcore band Black Flag, Henry Rollins, is featured on their 1981 record *Damaged* shattering a mirror with his bare fist. *Damaged* contains the requisite hardcore sound—breakneck tempos, rhythmic insistency, guitar distortion—and Rollins's signature growl. With songs about partying, beer, and women, at no point do we get a glimpse of an intimate timbre or the sensitive turn of a melodic phrase. Like all good hardcore, the musical emphasis is on speed and ferocity. However, one particularly revealing and vulnerable track, "Depression," begins with nebulous guitar feedback before launching into this typical hardcore punk sound. Rollins shouts the lyrics "Right here, all by myself / I ain't got no one else / the situation is bleeding me / there's no relief for a person like me." Yet the desperation in the lyrics is drowned out by the raw aggression of the music. Similarly, the catalogue of 1980s hardcore masters Minor Threat, in keeping with the hardcore aesthetic, does not contain one song over about two minutes and is monothematic in its overall soundscape. The band members throw themselves from the stage, destroy equipment, spit and scream static, monotone vocal lines, and write songs with tempos pushing 184 bpm. Yet the blatant self-consciousness of the lyrics begins to seep through in songs like "Little Friend." The lyrics describe a man on the edge: "No description / For what I feel / It's a non-emotion / It's something gray / Way down / Inside of me." After the third repetition of lead singer Ian McKaye's list of possible descriptors for his feelings—"anger," "fear," and "frustration," which is accompanied by a primal scream—we experience an uncharacteristic decrease in energy and tempo in a wash of guitar feedback. McKaye and his band mates convey a sense of emotional authenticity in their lyrics despite musical characteristics that would incite the most fervent slam dancing and stage diving.

Like any punk genre, technical proficiency and musical display is not essential in the construction of style. As hardcore chronicler Steven Blush notes, hardcore focused on "speed and anger" without any reference to the experimental or avant-garde.[25] Lacking the self-indulgent guitar solos of heavy metal or classic rock, tempos were as fast as possible and vocals were aggressive and abrasive, bordering on speech-song monotonal growls. Hardcore was very much about a preservation of this musical style wherein the communication of aggression, anguish, frustration, and even emotional vulnerability were relegated representation through breakneck tempos, harsh, gritty vocal timbres, and very little deviation from simple formal structures. It was a step forward, however, from the unemotional, asexual working-class British punk whose image of authenticity and energy hardcore artists strove to recreate. Late 1990s emo rock was inspired by the musical ferocity of hardcore and its struggle to reconcile more complex human emotions with a wider palate of musical signifiers.

Punk's Softer Side

Emo rock, and even some of the more mainstream hardcore artists, creates musical paradoxes that mimic the "masculine mystique" that is widely discussed in current academic and popular discourse. Musical expressions of sex, gender, and sexuality are contingent on the perpetuation of gender stereotypes and social roles. As we experience shifts in our culture and those social roles come under increasing scrutiny, these conflicts and changes can manifest themselves in artistic representations like popular music and art.[26] Through the mix of punk styles and the occasional use of musical signifiers normally reserved for more "sensitive" or "feminine" styles of music—acoustic guitars, stringed instruments, intimate vocal styles—emo musically presents a conflicted, but evolving, portrait of modern manhood. This portrait has, for many years, brewed beneath the surface of the aggressive veneer of punk rock genres; the more mainstream musical sensibilities of emo bring this punk-related genre, and its program of honest vulnerability, to the forefront. To achieve this feat, emo captures the changes in cultural attitudes about masculinity and the musical signifiers of emotional weakness—that is, such "undesirable" qualities like vulnerability, femininity, weakness—while attempting to retain the musical signifiers of aggression that are the bedrock of the punk/hardcore musical style. The struggles and seemingly contradictory combinations that characterized the 1980s underground subgenre of hardcore paved the way for a new, more multifaceted representation of masculinity in modern emo rock that captures, and perhaps even encourages, the current metamorphoses of social sex roles.

Emo, as an underground genre, was created from a merging of hardcore and indie rock after the last gasp of the grunge movement and before the Britneys and boy bands of the late 1990s. Andy Greenwald describes the inception of this genre as a sort of "kinder and gentler" punk: "The songs were smoother, and the chords were chunkier and corralled into sloppy melodies. The voices weren't accusing, they were yearning."[27] Emo still displayed the fast tempos, double time drumbeats, and declamatory vocals, but the style was not as homogenous as hardcore. Emo has become a broader genre that now encompasses acoustic rock, thrash, metal, rap, and country. Exploring the addition of instruments like acoustic guitars, pianos, even violins and cellos, evocative sonorities like major seventh chords, and deceptive terrace dynamics, emo began to expand the musical possibilities for punk and hard rock genres. The lyrical content and program as well have shifted beyond the anguish of hardcore and the "general pain of being an outsider to the specific hurt of a bad relationship."[28] It was the voice of disempowered, misunderstood teenagers across the country. In blunt, nonpoetic terms, the mission of the emo artists was to articulate the collective shortcomings, fears, and miseries of the masses through their music.

Emo is teen-centric. Regardless of the lead singer's age, the desired vocal timbre is a slightly prepubescent nasal quality with a diaphragmatic push that resembles the arrogant vocalizations of British punk. Emo music videos depict teen rites of passage such as proms, house parties gone wild, and anxiety over graduation. The album art for the band Saves the Day's *Through Being Cool* (1999) features the bored, disaffected, and slightly nervous artists as social outcasts, awkwardly lounging on a sagging futon while a high school house party rages in the background. Targeting music consumers in the midst of adolescence built emo a loyal, fanatic subcultural fan base.[29]

Jimmy Eat World, a certified platinum emo band from suburban Phoenix, is the perfect poster child for this burgeoning punk subgenre. The band members, regardless of their age, connect with the audience by casting themselves as equally awkward and gangly thirty-year-old men:

> Onstage [frontman Jim Adkins] is more craftsman than character, old and maybe gawkier than his fans but otherwise not that different from them. In "Pain," a lament delivered as if it were a call to arms, he sang as if he were trying to dissolve into the crowd of teenagers who were singing along.[30]

Musically, Jimmy Eat World displays a wider array of instrumentation, tempos, and structural forms than typical two-minute hardcore rants. In a song on their 1999 album *Clarity,* Adkins and fellow band members cater to their base with "Crush," a song about adolescent insecurity and regret. The lyrics read like a page from a high schooler's diary about a failed first goodnight kiss: "Hands around your waist / Take in restraint like a breath

/ It's your move / Settle for less again." Typical punk conventions such as repeated low guitar and bass eighth notes under short, detached vocal phrases accompany the verse sections, while the chorus and bridge sections are more melodic, eventually leading to a section in which the drums drop out and the vocals repeat "like a breath" amidst a distorted haze of feedback. This brief, but incredibly charged, pause occurs here leading to a more energized version of the chorus section, like the "restraint" of this transition section breaking free. This conceit—that is, the cathartic climax and release of this charged pause—is fairly common in modern emo songs. It could be considered indicative of signifiers of the climax-arousal song format that has historically signified masculine sexuality. However, given the lyrical content and other musical indicators such as instrumentation and complexity of form, it seems emo is beginning to challenge the rigid constraints of what it means to make music within a historically male-dominated subculture. Addressing the similar subject of unrequited love, The Get Up Kids' "Martyr Me" (2004) features the same type of subdued transition section, paring the instrumentation down to only vocals and acoustic guitar. A desperate "balcony scene-style" plea for what would presumably be a female savior from his life of ennui, the lead singer croons in almost affected youthful strains: "It's a good fight / Thrown in the towel / I'm just sinking water deep / But if all I have is defeat / [Chorus] Tonight if you're awake at all." After a build in momentum to a deceptive terrace dynamic—at the point we would expect the triumphant return of the chorus—we hear in fact a rather restrained section where we hear only the lead singer's voice accompanied by the earnest strum of an acoustic guitar. We are offered perhaps a window of vulnerability here—a point at which our troubadour would stand in a solitary spotlight and metamorphose the concert dynamic from one of raucous arena to intimate coffeehouse. Yet this window slams quickly after no more than a taste of this curious shift in aesthetic when the final restatement of the chorus returns at the original dynamic accompanied by the full electric instrumentation.

The darling of the emo movement, Dashboard Confessional lead singer Chris Carrabba, frequently strums an acoustic guitar with the same vehemence and aggression as any hard rocker plays an electric. A visual contraction, Carrabba's much-discussed good looks—with a perfectly coiffed 1950s-style James Dean, greaser haircut—are paired with intricate and elaborate tattoos up and down both arms, traditionally a social symbol for a punk or "deviant." Dashboard Confessional's fans are legendary in their fervent loyalty to the group and their almost cultlike behavior at live concerts. Obscuring Carrabba's own amplified vocals, scores of pathos-ridden teenagers scream the catalogue of lyrics, word for word, like a cathartic musical group therapy session. The band catapulted into the mainstream with their 2001 release, *The Places You Have Come to Fear the Most,* despite the fact that it was a stylistic departure for both the band and the genre itself. Although still containing songs that carried fairly active, punk-inspired drum beats and Carrabba's noticeably youthful tenor voice, the instrumentation was pared down to only, at times, Carrabba's voice and acoustic guitar. Historically the milieu of the sensitive, yet sexless, singer/songwriter, Carrabba appropriates this "feminine" instrument and refashions it for emo as a symbol of sincerity.[31] Relentless and rhythmic, Carrabba's guitar accompanies the lyrics to "Again I Go Unnoticed," the story of a stagnant relationship: "Another wasted night, / the television steals the conversation. / Exhale, another wasted breath, / again it goes unnoticed." Carrabba's voice still carries the punk/hardcore edgy grunt, but the symbolic sincerity of the acoustic guitar begs one to pay attention to the sentiments of vulnerability and pain in the lyrics. Appropriating the energy and rhythmic intensity of punk, Dashboard Confessional's subject matter and even the vocal timbre of its lead singer seems to betray its hardcore roots, a genre that has traditionally required *musical* aggression and machismo. Carrabba effortlessly shifts between a more guttural vocal style reserved for sexually aggressive and arrogant genres like punk and hard rock, and, with eyes closed and lips to microphone, a sweetly intimate falsetto croon.

On the more recent and amplified album *A Mark, A Mission, A Brand, A Scar,* Carrabba continues to vacillate between these aggressive, declamatory vocal styles and a more intimate falsetto on "Ghost of a Good Thing." Built on an accompaniment of acoustic guitar "power chords"—the root-fifth-octave voicing and preferred chord structure of heavy metal and hard rock—Carrabba warbles his way through the majority of the song in a delicate voice, so beautifully fragile one nervously waits for a prepubescent crack. In a brief return to the chorus, the "grain" of Carrabba's voice suddenly shifts, for the first and only time in the song, to a more nasal, declamatory vocal style accompanied by these assertive power chords. John Shepherd equates these nasal timbres to "reproducing physiologically the tension and experiential repression encountered as males engage with the public world," whereas the more thin, softer tones, produced in the head instead of the chest cavity, come to represent "male vulnerability" in hard rock genres.[32] Whether or not Carrabba or his fans are aware, these subtle vocal shifts project different characterizations and aid in the representation of not only this specific lead singer but also the set of characteristics that define emo as a genre. After this brief and jarring vocal episode, Carrabba returns to his softer style, later adding gentle acoustic guitar strums and arpeggios, tambourine, and even a Db major seventh chord—all signifiers of the more emotionally charged singer-songwriter style, *not* hardcore or hard rock.

Dashboard Confessional's title track to their 2001 acoustic album, "The Places You Have Come to Fear the Most," exhibits many of the aforementioned palate-broadening characteristics of the modern emo genre—including a charged pause for dramatic effect preceding the triumphant return of the chorus. However, this time, instead of reinforcing the musical conventions of punk and hard rock by launching back into a ragged vocal timbre after a softer transition section and charged, anxious pause, Chris Carrabba jumps immediately into the final chorus material one octave higher, at the edge of his vocal range. In a voice that resembles sobbing rather than screaming, Carrabba cries: "This is one time that you can't fake it hard enough to please everyone, or anyone at all." In perhaps the most revealing moment in emo rock, audible gasping cries punctuate these lyrics and mimic the hysteria of weeping as Carrabba struggles for air while ferociously strumming his acoustic guitar. Although the lyrical content here does not deal with unrequited love or the pain of a breakup, Carrabba pens a sentiment similar to that of the hardcore bands that inspired his music-making—that is, the frustration with inauthenticity and the tribulations of living a "genuine" existence. Appropriating the acoustic guitar as a symbol of sincerity and honest poetics, Dashboard Confessional, and other emo bands, attempt to musically depict masculinity and the genre of emo as multifaceted. The semiotics of emotional pain, frustration, anger, love, arrogant masculinity, and aggression are sometimes seamlessly united and, at the same time, jarringly juxtaposed.

Conclusion

The so-called crisis of modern masculinity in America manifests itself in numerous ways. From changing attitudes toward male and female roles in the workplace and home to the types of instruments that are appropriate for use in certain popular music genres, these social and artistic shifts are always tenuous and self-conscious at the outset. Many emo bands and fans resent, subconsciously perhaps, the genre label itself because of the gender implications it implies. Riley Breckenridge of the emo band Thrice explains that "people run from the emo tag because being emotional entails being sensitive and crying and stuff like that. Most sixteen year olds or eighteen year olds don't want to admit that they ever cry or that they ever are sensitive."[33] Yet these artists seem to be caught between expressing a kind of populist sentiment—that is, most teenagers in America, including males, can relate to being dumped, feeling invisible, or dealing with bullies—and representing the firmly entrenched ideas of what it means to make male-centered rock music. Emo rock and hardcore first reinterpreted these signifiers of male sexual aggression—pounding, repetitive guitar chords, declamatory vocal styles—as representative of emotional pain, adolescent angst, and the frustration of a world bent on misunderstanding its non-conformist youth. The relentless strumming of the electric guitar coupled with driving drumbeats is straying from its original indicators of sexual frustration and aggressive, violent masculinity depicted by punk genres. Rather, the expansion of musical ideas, lyrics, and instrumentation are slowly becoming acceptable as an indicator of emotional turmoil, insecurities, vulnerability, and other emotions beyond one-dimensional stereotypes of men's experiences. By slowing down and addressing the changing emotional landscape of American men, emo has connected with its fan base in a way hardcore and punk artists were unable to accomplish. Fans of this more introspective version of hardcore still require the energy, authenticity, and volume that is expected of any subgenre of punk; however, now that the sonic landscape has grown to represent more faithfully the sentiments of the lyrics, emo bands are finding that their fans have stopped stage diving, and started listening.

Notes

1. Versions of this paper were presented at the International Association for the Study of Popular Music in Charlottesville, VA, in October 2004 and the Hawaii International Conference on Arts and Humanities in Honolulu, HI, in January 2006. I am grateful for many conversations on masculinity and rock music, emo in particular, with Dr. Jennifer Walshe, Dr. Jean Little-john, John Williams, Prof. Scott Lipscomb, and Joe Cannon whose insights and encouragement inspired this paper. I am also grateful for the comments and suggestions of those at IASPM, specifically Griffin Woodworth, Daniel Party, and Prof. Richard Peterson.
2. Betty Friedan, *The Feminine Mystique* (New York: W. W. Norton, 1963), 368.
3. Andy Greenwald, *Nothing Feels Good: Punk Rock, Teenagers, and Emo* (New York: St. Martin's Griffin, 2003).
4. See, for example, Simon Reynolds and Joy Press, *The Sex Revolts: Gender, Rebellion and Rock 'n' Roll* (Cambridge, MA: Harvard University Press, 1995); Lucy O'Brien, *Annie Lennox: Sweet Dreams are Made of This* (New York: St. Martin's Press, 1993), 77–79; Robert Walser, "Prince as Queer Post-structuralist," *Popular Music and Society* 18, no. 2 (1994): 79–90, and *Running With the Devil: Power, Gender and Madness in Heavy Metal Music* (Hanover, NH: University Press of New England, 1993); Robert Walser and Susan McClary, "Start Making Sense! Musicology Wrestles with Rock," in *On Record: Rock, Pop, and the Written Word*, ed. Simon Frith and Andrew Goodwin (London and New York: Routledge, 1990 [1988]), 277–300 (283). See also Simon Frith and Angela McRobbie, "Rock and Sexuality" in *On Record: Rock, Pop and the Written Word*, ed. Simon Frith and Andrew

Goodwin (London and New York: Routledge, 1990 [1978]), 371–389 (374); Sheila Whiteley, *Women and Popular Music: Sexuality, Identity and Subjectivity* (London and New York: Routledge, 2000), "Little Red Rooster v. The Honky Tonk Woman: Mick Jagger, Sexuality, Style and Image," in *Sexing the Groove*, ed. Sheila Whiteley (London and New York: Routledge, 1997), 67–99, and *The Space Between the Notes: Rock and the Counter-Culture* (London and New York: Routledge, 1992); Lisa Lewis, *Gender Politics and MTV* (Philadelphia: Temple University Press, 1990), 43–54, 129–151; Susan McClary, *Feminine Endings* (Minneapolis: University of Minnesota Press, 1991), 148–168; Mark Simpson, "Dragging it Up and Down: The Glamorized Male Body," in *Male Impersonators: Men Performing Masculinity*, ed. Mark Simpson (London and New York: Routledge, 1994), 177–196; Gareth Palmer, "Bruce Springsteen and Masculinity," in *Sexing the Groove*, ed. Sheila Whiteley (London and New York: Routledge, 1997), 100–117.

5. See also Ian Biddle's chapter in this volume, Chapter 6.
6. Susan Faludi, *Stiffed: The Betrayal of the American Man* (New York: Harper-Collins, 1999), 38.
7. This idea of a "crisis" of masculinity and male identity is discussed by M. S. Kimmel in "The Contemporary 'Crisis' of Masculinity in Historical Perspective," in *The Making of Masculinities*, ed. H. Brod (Boston: Allen & Unwin, 1987), 121–154, and in "Rethinking 'Masculinity': New Directions in Research," in *Changing Men: New Directions in Research on Men and Masculinity*, ed. M. S. Kimmel (Newbury Park, CA: Sage, 1987). See also P. Hodson, *Men: An Investigation into the Emotional Male* (London: BBC/Ariel Books, 1984). These texts receive further commentary in David H. J. Morgan, *Discovering Men* (London and New York: Routledge, 1992), 6–23. For more popular psychology ruminations on the subject, see Robert Bly, *Iron John: A Book About Men* (New York: Vintage, 1992); Warren Farrell, *The Myth of Male Power* (New York: Berkley Publishing Group, 2001).
8. Morgan, *Discovering*, 7.
9. Faludi, *Stiffed*, 6.
10. E. Anthony Rotundo, *American Manhood* (New York: Basic Books, 1993), 13. See also Herb Gilmore, *The Hazards of Being Male* (New York: Signet, 1987), x.
11. See David Riesman, *The Lonely Crowd* (New Haven: Yale University Press, 1950), 18–41. Riesman's study focuses more on the effects of conformity in American society and the rise in white-collar labor. See also Barbara Ehrenreich, *The Hearts of Men: The American Dream and the Flight from Commitment* (Garden City, NY: Anchor Press, 1983), 34–35 for a detailed discussion of this work.
12. Faludi, *Stiffed*, 34–35.
13. See Ehrenreich, *Hearts*, 11–41, 169–182 for a discussion of what she refers to as the "breadwinner ethic."
14. Morgan, *Discovering*, 7.
15. Ibid., 18.
16. Philip Rice, "On Being Male in America," *Voice* (Spring 1981): 1.
17. Ehrenreich, *Hearts*, 127.
18. Ibid., 128. For more on the early men's liberation movement, see also Roger Horrocks, *Masculinity in Crisis: Myths, Fantasies and Realities* (London: St.

Martin's Press, 1994), 89–91; Joseph H. Pleck, "The Male Sex Role: Definitions, Problems and Sources of Change," *Journal of Social Issues* 32 (1976): 155–164 (155); Jack Sawyer, "On Male Liberation," *Liberation* 15 (1970): 32–33 (32); Robert Brannon, "The Male Sex Role: Our Culture's Blueprint of Manhood, and What It's Done for Us Lately," in *The Forty-Nine Percent Majority,* ed. Deborah S. David and Robert Brannon (Reading, MA: Addison Wesley, 1976), 4–15.

19. Morgan, *Discovering,* 67.
20. See Walser and McClary, "Musicology," 277–292, for a discussion on musicology and its adaptations to include popular and rock music.
21. See Frith and McRobbie, "Rock," 371–373.
22. See Bernard Perusse, "Shouldn't All Music Be Emotional?," *The Gazette* (Montreal, Quebec), May 8, 2004, D1.
23. See Steven Blush, *American Hardcore: A Tribal History* (New York: Federal House, 2001), 29; Steven Taylor, *False Prophet: Field Notes from the Punk Underground* (Middletown, CT: Wesleyan University Press, 2003), 72. A similar situation occurred in England that spurred the British punk scene. See Jon Savage, *England's Dreaming: Anarchy, Sex Pistols, Punk Rock, and Beyond* (New York: St. Martin's Griffin, 1991), 108–110, for commentary on the social and economic conditions in England at the time punk surfaced in the late 1970s.
24. New Wave was, in many ways, an "art school" version of punk and hardcore youth sought a music that would reclaim the DIY authenticity and raw energy of punk without the cumbersome, intellectual baggage of New Wave. For more on the comparisons of New Wave to punk, see Dave Rimmer, *Like Punk Never Happened: Culture Club and the New Pop* (London: Faber & Faber, 1985), 7–23; David Szatmary, *A Time to Rock: A Social History of Rock and Roll* (New York: Schirmer Books, 1996), 236, 274–275; Legs McNeil and Gillian McCain, *Please Kill Me: The Uncensored Oral History of Punk* (New York: Grove Press, 1996), 405; Taylor, *False Prophet,* 71; Lawrence Grossberg, "Is There Rock after Punk?" in *On Record: Rock, Pop, and the Written Word,* ed. Simon Frith and Andrew Goodwin (London and New York: Routledge, 1990), 111–124; Simon Frith and Andrew Goodwin, "New Pop and its Aftermath," in *On Record: Rock, Pop and the Written Word,* ed. Simon Frith and Andrew Goodwin (London and New York: Routledge, 1990), 466–471; Blush, *American,* 12–14, 35–37.
25. Blush, *American,* 37.
26. See Blush, *American,* 35, for a commentary on hardcore as a male-dominated subgenre and its relationship to the beginnings of the Riot Grrrl feminist punk movement that began primarily in Olympia, Washington.
27. Greenwald, *Nothing,* 34.
28. Josh Tyrangiel, "Emotional Rescue," *Time* (May 27, 2002): 60. See also Alex Pappademas, "The Heartbreak Kid," *Spin* (October 2003): 66–69.
29. The particulars of emo's fan base are a topic beyond the scope of this current study. However, Andy Greenwald discusses the demographics and dynamics of emo fans at length in his book *Nothing Feels Good.* It is interesting to note that unlike punk and hardcore, there are nearly equal numbers of men and women at emo concerts and the participatory aspect of these live events—for example, singing the lyrics along with the band—are not specific to any one gender.

30. Kelefa Sanneh, "Are We Not Sensitive? We Are (Arena) Emo," *The New York Times,* April 16, 2005, 7. See also Aldin Vaziri, "Don't Say Emo to Jimmy Eat World," *The San Francisco Chronicle,* November 3, 2004, E2.
31. For commentary on the symbolic properties of rock instruments, specifically the guitar, see for example Steve Waksman, "Black Sound, Black Body: Jimi Hendrix, the Electric Guitar and the Meanings of Blackness," in *Instruments of Desire* (Cambridge, MA: Harvard University Press, 1999), 167–206; Mavis Bayton, "Women and the Electric Guitar," in *Sexing the Groove,* ed. Sheila Whiteley (London and New York: Routledge, 1997), 37–49.
32. John Shepherd, "Music and Male Hegemony," in *Music as Social Text* (Cambridge: Polity Press, 1991), 166.
33. Perusse, "Shouldn't," D1.

8

"Don't Cry, Daddy"

The Degeneration of Elvis Presley's Musical Masculinity[1]

FREYA JARMAN-IVENS

From his threateningly virile youth to his comparatively impotent crooning middle-age, Elvis Presley has come to represent a wide spectrum of
masculinities.[2] Although it is the Presley of early years that most obviously toyed with constructions of gender identity—his long, carefully
tended hair and eye makeup juxtaposed with an infectious bodily expression—the same incarnation is also that which has come to symbolize the
epitome of unbridled masculinity. The young Presley functions as a site
of both desire and identification, with each of these processes operating
along stereotypically gendered lines: Sue Wise writes, "Elvis's appeal is traditionally depicted as an appeal to young girls who, overwhelmed by his
animal magnetism, were able to lose their sexual inhibitions and, albeit
in the safety of a concert hall, 'respond' to being turned on by the male
sexual hero."[3] His male audience, on the other hand, "identified with him
and his supposed ability to 'lay girls' easily and without consequence."[4] So,
although young women are clearly intended to desire this Presley sexually
(although remaining subject to his sexual powers), young men are figured
as exalting him as a heroic representative of their own sexual potential,
and to desire only his capacity in this regard.

There is a crucial paradox at the heart of the objectified male, the kind
of male-on-display that Presley seemed to embody particularly through
his pre-army and Hollywood work. That paradox is also implicit in Laura

Mulvey's seminal formulation of the gendered structures of classic Hollywood cinema, in which the male viewer's identification with the male star is facilitated by the cinematic process, just as Presley's male audience is figured as identifying with him: Mulvey's article underlines the particular construction of *women* as "to-be-looked-at."[5] In classic Hollywood cinema, Mulvey postulates, it is women who are fetishized and put on display for the male gaze. The male body on display, positioned or positioning itself as "to-be-looked-at" is thus a particularly feminizing subject position in these terms. Arguably, as Richard Dyer suggests, the male body in action, deflecting the erotic gaze by "doing something"[6] may just about maintain the masculinized subject position in Mulvey's model: "A male movie star's glamorous characteristics are . . . not those of the erotic object of the gaze, but those of the more perfect, more complete, more powerful ideal ego."[7] Yet the singing and dancing that constitute Presley's "doing" are hardly traditional exemplars of masculine activity. Quite the contrary: each activity has a cultural history of association with the "feminine," and specifically with a negativized, sexually troublesome femininity.[8] Moreover, the theory here does not overcome the experience: Presley—particularly the censored body of the young Presley—is still highly charged as an eroticized object of desire. The male body on display is a curious thing, and Presley offered a particularly interesting example of this in different ways throughout his career. Furthermore, his physicality is often described in specifically feminizing terms, outlining his ability (conscious or otherwise) to cross boundaries of gender representation. In his youth, he is described as having been obsessively concerned with his appearance, as having a great fondness for stylish clothes, and his penchant for eyeshadow is also well documented.[9] In addition, it seems his hair was a particular site for an expression of vanity, a stereotypically feminine concern: "He was constantly fooling with his hair—combing it, mussing it up, training it, brushing the sides back."[10] And this long, constantly groomed hair was, it seems, tended to by a beautician, not a barber.[11] Thus, even this supposed epitome of rampant, uncontrollable virility already occupies a fluidly gendered position.

Yet these gendered paradoxes implicit from the start of Presley's career do not align easily with the story of his supposed "degeneration" into a comparatively ineffectual masculinity. A preamble to this putative degeneration can be sensed as early as his performances on *The Ed Sullivan Show*,[12] when his sexualized body was apparently forced into inhibition for public viewing, signified by an executive decision not to film the problematic pelvis. Similarly, when he appeared on *The Steve Allen Show*,[13] it was understood that the eponymous presenter would only accept Presley's presence if he "cleaned up his act,"[14] and so the singer appeared in a tuxedo to perform the comparatively unthreatening ballad "I Want You, I Need

You, I Love You." He followed "I Want You" with a performance of "Hound Dog" that was quite clearly intended to placate his critics: in June 1956, after his performance of the song on *The Milton Berle Show,* the *Daily News* had reported "an exhibition that was suggestive and vulgar, tinged with the kind of animalism that should be confined to dives and bordellos"[15]; on *Steve Allen,* a month later, his performance was far safer, as he sung the song to a live basset hound. Moments such as these are often described as stories of two characters: the uncontrollably physical Presley and the sexually conservative authorities who tried to tame him. With the early Presley figured as so inescapably virile, despite his potential for gender fluidity, it is the Presley of later years who has been most commonly described in terms of a neutered masculinity, the spirit of a wild stallion overmarketed, constrained and "castrated" by Tom Parker.[16] It is Parker who is cast as the great catalyst in this story, with the U.S. Army and the Hollywood star system as two of his henchmen. Taking on the role of Presley's manager in 1955, Parker quickly established an Elvis brand that was founded less upon the young man's physical expressivity and more on the effect he was capable of having on his (female) audience. The story tells of Presley's easily avoidable conscription to the army and the making of films much-criticized for being formulaic. The character that emerged from the U.S. military and the Hollywood studios, ready to make a musical "comeback" in 1968, is frequently configured as radically different from the young "untameable" Adonis who, ten years previously, had been billed as being happy to do his "national duty" for two years.[17] The army conscription in particular appears to be a turning point in the story of Presley's degenerating masculinity,[18] and Parker is blamed for the effects of Presley's service. Rogan Taylor writes:

> Indeed, fantastic though it sounds, it appears that Parker was the chief mover to instigate Elvis's disastrous call-up into the armed services in 1958. As John Lennon said, when he heard of Elvis's death, "Elvis died when he went into the army." It looks as if it was the Colonel who 'killed' him in this way, purely to further his manipulative intentions.[19]

Taylor goes on to accuse Parker of using the two years of Presley's absence from direct cultural activity to concoct "the perfect plan for translating Elvis the Pelvis into a watered-down combination of Dean Martin and Bing Crosby."[20] Richard Corliss sums up the transformation and sets Parker at the center of the story: "Parker's determination to slip Elvis into the old show-biz mainstream effectively neutered the emperor of sexual and musical threat."[21] What such comments demonstrate is the sense in which not only Presley's physicality but also his creativity and musicality are seen to have "degenerated" into a neutered form, and it is the musical elements of this story that form the focus of this chapter.

Musical Masculinity

Intertwining with the tale of Parker-the-great-castrator is a musical tale in which another henchman is cast: the record company RCA. In this layer of the story, the early Sun recordings (to 1955) are figured as culturally superior to the RCA catalogue, as Richard Middleton notes: "All too often commentators stress a change in 'sound' (for example, the 'primitive'—hence 'authentic'—acoustic of the Sun records giving way to the 'sophisticated'—hence 'manipulative'—methods of RCA, with their more elaborate use of amplification, vocal backing groups, strings)."[22] Thus, the musical differences between the Sun and RCA sessions can be situated in a wider story of corporate "castration," with Parker as the orchestrator: "most rock critics [see] Elvis's career as a progressive sell-out to the music industry, a transition from 'folk' authenticity . . . to a sophisticated professionalism . . . in which the dollars multiplied but musical values went by the board."[23] Middleton is careful to identify how particular vocal styles run more coherently through Presley's career than is usually allowed for, across the supposed divide between the Sun and RCA output, and the vocal characteristics of the middle-aged ballad-singing Presley are indeed perceptible in the mid-50s recordings. Moreover, this is not an impression that is only found with the benefit of hindsight: Marion Keisker, receptionist at Sun records when Presley came to make his very first recordings—two ballads—noted, "Good ballad singer. Hold."[24] However, the point from which Middleton starts clearly demonstrates the weight carried by the dominant interpretation, of an undesirable shift in musical sound and style heralded by the move to RCA that was facilitated (of course) by Parker.[25]

Although Presley continued to perform many of his early hits until the end of his career, the way in which he performed them changed significantly, and they offer good points of comparison. Robert Matthew-Walker sums up Presley's relationship in the 1970s with his early hits, by commenting on his performances in June 1977, in Rapid City, "one cannot escape the suspicion that some of the earlier rockers are put in—in very abbreviated form—for old times' sake; the performances are little more than sketches, with hectic, garbled words."[26] Even the earlier, much-exalted *Aloha From Hawaii* show (1973) hints at this perceived tokenism. A useful point of comparison may be the performance of "Hound Dog," first released in 1956. The song in its original manifestation is an excellent example of what Middleton has called "boogification,"[27] the disjointing rhythmic effects of Presley's early vocal style, with its falsetto interjections and disruption of normal lyrical scansion by way of strategic "-huh-"s in the middle of words. By comparison, the 1973 performance operates at an increased tempo that disallows such intricate vocal work. Combined with the fact that the later performance is reduced to a threefold repetition of the song's first verse, and consumes only forty-five seconds of the show, the result is a performance that points nostalgically to the original release while also elevating Presley's lyrical vocal style over his earlier almost scattish technique. With a reduced performance time courtesy of the increased tempo and loss of material, "Hound Dog" is not representative of the *Aloha* show's general musical modus operandi. Presley states early on in the show, "We're gonna try to do all the songs you wanna hear," but the statement is immediately followed by his rendition of the Beatles' "Something": the earlier hits such as "Hound Dog" are, as Matthew-Walker suggests, relegated to token skits.

Moreover, despite his continued performance of early hits in later shows and a certain continuity in vocal style, it cannot be denied that there occurred a generalized shift in the musical styles on which he focused. Many of his live performances throughout the 1970s foregrounded motivational ballads (such as "My Way," "American Trilogy," or "Danny Boy"), and songs that allowed him to showcase his powerful vibrato (such as "Spanish Eyes," "My Boy," "And I Love You So," or "Unchained Melody").[28] Yet, while the last years of Presley's life may epitomize what is thought to be his musically emasculated state, the change was of course a gradual one. The roots of the so-called degeneration can be traced back such that they align with another corporate system cast as Parker's accomplice—Hollywood—and this is another example of a broader discourse that prevails in (popular) music histories, one that pits the corporate machine against the "authentic" and "genuine" performer. Any underlying gendered connotations of this discursive binarism are arguably not inherent, but what emerges from an exploration of Presley as a case study is that the gendering does occur at some level, and while a simplistic figuration might be to suggest a masculinized domination by the corporation of the "weak" performer victim, what is also apparent is that the *effect* of that putative domination is precisely to de-masculinize the so-called victim artist. As such, while in a simplistic formulation we might articulate this relationship in terms of the "masculine corporation," the important part of the discourses here is that "corporate influence" has a result that is commonly figured as emasculated, certainly in the case of Presley.

Presley started his acting career prior to his military service, his first film being *Love Me Tender* (dir. Robert D. Webb, 1956). In the context of conservative fears about the excessive sensuality that the young Presley seemed to exude, even this first film enabled a certain containment of the perceived threat: "His first brush with Hollywood had surfaced the softer side of Elvis's personality. According to [*New Republic* critic Janet] Winn, 'in this movie Elvis demonstrates once and for all how downright unfair it is to call him a teenage menace.'"[29] Presley completed three other films prior to commencing his military service in 1958,[30] but it was his postmilitary period in which the majority of his films were produced. From 1960, on his release from the armed forces, to 1969 and the release of his last Hollywood movie *Change of Habit* (dir. Joe Connelly), many of Presley's recording sessions were given over to soundtrack recordings. From the description given by Robert Matthew-Walker, who describes each recording from Presley's career individually, a sense quickly comes across that much of the Hollywood material achieves some kind of "novelty value," dependent on the theme of the film for which they were being recorded, and further removing a sense of agency from Presley. Interspersed with songs for films, Presley also recorded collections of religious songs that—chronologically—loosely frame the "movie years": *His Hand in Mine*,[31] and *How Great Thou Art*.[32] Furthermore, leaving to one side "themed" film songs (such as "Flaming Star,"[33] "Guadalajara,"[34] or "Kismet"[35]), a number of Presley's single releases can be characterized as either "mannerist rock and roll" or "up-tempo ballads,"[36] examples of which include "Good Luck Charm,"[37] "She's Not You,"[38] and "Return To Sender."[39] Arguably, the direction in which Presley's music was headed was significantly removed from that which was about to become most popular. Rather than aligning musically with groups such as the Beatles—whose music has continued to be represented as "worthy" or "great" popular music—or with embryonic forms of prog and psychedelic rock, Presley's music throughout the sixties gradually tended more towards the "romantic lyricism"[40] so central to his later focus on ballad material, and any "boogification" present was on the whole more stylized than before. What this shift from his earlier rockabilly style enabled was the foregrounding of Presley's powerful baritone vibrato in his music—a voice that was always peeking through, or was used to less obvious extents—and it is this voice that is most associated with the supposedly less "masculine" music of the last years of his life.[41]

The problems of masculinity in songs from the post–army period are alluded to briefly by Robert Matthew-Walker, who expresses his concerns about Presley's fading musical masculinity in his comments on "Love Letters" (1966), a cover of a Ketty Lester song from 1962: he describes it as "a magnificent performance" but concludes that "it is difficult to accept this as a man's song."[42] Matthew-Walker offers no justification for this gendering of the song, although some presumptions could be made as to his reasoning. It can easily be argued, for instance, that the narrative of the song is outside of normative constructions of a male subject position. Similarly, Matthew-Walker uses the term "manly" to describe Presley's recording of "Indescribably Blue" in 1966, although again he offers no definition of or justification for this term. Could a more "manly" performance have "saved"

"Love Letters" from the gender mismatch he perceives? It seems that it did manage to save "In the Ghetto," in which, Matthew-Walker writes, "Presley's manly voice has both authority and tenderness."[43] Arguably, "In the Ghetto" could just as easily have been described instead as "mawkishly sentimental," the words used to describe "Don't Cry, Daddy,"[44] recorded at the same session in 1969, but somehow the "manliness" prevails. In the same recording session, Presley "reveals unsuspected depths in the lyrics of the Dean Martin hit 'Gentle on My Mind.' Presley is rugged as opposed to the bland sophistication of Martin."[45] The gendered codes at work here are easy enough to sense. Once again, "sophistication" is figured as a negative description, presumably at least partly on the basis that it reveals the influence of corporate systems through increased technological intervention and adornment, and having the effect of precluding the "rawness" of recordings such as Sun would release. Analogously, Matthew-Walker uses the authority of Sun to mark positively "Whole Lotta Shakin' Goin' On" (1970): "Sam Phillips would have approved," he writes.[46] A certain "tenderness" is allowed in the "manly" "In The Ghetto," but the presence of "authority" is also obviously important. This is arguably a "mature manliness," in which empathy and emotions are permitted, although sentimentality and unnecessary emotional wallowing are not. Similarly, a connection is drawn between expressive sexuality and the earlier recordings. Of "Power of My Love" (1969), Matthew-Walker writes: "Solid and raunchy, Presley's performance is irresistible: full of sly innuendoes and *double-entendres*. There are a few singers who can manage this, yet it stems from the Presley of 1954/1955."[47] Overall, it is clear to see a general conflation in perceptions of Presley's work between the early (Sun) recordings and a raw sensuality, and similarly between the later (RCA) recordings or live performances and over-sentimentality. At the same time, these distinctions are mapped onto a gender binary such that a perceived general deterioration of masculinity over the course of Presley's career is synonymous with a construction of a loss of musical value.

The Campness of the Aural Spectacle

One of the central conditions of the story of Presley's degenerating masculinity is the change of physical style over the course of his career. The terms in which his genderedness is described are strongly associated with his various physical formations. Images of Presley in the early stages of his career, as the handsome rebel youth in "cool" suits, are associated with the hypermasculine sexual threat that he was seen to pose to the conservative establishment, and the rock 'n' roll soundtrack that accompanied those images. Similarly, the ostentation of his sequined jumpsuits from the

1970s and the Vegas shows is linked with an increasingly bloated body and the comparatively "safe" music that he was performing more, especially in the final few years of his life. It is particularly these later images that have been adopted by Elvis impersonators in the years since his death, and the phenomenon of Elvis impersonation combines with the spectacle of the middle-aged Presley himself to allow a continued injection of camp into the sustained Idea-of-Elvis. Presley himself may not have embodied the same kind of camp performed by Larry Grayson, Kenneth Williams, or Mr. Humphries[48] but his multivalent brand of gender—that which was always present in the fluidity and performativity of gender in his earlier years—may well be what has allowed a camp element to be imported into subsequent recycled versions of his image, and which is now reimported into the Presley-original.

Susan Sontag has usefully theorized the notion of camp, writing that it "incarnates a victory of 'style' over 'content,'"[49] while Clement Greenberg describes the closely related kitsch as "ersatz culture," the art of "vicarious experience and fake sensations."[50] The spectacle offered by Presley himself, especially throughout the Vegas performances, undoubtedly deserves to be called "camp," and it is almost certainly no accident that it is the Presley of the 1970s that is most often appropriated for the kitsch phenomenon that is Elvis impersonation. From 1969, Presley's career was primarily devoted to live performances across the United States, with repeated two- and four-week bookings in Las Vegas. These shows were characterized by their extreme spectacularity. The jumpsuits that Presley had started wearing in 1970[51] became progressively more overstated in style with elaborately sequined decorations, and they frequently incorporated a silk-lined cape, reminding the knowing viewer of the poses of Liberace, another great icon of high camp.[52] His performances involved grand physical gestures derived from the martial arts he studied. Peter Guralnick describes the effect of Presley's shows by the end of 1971:

> [They had] taken on an overt grandiosity which was only accentuated by Elvis' hyperbolic readings of 'How Great Thou Art,' 'Bridge Over Troubled Water,' and 'The Impossible Dream.' His costumes, his jewelry, and the poses that he struck only added to the sense of iconography increasingly attendant upon his performance, consciously contributing to the impression that he was larger than life.[53]

What is quite clear about Presley's shows from the 1970s is that they enact precisely the "victory of 'style' over 'content'" that Susan Sontag cites as a significant feature of camp.[54] Indeed, this seems to have been a source of discontent among some of Presley's musicians, who "grumbled that there was nothing to follow the opening with, [and] that more time and effort had been put into the effects than the substance."[55] From all that has been said about the flamboyance and extravagant style of the shows, and with this complaint coming from the musicians, it might be inferred that the comment is pointing to a lack of specifically musical substance, when compared with an abundance of visual effect. Beyond the undeniable prevalence of the visual display of camp, though, it is also worth opening up the possibility that there may have been a kind of *musical* camp at work in Presley's later work in an attempt to uncover further explanations for the tale of deteriorating masculinity over the course of his career. The "opening" mentioned above is Strauss's *Also Sprach Zarathustra,* which became a standard show-opener for Presley from about 1971. The cosmically grandiose music was most famously utilized in a scene in *2001: A Space Odyssey* (dir. Stanley Kubrick, 1968), and this scene apparently inspired Presley to request its adaptation for his shows.[56] The same set of connotations undoubtedly underpins each usage: as Presley's music director Joe Guercio put it, "he didn't want to be just a guy walking out there, he wanted to be a god."[57] Peter Guralnick summarizes: "with the *2001* theme, he was."[58] The music of *Zarathustra* easily paints an image of hyperbolic grandiosity. Strauss's major brass chords move proudly upwards in perfect fourths and fifths, carving out an unquestionably confident octave. The brass is solidly grounded by pounding timpanis that further establish the tonal region, nearly to the point of arrogance. Finally, after just less than a minute of subtle oscillation between tonal stability and tension, the brass is joined by the rest of the orchestra in a glorious and extravagant crescendo to a gaudy mass of C major. Strauss's *Zarathustra* was augmented in Presley's show by a chorus of "aahs," and the overall effect is almost an aural equivalent of the sequins that adorned the jumpsuit on the man who, after this "warm-up," could then appear on stage to be received and adored by his audience.

This particular example of "musical camp," though, is loosely containable within the realm of the spectacular show, insofar as it is part of the theatricality of the visual event itself, rather than a musical object specifically "of" Presley, or one that is itself inherently camp. Yet certain songs do provide examples of aural camp at the heart of Presley's musical catalogue. One such example can be found in the *Aloha* performance of "Something." After the first line of the second verse, support singer Kathy Westmoreland soars into an "aah" that starts on a warbling D^6 and falls through B^5 and $F\sharp^5$ in crotchets, landing on F^5 on the first beat of the next line's bar. The harmonic shift to G^7 is in this way made to be utterly inescapable. The Beatles' original[59] features increasing amounts of preparation for repeatedly satisfying harmonic shifts, initially courtesy of McCartney's prominent bassline and later supported by a lush string section. In Presley's performance,

McCartney's leading bass-line is taken up by a combination of strings, piano, and bass, and the harmonic progression is somewhat less inevitable instrumentally. However, Westmoreland's distinctive voice and the line that she sings lend an edge of tension to the moment, which is relieved perfectly giving the utmost harmonic satisfaction. The constructed inevitability of the harmonic progression is not exactly camp *per se,* but there is something about Westmoreland's warble and the harmonic work her vocal line achieves that allows for a camp reading. There is, I sense, a distinct similarity between the timbre of her voice, perhaps more specifically her vibrato, and the stylized vocalities deployed in certain Disney film tracks[60] and classic Hollywood film songs.[61] This loose connotation allows two potentially camp elements to emerge on listening to Westmoreland sing in "Something." First, the association with film as another kind of large-scale display underlines the implication of grandeur already present in Presley's own show. And second, perhaps more significantly, there is a time gap between this performance (1973) and the classic films (animated or otherwise) which her voice may gesture towards (of the 1930s, 1940s, and 1950s). Sontag is quite explicit about what she understands to be the importance of nostalgia and retrospection in camp: " . . . so many of the objects prized by camp taste are old-fashioned, out-of-date, *démodé.* It's not a love of the old as such. It's simply that the process of aging or deterioration provides the necessary detachment. . . ."[62] Such a notion might suggest that, in the particular example of "Something," a camp space is opened up by the vocal allusion to these "*démodé*" cultural forms. Moreover, it also raises (and goes some way to answering) a question which I have not yet addressed: to what extent is my reading of the performance as camp based on the operations of the musical text in 1973, and to what extent does it reveal a retrospective injection of camp, from a twenty-first-century writing position? Certainly, there is an extent to which it is true that the thirty or so years' distance between me and *Aloha* is informing my reading of the music. Yet there is also a sense in which the performance in itself might have alluded to already outmoded cultural forms. Moreover, the point I am ultimately trying to make is that the figuration of Presley's later work as unconvincingly masculine is precisely one that has emerged in discourse, and one that therefore precisely has developed *over time.*

Musical camp arguably makes another appearance in "What Now My Love,"[63] also performed in *Aloha.* There is persistent compound triple-time rhythm (played mostly in Presley's performance on side-drum and piano)—very similar to the famous side-drum part that characterizes Ravel's *Bolero*—that propels "What Now" and gives it inescapable momentum. Again, this momentum in itself is not exactly "camp," but it is crucial to the effect of theatricality in the piece, and that theatricality in turn is central to the camp potential of the song overall. The edge is taken off this driving rhythm in parts of the *Aloha* performance with the introduction of other percussion, strings, and brass, which generally bring about a smoother effect, yet other elements still maintain the camp potential. Kathy Westmoreland's trademark warble leads a chorus of backing vocalists through harmonic changes that are made to feel as inevitable as they did in "Something." Once again, although the harmonic changes themselves have little to do with a "camp" effect, their inevitability becomes part of the aural spectacle being presented in the performance. Over the course of "What Now," dynamic changes and rhythmic devices are used in combination to construct carefully a sense of aural spectacle. The driving rhythmic motif, in $\frac{12}{8}$, works mostly by oscillating between triplet quavers and dotted crotchets:

$$\text{♩.♩♪♪♩.♩♪♪}^{64}$$

At the final iteration of the question "What now my love?," the performance works with the implicit potential for shifting rhythmic emphasis, and transforms what would normally be two groups of three quavers into three crotchets, after a short caesura:

$$\text{♩.♪♪♩♩.♪♪♩|♪♩♩♩.♩♩♩}$$

At the same moment, a sudden increase in volume and a shift to a completely homophonic texture herald a finale that enacts the glorious emotional pain of the narrator: "Now there is nothing / Only my last goodbye." These three crotchets, with Presley singing "What now my," backed by the force of the entire musical ensemble, thus encapsulate the latent camp of the song: at this moment, grandeur and personal anguish are fused into a flamboyant aural spectacle of suffering.

What such musically camp moments represent in the story of Presley's degenerating masculinity is a change in the nature of the spectacle. His earlier performances had been concerned with (or at least had been read as) the spectacle of masculinity, and it was the display of masculine excess that so disturbed contemporaneous conservative critics. These examples of musical camp, on the other hand, might more accurately be described as a "spectacle of the spectacle," and a specifically aural spectacle at that. They are the musical elements of a Great Show, and in this way demonstrate something of the influence of Tom Parker, ex-carnie[65] and creator of Great Shows such as *Aloha*. Thus, not only does their very campness suggest an "inferior" masculinity, but insofar as they imply Parker's influence they also form part of the story of Presley's "castration" by the "evil" Parker. It is also worth remembering here the potential for gender fluidity in the young Presley that was not quite recognized by his early critics. There is arguably intricately gendered work being undertaken over the course of his career and in the subsequent discourse. That is to say, whereas on the surface we might see Presley's work as part of a narrative in which he and his work are gradually emasculated from a starting point of heightened virility, it may be that the fluidity that was present in the young Presley's gender performances in some way allowed for the subsequent figurations of his later work as camp. As such, the "emasculation" is not only part of a story of "deteriorating masculinity," but also of a process of normalization: it is not only a question of "containing" the "threat" of "*hyper*-masculinity," but also that of "*antinormative*" masculinity.

Blackface, White Music, and Masculinity

The final part of the story of Presley's ostensibly vanishing virility that I wish to delve into has to do with the discursive networks woven between race and masculinity. In particular, I want to conclude by arguing that discourses of race provide a kind of ground bass to the contrapuntal stories of degenerating masculinity and deteriorating musical value. It is widely accepted that the young Presley was, by virtue of his habitat, subjected to large quantities of "black" musics, particularly blues.[66] It is also understood that Presley's early musical style was heavily influenced by "black" musics, and a common reading of his relationship with the racialized history of music is of him as an unblacked blackface performer, colonizing and appropriating black musics for personal gain.[67] As Eric Lott summarizes, "Presley's not-quite and yet not-white absorption of black style was inevitably indebted to a musical tradition of racial impersonation,"[68] by which he means the nineteenth-century tradition of blackface performances. Bill C. Malone offers a similar explanation: "Elvis's fusion of black and white music was merely the most recent phase in a process of interaction that . . . has been manifested in American professional entertainment since at least the appearance of the blackface minstrels after 1830."[69]

Yet a more complex set of musical and racial connections is formed over the course of Presley's career, and indeed Malone hints at this in the word "interaction." In the first instance, as Charles Wolfe observes, the gospel quartets that so inspired Presley, and in time formed a significant part of his backing vocals group—J. D. Sumner and the Stamps; the Imperials; and the Jordanaires—were from a particularly white musical tradition.[70] James Goff Jr. also argues that "southern gospel has remained predominantly a white phenomenon," and that this is distinct as a genre from "traditional 'black gospel.'"[71] Writing about Presley's musical life in the late

1940s, Peter Guralnick describes the influence of white gospel music on the young Presley:

> He became a regular at the All-Night Gospel Singings, which had started at Ellis Auditorium up the street and all through the South in the previous two or three years . . .—he rarely missed a show. Once a month Ellis was filled for what amounted to a marathon sing-off . . . among the top white gospel quartets of the day. He sat there mesmerized. . . . There was probably no type of music that he didn't love, but quartet music was the center of his musical universe.[72]

Of course, it is not as simple as the suggestion that white gospel music is utterly distinct from black gospel traditions, and it ought to be noted that (of course) white gospel owes much to the black history of the genre. Wolfe is quite specific about some of the stylistic influences that occurred in the middle of the twentieth century, writing that certain harmonic and melodic devices, as well as the melody/harmony structure of the quartets, were "appropriated" by white quartets, techniques that were "probably borrowed from popular black 'jubilee' groups."[73] Those groups, of course, have their own black cultural history that is commonly traced back to the "Negro spirituals" of the nineteenth century, which in turn were influenced by both African and white musical traditions, and so the white gospel quartets admired by Presley were part of a long history of cultural exchange. Nonetheless, the point of reference for Presley was the white expression of gospel music, as promoted by the likes of J. D. Sumner or the Imperials. Furthermore, Presley's capacity for the operatic in his vocal performances reveals the legacy of white "light-opera" tenors such as Mario Lanza—a singer to whom Presley himself had attributed influence on his singing style[74]—and Enrico Caruso. Despite the ways in which these white musical elements impact significantly on Presley's early musical output, the general understanding that is taken from his earlier work is that it evidences more clearly a black musical heritage, and that white influences were foregrounded later in his career. With that in mind, it might be suggested that there is described a trajectory of decreasing importance of black musical elements in Presley's work that intertwines with the story of masculinity that is told.

This, of course, is no accident. Racial discourses have important gendered operations within them, and gendered discourses have ways of being articulated through a prism of race. On the subject of eroticism in popular music, for instance, Richard Dyer explains: "Typically, black music was thought of by the white culture as being both more primitive and more 'authentically' erotic. Infusions of black music were always seen as (and often condemned as) sexual and physical."[75] These associations of course have a long cultural history, in which the black body has been fused in the cultural consciousness with "excessive" eroticism and increased libido; and this correlation stretches back most (in)famously to late nineteenth-century colonialist discourses,[76] and further, to the earlier nineteenth-century minstrelsy.[77] As bell hooks graphically summarizes, the black man is figured as "the embodiment of bestial, violent, penis-as-weapon hyper-masculine assertion."[78] If we start with the understanding that, in music and elsewhere, blackness is believed in some way to be synonymous with a sexual element, the analogous perspective ought also to be proposed. That is to say, if black musical elements suggest a space for—or in some way infuse music with—a concentrated sexual component, would musical "whiteness" conversely defuse or forestall this sexual threat, or in some way limit the sexual potential of the music?

Almost certainly, this gendered-racialized nexus is centrally operative in the story of Presley's degenerating masculinity. When Robert Matthew-Walker suggests a correlation between the influence of Sun records and a "masculine" (read: "good") quality to the music, what is also at stake is the black musical legacy that has long been considered central to that early catalogue. Furthermore, when Matthew-Walker writes of Dean Martin's "bland sophistication," it is significant that Martin is representative of a particularly "white" musical genre. The capacity for ballad singing Presley favored in later recordings and performances may have been always present under the surface, as Middleton describes. Yet in allowing it to come to the fore, Presley missed the change in popular music heralded by the Beatles and ended up existing musically more in the manner of Bing Crosby or Dean Martin, as Rogan Taylor argues: indeed, it is surely no coincidence that Presley recorded "Gentle on My Mind," previously recorded by Dean Martin,[79] or songs associated with cognate artists such as Frank Sinatra ("My Way"[80]), or Matt Monro ("Spanish Eyes"[81]). These artists and the music they epitomize have come to signify a particular brand of masculinity in popular music history. Of course, much may be said about the masculinity of Sinatra and other similar artists: the masculinity that they signify has a certain respectable roguishness to it, and it does not possess any obviously self-aware camp element to it, or any other factor that would in and of itself suggest an ineffectual or antinormative masculinity. John Gennari describes Sinatra as "setting the standard for stylish virility," both in his music and his image.[82] Nonetheless, when the gendered operations of Sinatra, Monro, et al. are compared with those of male artists from other more explicitly "masculine" genres, they fall short. Sinatra's vocal style was the next branch of the family tree of crooning, although he did seek "expressly to distinguish his singing style from [Bing] Crosby's relaxed crooning."[83] Arguably, Sinatra's "stylish virility" was a further move towards reassuring audiences of the normative masculinity of the genre's exponents. Crosby's own style was a step in the right direction here, as he in turn distinguished himself from classic crooners such as Rudy Vallee. Writing about the early days of crooning—the late 1920s and early 1930s—Allison McCracken writes, "The romantic, soothing sound of the male crooner represented popular music's furthest step yet away from dominant standards of white masculinity."[84] She goes on to note that Crosby represented a "more masculinized crooning" than that which Vallee had espoused, and that this was in part signified by a lower emphasis on his vibrato.[85] In short, a general (although not necessarily totally thoroughgoing) process of masculinization seems to have occurred over a few decades in this genre, such that the "vulnerable," "feminized" Vallee is superseded by the "masculine 'cool'"[86] of Crosby. The legacy of Crosby's crooning was, in turn, arguably realized by the likes of Sinatra and Martin, who further legitimized the music "by connecting it to traditional notions of white masculinity," as McCracken argues of Crosby.[87] At the same time, the music with which Sinatra and his colleagues are associated can be positioned as diametrically opposed to rock styles, which are—so the story goes—the musical manifestation of the essence of masculinity, and (again, no accident) the logical descendents of the musical watershed that Presley's early work represented.

One of the most common stories that is told of Elvis is undoubtedly one of degenerating masculinity, with Tom Parker, Hollywood, RCA, and the U.S. military figured as conspiring to contain the perceived threat of excessive masculinity by limiting and controlling the vehicles for his creative work. A similar story is told of a qualitative deterioration in Presley's creative output, such that the "bland" and "glossy" 1970s work is severely devalued when compared with the "energetic" and "edgy" work from the 1950s (particularly the pre-RCA work). Yet these two narratives have a great deal more points of connection than is typically recognized in such Faustian tales. This is, as I have argued, perceptible in the camp potential in certain musical moments, and perhaps the increased focus on vibrato in his work (that same vocal device that signified a difference between the styles and effects of Rudy Vallee and Bing Crosby). Also deeply significant is the link that discourses of race facilitate between music, sexuality, and gender performance. What the racial element allows for is a way of explaining the connections constructed in these stories between music and masculinity, and how they can be seen to work—to deteriorate—almost in parallel: that which affords "value" to music that references black musical history is the same thing that affords "empowerment" to masculinity, even as the "worth" may conversely be used to describe a threat, either musical or masculine. It is as if race acts as a pair of 3-D glasses, bringing together the complementary, different-colored pictures that together make up a more substantial whole: what ultimately arises from layering music, race, and masculinity over Elvis, is that the multiple stories told of Elvis—musical, gendered, and racialized—are also, perhaps more effectively, able to be told as one.

Notes

1. Sincere thanks go to Richard Middleton (University of Newcastle upon Tyne) for his insightful comments on drafts of this work.
2. Broadly speaking, I use "Elvis" in this chapter to suggest a certain set of culturally constructed and sustained ideas of what Elvis is, while "Presley" is used generally to denote the living being that was Elvis Aron Presley. It is not a strict division (either in this chapter or in a broader sense) and sometimes the lines are blurred, but this rough distinction is, I believe, useful nonetheless.
3. Sue Wise, "Sexing Elvis," in *On Record: Rock, Pop, and the Written Word*, ed. Simon Frith and Andrew Goodwin (London and New York: Routledge, 1990 [1984]), 390–398 (392).
4. Ibid., 392.
5. Laura Mulvey, "Visual Pleasure and Narrative Cinema," in *The Sexual Subject: A* Screen *Reader in Sexuality*, ed. *Screen* (London and New York: Routledge, 1992 [1975]), 22–34.
6. Richard Dyer, "Don't Look Now: The Male Pin-up," in *The Sexual Subject: A* Screen *Reader in Sexuality*, ed. *Screen* (London and New York: Routledge, 1992), 265–276 (270).
7. Mulvey, "Visual," 28.
8. Singing women may be the alluring and deadly sirens, whereas "dancing girl" was a nineteenth-century euphemism for "prostitute" and arguably remains associated with various sexualized acts of display, such as pole- or cage-dancing. See Lucy Green's work on the mask and musical display, with particular reference to singing and femininity. Lucy Green, *Music, Gender, Education* (Cambridge: Cambridge University Press, 1997), 21–22.
9. Peter Guralnick, *Last Train to Memphis: The Rise of Elvis Presley* (London: Abacus, 1995), 108, 124.
10. Guralnick, *Last*, 51. So concerned was Presley with his hair that in his early touring days, he apparently used three different hair products to achieve the desired effect. Guralnick, *Last*, 172.
11. Richard Middleton, "All Shook Up? Innovation and Continuity in Elvis Presley's Vocal Style," in *Elvis: Images and Fancies*, ed. Jac L. Tharpe (London: W. H. Allen & Co., 1983), 155–166 (165).
12. In 1956 and 1957.
13. July 1, 1956.
14. *Elvis: The Great Performances, Volume 1: Center Stage.* Dir. Andrew Solt. Distributed by Direct Video Distribution Ltd. 2002.
15. Quoted in Guralnick, *Last*, 285.
16. See Rogan Taylor, *The Death and Resurrection Show: From Shaman to Superstar* (London: Anthony Blond, 1985), 183; Wise, "Sexing."

17. See David E. Stanley, *The Elvis Encyclopedia: The Complete and Definitive Reference Book on the King of Rock & Roll* (London: Virgin Books, 1998), 45.

18. The paradox of the army having a demasculinizing effect on Presley is noted by Richard Middleton in this volume. As a thought to add to his observations, it strikes me that the hair especially adopts an interesting role here. After the significance that it had come to possess, a justifiably significant amount of attention was given to the ceremonial shearing of Presley's quiff necessitated by his conscription. In a normative version of events, the removal of this "feminizing" accessory ought to have had an overall masculinizing (or at least de-feminizing) effect. Yet in this particular instance, the tale is closer to that of the unfortunate Samson, whose strength—contained in his hair—was destroyed by Delilah and her shears. See Judges 16.

19. Taylor, *Death*, 183.

20. Ibid., 183.

21. Richard Corliss, "The King is Dead—Or Is He?" in *The Elvis Reader: Texts and Sources on the King of Rock and Roll,* ed. Kevin Quain (New York: St. Martin's Press), 79–81 (81).

22. Middleton, "All," 156.

23. Ibid., 155.

24. Guralnick, *Last,* 64.

25. Ibid., 224–227, 229.

26. Robert Matthew-Walker, *Elvis Presley: A Study in Music* (Tunbridge Wells: Midas Books, 1979), 106.

27. Middleton, "All," 157.

28. The same emphasis that was placed on these styles in live performance was largely reflected in his vinyl releases throughout the 70s. Examples include: "You'll Never Walk Alone" and "I Believe" (*You'll Never Walk Alone,* 1971); "Love Letters" (*Love Letters From Elvis,* 1971); "You Don't Have to Say You Love Me," "Wonder of You" and "Young and Beautiful" (*The Other Sides—Worldwide Gold Award Hits Volume 2,* 1971); *Elvis Sings The Wonderful World of Christmas* (1971); "Help Me Make it Through the Night" and "Hey Jude" (*Elvis Now,* 1972); *He Touched Me* (1972); "American Trilogy"/"First Time Ever I Saw Your Face" (Single, 1972); *Separate Ways* (1973); "My Boy" (Single, 1975); "And I Love You So" (*Elvis Today,* 1975); "Danny Boy" (*From Elvis Presley Boulevard, Memphis, Tennessee,* 1976); and "Unchained Melody" (*Moody Blue,* 1977).

29. Stephen R. Tucker, "Visions of Elvis: Changing Perceptions in National Magazines, 1956–1965," in *Elvis: Images and Fancies,* ed. Jac L. Tharpe (London: W. H. Allen & Co., 1983), 37–50 (44).

30. *Loving You* (dir. Hal Kanter, 1957); *Jailhouse Rock* (dir. Richard Thorpe, 1957); *King Creole* (dir. Michael Curtiz, 1958). Famously, Presley was granted a 60-day extension on the date when he was due to report for military service in order that he could complete filming for *King Creole;* see Stanley, *Elvis Encyclopedia,* 43.

31. RCA LSP-2328, 1960.

32. RCA LPM-3758, 1967.

33. 1960. Available on *Elvis In Hollywood* (RCA DPL2–0168), 1976.

34. 1963. Available on *Fun In Acapulco* (RCA LPM-2756), 1963.

35. 1965. Available on *Harum Scarum* (RCA LPM-3468), 1965.
36. Middleton, "All," 164.
37. 1961. Available on *Elvis' Golden Records—Volume 3* (RCA LSP2765), 1963.
38. 1962. Available on *Elvis' Golden Records—Volume 3*.
39. 1962. Available on *The Top Ten Hits* (RCA 6383-1-R), 1987.
40. See Middleton, "All Shook Up?" on this term.
41. Richard Middleton specifically describes how the vibrato style can be detected in brief moments of even "That's Alright, Mama," Presley's first release. Middleton, "All," 163. Yet, without a doubt, it is gradually allowed much more musical space throughout his career.
42. Matthew-Walker, *Elvis Presley*, 69.
43. Ibid., 79.
44. Ibid., 78.
45. Ibid., 79.
46. Ibid., 89.
47. Ibid., 81.
48. *Are You Being Served?* BBC1, 1972–1985.
49. Susan Sontag, "Notes on 'Camp,'" in *Camp: Queer Aesthetics and the Performing Subject—A Reader*, ed. Fabio Cleto (Edinburgh: University of Edinburgh Press, UK, 1999 [1964]), 53–65 (60).
50. Quoted in Chuck Kleinhans, "Taking out the Trash: Camp and the Politics of Parody," in *The Politics and Poetics of Camp*, ed. Morris Meyer (London and New York: Routledge, 1994), 182–201 (182).
51. Presley favored his self-designed jumpsuits because they were practical for performances, as well as flattering of his fluctuations in weight. Stanley, *Elvis Encyclopedia*, 94.
52. Marjorie Garber makes a direct comparison between the styles of Presley and Liberace in *Vested Interests: Cross-Dressing and Cultural Anxiety* (London: Penguin, 1992), 353–374. The similarity has also been briefly noted by Georges-Claude Guilbert in *Madonna as Postmodern Myth: How One Star's Self-Construction Rewrites Sex, Gender, Hollywood and the American Dream* (Jefferson, NC: McFarland & Company, 2002), 118. It is also worth noting that Presley and Liberace met in 1956 and performed informally in each others' jackets, and on each others' "native" instruments. Liberace's was a gold cutaway jacket, and may have been the inspiration for Presley's famous gold lamé suit that he donned in 1957, suggesting that some direct influence may have been at work in the later outfits. The two artists maintained a friendship after that first meeting. See Marie Clayton, *Elvis Presley: Unseen Archives* (Bath: Parragon, Avon, England, 2005), 61.
53. Peter Guralnick, *Careless Love: The Unmaking of Elvis Presley* (London: Abacus, 1999), 452.
54. Sontag , "Notes," 60.
55. Guralnick, *Careless*, 444.
56. Ibid., 443.
57. Quoted in Guralnick, *Careless*, 443.
58. Ibid.
59. "Something," *Abbey Road* (Apple PCS 7068), 1969.
60. See "Someday My Prince Will Come" sung by Adriana Caselotti in *Snow White and the Seven Dwarfs* (1937). See also the backing vocals in "When

You Wish Upon a Star" in *Pinocchio* (dir. Hamilton Luske and Ben Sharpsteen, 1940).

61. See "If You Haven't Got Love" sung by Gloria Swanson in *Indiscreet* (dir. Leo McCarey, 1931). See also Ann Blyth singing "Stranger in Paradise" with Vic Damone in *Kismet* (dir. Vincente Minnell and Stanley Donen, 1955).

62. Sontag, "Notes," 60.

63. It may be of note that the kitsch-camp potential of this song has successfully been realized by the Muppets. See *The Muppet Show: Music, Mayhem, and More!* (Rhino), 2002.

64. In the *Bolero* of which this motif reminds the knowing listener, an extra beat of quavers is interspersed with the above motif, such that every fourth bar is rendered thus: ♩.♫♫♫

65. A term abbreviated from the word "carnival," to denote someone involved in the carnival business. Usually used in a derogatory sense.

66. See Bill C. Malone, "Elvis, Country Music, and the South," in *Elvis: Images and Fancies,* ed. Jac L. Tharpe (London: W. H. Allen & Co, 1983), 123–36 (135); Charles Wolfe, "Presley and the Gospel Tradition," in *Elvis: Images and Fancies,* ed. Jac L. Tharpe (London: W. H. Allen & Co, 1983), 137–154 (137).

67. This reading continues to manifest itself in contemporary popular culture. Eminem raps: "I'm the worst thing since Elvis Presley / To do black music so selfishly / And use it to get myself wealthy." Eminem, "Without Me," *The Eminem Show* (Interscope 4932902), 2002.

68. Lott, "All," 203. Specifically, Lott notes that "Dixie," which formed part of Presley's "American Trilogy," had been a "blackface standard"; Lott, "All," 203. See Lott, "All," 204–209, for an excellent analysis of how blackface, "blackness," and "whiteface" are negotiated in the idea of Elvis, particularly through Elvis impersonation.

69. Malone, "Elvis," 124.

70. Wolfe, "Presley."

71. James R. Goff Jr., "The Rise of Southern Gospel Music," *Church History* 67, no. 4 (December 1998): 722–744 (725–726).

72. Guralnick, *Last,* 47.

73. Charles Wolfe, "'Gospel Boogie': White Southern Gospel Music, 1945–55," *Popular Music* 1 (1981): 73–82 (77).

74. See Guralnick, *Last,* 52.

75. Richard Dyer, *Only Entertainment* (London and New York: Routledge, 1992) 153. The condemnation of which Dyer writes could easily be evidenced by conservative and/or religious responses to Presley's work in the 1950s.

76. One specific manifestation of this model was to be found in beliefs about genitals, such that black women were believed to possess unusually large clitorises and/or labia, and black men to be unusually well endowed. See Sander L. Gilman, *Difference and Pathology: Stereotypes of Sexuality, Race, and Madness* (Ithaca, NY: Cornell University Press, 1985), 81–83. This last belief in particular persists in modern culture, as evidenced for example by a large number of jokes in which the punchlines are dependent on the supposed size of black penises.

77. See William J. Mahar, *Behind the Burnt Cork Mask: Early Blackface Min-*

strelsy and Antebellum American Popular Culture (Urbana and Chicago: University of Illinois Press, 1999). For example, Mahar cites the character "Dandy Jim," the subject of various versions of a song by that name. He does note that the character was neither solely a depiction of what was understood to be *black* masculinity at the time, nor always a sexual predator. However, the song "Dandy Jim" is, as Mahar writes, "considered a paradigm of the negative, demeaning, stereotypic songs characteristic of minstrelsy's worst racist perceptions about African American men," (228) and this is manifested in part in the "presentation of a character possessing great sexual prowess" (214).

78. bell hooks, *We Real Cool: Black Men and Masculinity* (London and New York: Routledge, 2004), 79.
79. Dean Martin, "Gentle on My Mind," *Gentle on My Mind* (Reprise RS6330), 1968. Elvis Presley, "Gentle on My Mind," *From Elvis In Memphis* (RCA LSP 4155), 1969.
80. Frank Sinatra, "My Way," *My Way* (Reprise RS20817), 1969. Elvis Presley, "My Way," *Aloha From Hawaii Via Satellite* (RCA VPSX 6089), 1973.
81. Matt Monro, "Spanish Eyes," *These Years* (Capitol T2801), 1967. Elvis Presley, "Spanish Eyes," *Good Times* (RCA CPL 1 0475), 1974.
82. John Gennari, "Passing for Italian: Crooners and Gangsters in Crossover Culture," *Transition* 72 (1996): 36–48 (36).
83. Ibid., 46.
84. Allison McCracken, "'God's Gift to Us Girls': Crooning, Gender, and the Recreation of American Popular Song, 1928–1933," *American Music* 17, no. 4 (Winter, 1999): 365–395 (368).
85. Ibid., 386.
86. Ibid., 386.
87. Ibid., 389.

SECTION **3**

Boys Will Be . . . ?
Other Modes of Masculinity

9

Queer Voices and Musical Genders

JUDITH HALBERSTAM

This chapter uses two eccentric musical examples from Black cultural history in order to trace the kind of gender variance that peppers popular culture on the one hand and racial formations on the other. By writing about Big Mama Thornton and Sylvester, furthermore, I forge an alternative genealogy of music by linking two performers not in terms of genre or period but in terms of the vocal innovations that attend their queerly gendered performances. I present each case separately and then conclude with some thoughts about how to create a history of "musical genders."

Hounding History: Big Mama Thornton and Elvis

When I was engaged in research from 1995 to 1998 on drag kings, it became clear to me that a number of African-American performers turned for inspiration to blues singers from the 1930s and 1940s. There are good reasons for contemporary queer black performers to dig through this rich performance archive if only because the history of female blues singers, according to Angela Davis and others, must be told in terms of the politicization of sexuality, the emergence of Black feminism and the production of an affective discourse on freedom, community, and domesticity.[1] However, the drag king performances made explicit what histories of the blues tend to repress: namely the very queer and specifically masculine or butch personas of a large number of female blues artists. I want to trace

183

some kind of lineage from twentieth-century female blues performers to contemporary drag kings in order to capitalize on Joseph Roach's notion of memory as a sort of "anti-museum."[2] For Roach, myth-making acts, like canon-formation, create archives out of some acts, performances and events only by wiping out countless others. A heteronormative history of the blues might bump into oblivion another, more obscure, queer history. But these lost and forgotten acts, performances and practices live on in space rather than in time according to Roach; they live on through gestures, song, the singing voice, the dance step and a whole suite of stylizations. Using Roach's complex methodology of subcultural reinvention, we can start at an eccentric place in history (the drag king for example) and work backwards to find the queer echoes of contemporary gendered performance.

We have considerable evidence that drag king cultures and male impersonation cultures have been particularly prevalent in women of color communities where so called role playing has been a subcultural dominant for far longer than in white lesbian communities, which have often favored an aesthetic of "androgyny." And so, alongside the multiple accounts of male to female transvestism in Harlem in the 1930s, there are also many accounts of women performing in drag in Harlem in the same period. Angela Davis, for example, writes of Ma Rainey in her book on *Blues Legacies and Black Feminism* that "Rainey's sexual involvement with women was no secret among her colleagues and her audiences." She also notes: "The ad for the release of 'Prove It on Me Blues' showed the blues woman sporting a man's hat, jacket . . . ."[3] If Ma Rainey wore and performed in drag, we can assume, then drag must have been an accepted style in the black queer community of Harlem. According to Bruce Nugent, George Chauncey, Eric Marcus and others, drag balls were pervasive in Chicago and New York in the 1930s and these African-American balls included male and female impersonators. Nugent writes: "The Ubangi Club had a chorus of singing, dancing, be-ribboned and be-rouged 'pansies,' and Gladys Bentley who dressed in male evening attire, sang and accompanied herself on the piano; the well-liked Jackie Mabley was one of Harlem's favorite black-faced comediennes and wore men's street attire habitually. . . ."[4] It is this tradition of female to male drag and early twentieth-century lesbian bar culture that provides the blues tradition that I want to track or at least imagine here through a consideration of the life and music of Willie Mae Thornton.

Willie Mae Thornton was born in 1926 in Montgomery, Alabama. In the 1950s Thornton had some success in the Texas music scene and she began playing and singing with Johnny Otis, Little Esther, and Mel Walker. After one show, Thornton was given the nickname "Big Mama," supposedly because she was large, tough and had a big voice. Most photographs of Thornton, however, reveal that her toughness was part of her overtly masculine style and one can assume that the moniker "Big Mama" was applied in part to domesticate her overtly butch style. In fact, it is hard to match the nickname at all with the image in the photos of a brash, confident woman in men's suits and shirts. Big Mama was known as a "shouter" and, like countless other African-American performers, she learned her style in Black churches as well as in clubs and bands. Her deep singing voice and her particular forms of vocalization arose out of African-American musical traditions and passed on both narratives of strength and persistence but also stories of loss, hardship and suffering. Thornton's toughness and its vocalization have to be considered in relation to what Lindon Barrett refers to as the way "the singing voice stands as one very important sign of the value of those lives and voices situated in the dark."[5]

In 1953, as is well known, Thornton had a hit with the song "Hound Dog." The single sold almost two million copies and Thornton received only $500 for her part in it. Thornton contested the authorship of this song for years and although she admitted that Lieber and Stoller had a hand in the writing of "Hound Dog," both she and Johnny Otis claim that they improvised a great deal when they recorded the song and that they deserved royalties for its use. Three years later, after hearing Thornton's recording, Elvis Presley recorded his own version of "Hound Dog" and his version made him a star and launched rock and roll history. Neither Thornton nor Johnny Otis received a penny in royalties from the massive sales of Elvis's first single.

While the history of Elvis has often been told as the history of cultural theft and in terms of the absorption of Black cultural influence into white cultural production, only rarely is this process described in terms of the "straight" absorption of "queer" cultural influence. Thornton, in her mode of dress, her affect, her phrasing, and her bluesy performance can easily be categorized as queer, and her effect on Elvis, his masculinity, his way of dancing, his singing, has yet to be assessed. The denial of authorship, which Thornton so bitterly decried in terms of the ownership of the song itself, can be extended to the style of masculinity that she crafted. In other words, in histories of rock and roll, Big Mama Thornton, like many blues women before her, is cast as a passive instrument: her voice, her rhythm, her moves are all interpreted as effects of the music handed to her by white authors rather than as the origins of a genre, a gender or a mode of expressive embodiment.

I want to examine the legacy of Willie Mae Thornton in three specific ways. First, we can consider her legacy in terms of the appellation "Big Mama": how does the term "mama" work in relation to Thornton's explicit masculinity? Why are so many blues women cast as "ma" or "mama"? What dramas of production and reproduction are set in motion by the apparent clash between female masculinity and the maternal? Second, we must think about Thornton's musical career in terms of the dramas of racialized concepts of authorship. Rather than categorizing Thornton as an under-appreciated blues singer who simply never got her due, as is common in many articles written about her, can we read Thornton as part of a sexual, gendered, and racialized history that must necessarily be repressed in order for white male culture, here in the form of Elvis, to authenticate itself? If we recognize Thornton's masculinity as authentic in some way, and as central to the music she produced and the aesthetic style she crafted then she can be cast as an influence rather than simply a precursor. This is an important distinction given the tendency in masculinist histories of rock to trace all-male genealogies for trends, genres, and music movements. Finally, the career of Big Mama Thornton, her successes and failures, her choices of song, venue, and self-presentation, convey important information about the meaning of the blues. Is there some important connection between the blues and female masculinity or butchness (*Stone Butch Blues* . . .)? Put another way, if the blues is literally and metaphorically about the psychic, political and social experience of what can broadly be termed "castration" in psychic terms or disempowerment in political terms, can we locate the butch blues singer (Ma Rainey, Gladys Bentley, Big Mama Thornton) at the very heart of this aesthetic enterprise rather than consigning her to its margins? Is the transition from the blues to rock and roll that comes to stark visibility in Elvis's cover of "Hound Dog," a musical transition from castration to phallicism, from not having to being, from loss to presence, from a searing critique of white patriarchy to a celebration of white manhood?

Nobody's Mama!

Big Mama Thornton never married, bore no children and was never romantically associated with a man. Johnny Otis speculated in an interview about her sexuality and he said: "I could never get a handle on Willie Mae sexually and that's not a judgment. If you're a homosexual or whatever, it's nobody's damn business what you do in your bed. But that doesn't stop you from being curious and I was." Otis says he was curious about her sexuality and immediately makes the link between sexual ambiguity and homosexuality. He continues: "People in the band heard these rumors she was gay. She was a big woman and sometimes wore suits or masculine kinds of clothes, but that might not mean anything. All I can honestly say is that she was a good, intelligent person. I personally never saw her with any men, but on the other hand I never saw her with any women either. So all I know is that I don't know much about it."[6] This is an interesting quote and one of the most direct statements about Willie Mae Thornton's sexuality. Otis is obviously afraid about damaging Thornton's reputation by making an open declaration about her queerness and so he retreats to the claim of "not knowing what there is to know." But at the same time, he gives all the relevant information about Thornton's sexuality: her size made her seem tough rather than maternal; her penchant for men's clothing added to her masculinity; she quite openly lived without a man.

Thornton's sexuality and gender, her explicit cultivation of butch style in other words, needs to be lined up alongside the term "Big Mama." In her study of blues women, Angela Davis comments: "The protagonists in women's blues are seldom wives and almost never mothers" and she explains, "the absence of the mother figure in the blues does not imply a rejection of motherhood as such, but rather suggests that blues women found the mainstream cult of motherhood irrelevant to the realities of their lives."[7] In the post-slavery era, as Davis argues, black women, like black men, articulated complex understandings of freedom in relation to mobility, sexuality and gender and in opposition to domesticity, marriage and family. The term "ma" or "mama" then when used in reference to rather masculine blues singers does not reference a domestic context; rather it should be read as a way of anxiously re-coding the non-femininity of these women: if a performer is conventionally feminine, in other words, petite, womanly and seductive, she is not going to be called "mama." Billie Holiday's nickname, for example, was "Lady Day" not "Mama Day."

The terms "mama" and "daddy," were and are used in African-American vernacular to express lover relationships as much as familial relations and in some blues lyrics, "daddy" could as easily refer to a butch female lover as to a male lover. The unmooring of parental labels from the function of parenting itself and the tethering of these terms to sexual roles implies that the domestic has been queered. Indeed, the patently anti-domestic sentiments found in the blues, whether expressed as defiance, disappointment, anger or refusal, lead almost inevitably to queer articulations of desire and affiliation. It is this queer politics of sexuality that scholars of the blues have overlooked. Davis, Hazel Carby and others all mention the fact that many blues women were lesbians, but they tend to cast lesbian lyrics in terms of "women loving women" and "sisterhood" thereby preserving the gender coherence to which the term "mama" also lays claim. In the case of Willie Mae Thornton, on account of her overt masculinity, her status as unmarried and her disinterest in men, the term "Big Mama" draws attention to rather than distracts from her unconventional gender.

Authorship

Narratives about women in rock, as many cultural critics have pointed out, inevitably locate women as artists who either come before or follow on from the main attractions in rock history. A woman might be a female

Dylan/Jagger/Lennon; she might play guitar like Hendrix, Beck, or who-ever. These temporal formats that always historicize female and queer musicians in the before or after of music history make it hard to assess properly what kinds of influence particular female artists may have had on male artists or queer genres may have had on hetero genres. Gayle Wald's work on Sister Rosetta Tharp, for example, casts Tharp as not simply an interesting gospel singer turned rock and roller, but rather tries to locate Tharp in a narrative about the emergence of rock and roll.[8] Tharp can be seen playing electric guitar in some video footage, and, as Wald points out, she pioneers certain styles of guitar handling that become de rigueur for male performers like Pete Townshend some twenty years later. Only rarely is a female musician cited, however, as an influence on a male per-former. One of the few times when this has happened is in the case of Little Jimmy Scott: Scott has a high voice for a man and instead of disavowing the connection between his voice and female vocalists, Scott often cites Ethel Waters and Bessie Smith as influences.[9] The relation of copy to origi-nal haunts the history of Willie Mae Thornton.

Big Mama Thornton had a moderate hit with "Hound Dog," a typical blues lament about a no good man who "ain't nothing but a hound dog, snooping round my door." The second verse casts the man as someone who has represented himself as "high-classed," but Thornton claims to see through that and she sums up: "yes, you told me you was high classed / but I could see through that / And daddy I know / you ain't no real cool cat." The song is fairly conventional in terms of its representation of male pro-miscuity and female disappointment. However, half-way through the song, Thornton begins to improvise and she lets the guitar pick up the melody while she plays the part of the dog, howling and hooting. Here Thornton inhabits multiple roles: she is the male lover or hound dog, the woman scorned and the band-leader directing her musicians. She slips easily between these roles and, with her husky voice and jaunty delivery, she can-not be simply identified as the jilted woman. The gender mobility within the song, presumably, made it appeal to male as well as female singers.

When Elvis took up "Hound Dog," he changed the lyrics. Obviously, he was not going to sing a song about a "hound dog" sniffing around his "door" and wagging a tail at him! So Elvis changed the lyrics, or rather simplified them into a gender-appropriate narrative. "You ain't nothing but a hound dog," he sings, "crying all the time / Well you ain't never caught a rabbit and you ain't no friend of mine." Elvis picks up the pace of the tune a little, adds a hiccup to "crying" so that it becomes "cry-hin" and then slurs his way through the now nonsensical lyrics. What Elvis takes from Thornton, however, is more than the song, more than the raw material. He takes the shout from Thornton, the defiance, the confident rejection of the "high class poseur." He takes her confidence, her rhythm, her phrasing even and her gender mobility. Thornton felt the sting of this cultural theft deeply and she said: "I've been singing before Elvis was even born. A white man jumps up and becomes a millionaire before me off of something that I made popular. They gave him that right . . . now, why do they do that? He makes a million and all this jive because his face is different from mine." Thornton's complaint should be heard here as an extension of the blues experience: this absorption of black cultural production into white performance *is* the blues; and the histories that locate Thornton merely as a singer who sang "Hound Dog" first as opposed to an artist who pioneered the form, the vocal style and the sexy masculinity that came to be essentially associated with Elvis's iconicity, reverse the relation between female and male masculinity, black and white cultural production, queer and hetero cultures and the blues and rock and roll.

The Blues

Finally, we need to retheorize the blues in relation to a kind of inevitable queerness that constitutes the form, the content and the biographies of blues songs and singers. If we were inclined to use psychoanalytic terms for the emotional experiences summarized as the blues, we would use the term: "castration." The blues theorize what has been lost, what remains irretrievable, what constitutes the self in terms of lack. Angela Davis says that the term the blues derives not only from the "musical scale containing 'blue notes' but also because it names, in myriad ways, the social and psychic afflictions and aspirations of African Americans."[10] If the blues provide a complex catalogue of the emotional legacy of slavery, the butch blues singer is particularly well situated to the role of narrator in this history. In terms of her dislocation from gender and sexual normativity, her unusual domestic arrangements, her status "between genders," the butch singer of the blues—and here we can think of Gladys Bentley in her tuxedo, Ma Rainey in men's clothing, Willie Mae Thornton wearing a pork pie hat, suit, and tie—embodies both the abjection of Black masculinity in white patriarchy and its triumph nonetheless. Thornton, for instance, was widely regarded as "tough" and as unfeminine, but she was respected everywhere by musicians and cast often as phallic. Byther Smith talks about playing for Thornton in the 1970s, and he describes her with a mixture of awe and confusion: "She was the kind of person that, nobody ever suited her. No musician could satisfy her, she was never pleased with what they did." Smith takes pride in the fact that he was able to satisfy Thornton's high standards and he says: " . . . the girl that was traveling with us and taking care of her told me: 'you're the only person that Mama likes.'" Apart from the fascinating reference to Thornton's female traveling companion here,

Smith's description of Thornton turns her into a kind of paternal figure whom no one can please. He tries, almost desperately, to restore a maternal quality to her and her talks about going up to Thornton and kissing "her on the jaw before she could get angry." But then he remembers ruefully that Thornton would just swat at him saying: "Get away from me, I don't want none of you young men."[11]

Nowadays in drag king clubs all around the United States, drag kings make Elvis a part of their repertoire. Elvis seems like an obvious drag icon given his performative masculinity and the widespread practice of Elvis impersonation; however, if we restore the history of Willie Mae Thornton's influence on Elvis, we can reread drag king performances of Elvis, particularly Black drag king performances, as a way of imagining the lost circuits of influence within which Elvis and other white male rock heroes are merely echoes of the forgotten Black butch musicians who preceded them and who were hounded from history by them.

"You Are My Friend": Sylvester's Falsetto and the Sound of Queer Friendship

In my second example of a queer genealogy of gendered voices that scrambles conventional popular music history, I want to turn to a performer who queered masculinity in a very different way from Big Mama Thornton and in a very different genre. Disco diva Sylvester offers a fascinating counterpoint to Big Mama Thornton's legacy of butch blues. While Thornton turned songs of loss and disaffection into the location for gender reinvention, Sylvester reveled in the opportunities that disco afforded him to occupy the feminine role of diva while queering gay masculinities. The much-documented "death of disco" was also the death of entire ecologies of gay femininities and masculinities. Indeed when the role of disco diva gave way to the more macho function of DJ, dance music lost more than just a mouthpiece. The disco queen, male and female, is a figure for an earlier moment of queer identity and queer culture, one less invested in normative masculinities and more rapturous about excessive femininities. Sylvester, with his flamboyant stage performances, his overt femininity, his close bond with his female back up singers and his extraordinary falsetto, represents an earlier moment of queer culture within which the drag queen and the disco queen were often one and the same. Like Little Jimmy Scott, another Black singer with a high voice, Sylvester cultivated both the unusual range of his singing voice and the connection it gave him with women and queer femininity. And like Little Jimmy Scott, Sylvester was not shy about listing women as his major influences. Just as Scott often cites Ethel Waters and Bessie Smith as influences, Sylvester would mention blues women as well as his grandmother, blues singer Julia Morgan. He might have mentioned Big Mama Thornton too, an icon of queer Black gender performance. This section will trace the wild and wonderful contours of a history, culture and aesthetic of black queer gender variance as it emerges from Sylvester's singing style and his live performances.

In an interview with R&B legend Patti LaBelle, Marc Anthony Neal asks the diva how she felt when Sylvester covered her 1977 song "You Are My Friend." "Oh," she answers, "that was awesome. And he was my buddy and he told me when he was going to record it and I said 'wonderful.' I loved his version of it—don't need those jewelries, don't need that hair." Patti LaBelle names Sylvester as her "buddy" when talking about him singing her song, "You Are My Friend." And she refers to the moment in the live version when Sylvester points to his female singers, Martha Wash and Izora Armstead, and says "these girls can sing, y'all . . . they don't need those dresses, they don't need those jewelries, they don't need no hair . . . these girls can sing." Patti LaBelle recognizes Sylvester's act of covering her song as an act of friendship, a tribute of sorts and she takes great pleasure in the femininities produced by Sylvester, Martha, and Izora. Sylvester's relation to LaBelle takes the form of tribute, and his bond with Wash and to Armstead constitutes a vocal companionship; these modes of friendship cannot be characterized in terms of the relation of the fag to the fag-hag; the song, and the falsetto in which Sylvester recreates it, stage black gay femininity as an interwoven history shared by black sissies and their diva icons. The falsetto also shifts the scale of gender and creates a soundscape within which all the voices sound queer.

Sylvester, Martha, and Izora do not wear their drag, they sing it. Sylvester's falsetto, nestled as it is between the soaring range of Martha Wash and the booming bass of Izora, speaks to the listener of discord, performativity, black history, and queer friendship. The falsetto, of course, takes multiple forms and plays a different sound in every throat: as the male diva strains to find the upper reaches of the male voice, his falsetto also cuts him loose from his anatomy and takes him into a sorority of female singers. Sylvester's falsetto connects him to black female divas, to the queen's throat, but it also highlights what Joon Lee calls "the joys of castration." Joon Lee's work documents the lively bond between women and gay male femininity and, in doing so, Lee adamantly refuses to think of castration as "something lost." By documenting and fully imagining the investments that, according to him, young effeminate boys of color often make in fabulous Black, feminine divas, Lee casts "castration" as this affirmative bond between marginalized characters.[12] Once in the oxygen thin air of operatic divadom, the queen must make his falsetto work, he cannot lounge in those high climes, he has to keep flapping to stay afloat: picture

Sylvester in one of his long flowing dresses, working his arms with the voluminous sleeves hanging down like giant wings; as his voice soars, he might tuck his elbows tight into his sides and move them up and down as if he is struggling to keep the high note buoyant.

Jake Austen has characterized Sylvester's voice as an "unnatural" falsetto and he makes a comparison, not unkindly, to the "natural" falsettos of Eddie Kendricks or Smokey Robinson; Austen means no slur on Sylvester, rather he emphasizes that Sylvester's voice is "strange" rather than silky, "thin" rather than full. He implies that the seemingly perverse qualities of Sylvester's voice overtly link it and Sylvester to queerness and to gender deviance; they also link him, in all kinds of ways, to women. So, while some falsettos become the mark of another kind of masculinity, Sylvester's, like Little Jimmy Scott's, deliberately marks him as having and indeed cultivating the voice of a woman. The falsetto, then, can be the trademark of a high-flying, an ecstatic even, masculinity, or it can be the telltale sign of a perverse identification. In the following examples of falsetto singing we will see that the singer is marked as more or less masculine but the falsetto places him in an affirmative relation to femininity: first, when Prince sings with Rosie Gaines on a live version of "Nothing Compares to You," his falsetto is situated by the song and by his interaction with Gaines as tortured, emotionally wrought, and only nominally heterosexual. Even the lyric, "nothing compares to you," suggests that femininity is both a place of desire *and* identification for Prince. Desire may play out in the lyric, but identification is legible in the voice. Maxwell, when he sings a version of Kate Bush's song, "This Woman's Work" similarly situates himself in a heterosexual matrix and in the place of the father. And yet, covering a woman's song, about woman's work, about child-bearing no less, and about the gulf between that work and the "craft of the father" leaves the listener with the impression that Maxwell partakes voluntarily in "this woman's work" as he takes his melancholy falsetto higher and higher, and further away from the seemingly solid ground of paternity.

Both Prince and Maxwell sing a falsetto in a way that situates femininity as something to which the male might aspire. In *Bedouin Hornbook,*[13] Nathaniel Mackey writes about precisely this aspirational quality of the falsetto: "What is it in the falsetto," he asks, "that thins and threatens to abolish the voice but the wear of so much reaching for heaven?" He goes on to link the falsetto to the moan and the shout. In his fantastic description, the falsetto partakes less in the unnatural and becomes the supranatural, the sound of "reaching," the strain of trying to go higher; the falsetto surpasses the word and takes the listener up into a new world, a new world we might add, of gender. Mackey cautions earlier in the same passage, however, that the falsetto also echoes through with the "legacy of lynching" and he describes Al Green on "Love and Happiness" as sounding as though "singing were a rope he becomes eternally close to be strangled by." The proximity of racial violence and transcendence quiver in the falsetto's throat as he strains to exceed the rope but finds himself caught nonetheless by its chords. But when the singer addresses himself to women, when he mingles his "unnatural" voice in friendship and in community with theirs, he turns the threat of castration into another kind of noise. Then the throat opens up, almost vaginally, and the queer disco diva revels in his femininity rather than keeping it phobically at bay.

The live version of "You Are My Friend" begins with a beautiful passage in which Sylvester makes the song his own. He strips Patti LaBelle's version down to a few repeated phrases and takes out some of the more narrative oriented lyrics. The song becomes a hymn to friendship lost and found and Sylvester's voice closes in on the song's emotional core. The queen dives into the sentimental heart of the song and he leaves the heterosexual narrative about lost love on the side for another songstress. "This song," he says before the music starts, "is dedicated to all of you," meaning the adoring San Francisco crowd, the listener, Martha and Izora. He then begins to circle around the phrase that will form the song's animating principle: "you are my friend . . . I've been around, I've been looking around and you were here all the time." Sylvester strains in this segment of the song to reach the high notes and the tension in his voice provides the song with its acoustic drama; when his voice thins, in the far corners of the song, it also punches through the potential corniness of the lyric to find a place of palpable emotion. After this opening phrase, Sylvester breaks to turn to the song's real subject, namely his relationship with Martha and Izora. He lovingly tells of how they met and of how the two women have stood by him, through everything. Finally, Sylvester invites each woman into the song, into the rhythm and he offers to share the stage with them. He sings first to Martha: "Martha, you've been around" until she picks the lyric up "I've been around . . . and you were there all the time." Following Martha's gorgeous solo, Sylvester, tells the audience "we love each other" and then turns to Izora: "Izora, you've been around . . . ." When Izora's voice answers the call, "I've been looking, you were here all the time," the male falsetto finds its female bass complement.

Izora begins her solo down low; she occupies the regions where we might reasonably have expected to find a male voice, but she turns her bass into something much more interesting than a male counterpart to Sylvester's "unnaturally" high range. Izora goes low so that Sylvester can soar, she grounds his flutey quavers and answers his occasional screech with a growl. She digs deep and finds a guttural response that is more of a low rumbling than a melodious bass. Izora's growl, tethered as it is to Syl-

vester's tuneful screams, reminds us of Mackey's placement of the falsetto
in the family of the moan and the shout. All of these sounds go far beyond
the word and in this place beyond language they create queer friendship
from noise unloosed from the gendered body, melody not bound to harmony. The song's finale features the three dueling divas pushing in and out
of each other's range and building to a quiet conclusion where Sylvester
confirms: "You are my friend."

In "You Are My Friend," Sylvester collaborates with his female singers
to create a compendium of gender within a specific history of racial formation. They do not sing, "we are family," they do not call each other brother
or sister: the term for this relation, this queer bond, is "friend" and it is
the music which brings their voices queerly together. Sylvester's brave and
open embrace of his femininity, by contrast with the defensive shoring up
of gay masculinity in contemporary queer communities, might well look
and sound anachronistic now, and yet, the utterly moving use of gay male
femininity to make female femininity sound and feel "mighty real" forces
us to reckon nostalgically with what has been lost to queer community
through recent, deep investments in normative masculinity. Izora's growl
and Sylvester's falsetto open up a space in language, in history, for us to
mourn the loss of two distinct voices and to celebrate the sound archive,
the queer archive of the falsetto and the contralto, that they left behind.

Conclusions

In a fanciful way, but in accordance with Roach's methodology for the construction of contrary genealogies for subcultural activity, we can link Big
Mama Thornton's butch blues singing to Sylvester's disco diva falsetto, and
we can use the framework of "queer friendship" and "queer voice" to link
the two within a network of lost legacies, subjugated histories and eccentric
lineage. Sometimes, the subcultural historian has to make a leap of faith in
order to assemble the jigsaw puzzle of queer affiliation and to rewrite even
seemingly alternative framings of the queer voice. For example, in her
fictionalized account of Big Mama Thornton and her influence on Elvis,
Alice Walker depicts Thornton as a conventionally feminine woman, a
mother, and a victim of a straightforward cultural theft.[14] To read Thornton as another Black female artist who has been culturally robbed by a
white man is to ignore the subtlety of influence—in other words, as Eric
Lott's work implies, no cultural theft leaves the thief unchanged.[15] While
theft, for Lott, implicates the borrower in a deep desire for the other, it
also utterly contaminates the "successful" performance with the presence
of the "original." In the two examples of queer vocalization and musical
genders that I have presented here, Thornton and Sylvester play out each

side of the theatrics of the cover version. While Sylvester uses his cover of Patti LaBelle to place himself within a sorority of Black female performers, Thornton's original song becomes the foundation for one of the most influential performances ever of Western masculinity. And while Thornton is hounded from history by Elvis, her queerly gendered legacy lives on in the booming bass with which Izora answers Sylvester's song to friendship.

Notes

1. See Angela Davis, *Blues Legacies and Black Feminism: Gertrude "Ma" Rainey, Bessie Smith and Billie Holiday* (New York: Vintage, 1999); also Ann DuCille, "Blues Notes on Black Sexuality: Sex and the Texts of Jessi Fauset and Nella Larsen," *Journal of the History of Sexuality* 3, no. 3 (January, 1993): 418–444; also Hazel Carby, "It Just Be's Dat Way Sometime: The Sexual Politics of Women's Blues," *Radikal Amerika* 20 (1986): 9–22.
2. Joseph Roach, *Cities of the Dead: Circum-Atlantic Performance* (New York: Columbia University Press, 1996).
3. Davis, *Blues*, 39.
4. See Bruce Nugent in *Hidden from History: Reclaiming the Gay and Lesbian Past,* ed. Martin Bauml Duberman, Martha Vicinus, and George Chauncey Jr. (New York: Plume, 1990).
5. Lindon Barrett, *Blackness and the Value: Seeing Double* (Cambridge and New York: Cambridge University Press, 1999), 57.
6. Johnny Otis quoted in Bill Carpenter, "200 Pounds of Boogaloo," *Living Blues* 106 (November/December, 1992): 29.
7. Davis, *Blues*, 13.
8. See Gayle Wald, *Shout Sister Shout! Rosetta Tharp—America's First Guitar Goddess and Gospel's First Superstar* (forthcoming from Beacon Press, 2007).
9. See also chapters in this volume by Richard Middleton (Chapter 5) and Shana Goldin-Perschbacher (Chapter 11), who both write about the influence of female vocalists on male singers.
10. Davis, *Blues*, 33.
11. Mark Lipscomb and Barbara Anderson, "Byther Smith: Came to Me Overnight, Something Like a Dream," *Living Blues* 97 (May/June 1991): 26.
12. Joon Lee, "The Joy of the Castrated Boy," *What's Queer About Queer Studies Now?,* special issue of *Social Text,* ed. David Eng, Judith Halberstam and Jose Muñoz, 23, no. 3–4 84–85 (Fall/Winter, 2005): 35–56.
13. Nathaniel Mackay, *Bedouin Hornbook* (Los Angeles: Sun and Moon Press, 1986).
14. Alice Walker, "Nineteen Fifty Five," *You Can't Keep a Good Woman Down* (New York: Harvest Books, 2003), 3–20.
15. Eric Lott, *Love and Theft: Blackface Minstrelsy and the American Working Class* (Oxford: Oxford University Press, 1995).

10

[Un]*Justified*

Gestures of Straight-Talk in Justin Timberlake's Songs

STAN HAWKINS

Subordinated to specific aesthetic norms, the pop star invites idolization and endless amounts of intrigue. In recent years, the male variant of this creature has become more transgressive as his body has appeared to be released from heteronormative constraints and racial divisions. Based around this assumption, the study undertaken in this chapter concentrates on a range of strategies that produce and sell pop. In whatever way we view the body, it emphasizes biographical materiality, symbolizing a site of struggle. This chapter not only looks at some of the causes for queering boundaries, but also considers the representation of male bodies and how they function in this process. The straight-queer pop idol, Justin Timberlake (from now on J.T.) takes center stage as I attempt to explore how his identity is packaged in various guises. Indeed, it seems that the space he occupies belongs to the world of queering, where gender travel through straight-play emphasizes the restrictions of masculinity while still clinging on to them.

Within No-Man's Land

What I want to suggest from the outset is a type of tourism that characterizes a new generation of white male pop stars within a no-man's land. Indisputably, J.T.'s personality is seductive through his musical style as much as his spectacle, and it is a combination of many elements that become the medium through which he expresses himself. Released in late 2002, his debut solo album, *Justified,* is in stark contrast to his earlier recordings with boy band, *NSYNC.[1] As such, the music's strong R&B style is largely attributable to the production skills of J.T.'s friends, Pharrell Williams and Chad Hugo of the Neptunes, and the producer, Timbaland.[2] That which instantly strikes one is the pleasures articulated in his performance, transported through the visual manifestation of movement and dance. In this sense, his appropriation of different styles raises a number of issues that can be linked to masculinity. For instance, J.T.'s construction turns his performance into a personal act of self-justification. Any guarantee of his own sense of authenticity is located in the way that he bridges an obviously artificial display (in the form of music video) into a personal space that validates an authentic self. By this I mean that outside the display of performance, there are qualities that endorse other values that the star embodies, which are narrated by interviews, gossip columns, articles, and so on.

Through bodily display, then, his way of musicking[3] becomes a central arena for consideration, which, in turn, is informed by the promo videos and live shows that have made J.T. one of the most popular solo male performers in the world. Camped-up mannerisms and a cute boyish look have sold his persona to millions. In all the songs on *Justified,* J.T. enters the symbolic world of lyrics from different positions. Assuming the phallus as a guarantor of his authority, the content of his songs are crammed with moments of passionate outburst. Significantly, the portrayal of masculinity through lyrical content and musical performance opens up a rhetorical space that is politically potent and, at the same time, entertaining. It is as if J.T. pardons his masculinity through a thoroughly queer aesthetic that accesses straight and gay audiences. All the indicators of this are as prevalent in his vocal style as in his videos as, quite effortlessly, his performance oscillates between activity and passivity.

Let us now turn to his voice and consider the connections between what we hear and what we see. Undoubtedly, the musical genre of the performer explains a lot. Although the description of countertenor is usually relegated to trained classical music singers, male pop singers have frequently turned to this vocal class. J.T.'s trademark falsetto extends well above Tenor C to the highest note of F^5, and his lowest pitch is around B^2. With a register of two and a half octaves, he deploys the *hautcontre* techniques used by countertenors who take the parts of castrati in baroque operas today. At the same time though, J.T. has an extraordinarily elastic and embellished style of singing that is found in the black styles of soul, blues, and gospel. There can be little doubt that his falsetto is highly coded, which brings up the matter of reception. Wayne Koestenbaum has noted: "Falsetto seems profoundly perverse: a freakish sideshow: the place where voice goes wrong."⁴ Historically as much as culturally, falsetto is coded in effeminacy, and, as Koestenbaum points out, cultures have long since ridiculed men who sing high. Yet, falsetto has its virtues, not least in pop. As Koestenbaum goes on to claim, it can provide "the illusion of truth,"⁵ and as a feigned sound, this type of voice, often mistaken for a "gay voice," possesses an "unnaturalness" that can signify shame and delight quickly. In other words, nuances in pitch and specific vocal mannerisms can be felt pretentious, loathsome, intimidating, and not least ironic. On the matter of pitch variability and the connections between phonetics and sexual orientation, Ron Smyth, Greg Jacobs and Henry Rogers have undertaken an extensive study into how listeners perceive voices. In order to understand why men's voices are experienced as gay(ish) or straight(ish), their results based on participant observation and interviews (within a North American context), reveal that the gay voice occurs within a homophobic culture. Furthermore, the "gay voice," they discovered, "can be stigmatized both within and outside the gay communit(ies)."⁶

Relating J.T.'s falsetto and his arguably affected vocal style to his stylized image, leads to general questions of performance and vocal deception. Simon Frith is explicit on this matter, claiming, "if a voice can be made to change to deceive other people, it can also be used to deceive ourselves."⁷ Indeed, our experiences of determining whether falsetto borders on the side of the effeminate or gay lies in how we hear voices and what we listen to in a song. Shamelessly, J.T. appropriates Michael Jackson's vocal falsetto and stylistic tendencies, almost pretending to be someone he is not. This is nothing new in pop music, as Frith verifies when he discusses the pleasures that derive from singers taking on other singers' voices. More specifically, Frith refers to the issue of race and sex:

> This is most obvious in the white use of black voices in rock and roll history, from Jerry Lee Lewis's "Whole Lotta Shakin' Goin' On," [. . .] to Mick Jagger's "I'm a King Bee," which, we might say, presents itself as white-boy-lasciviously-slurring-and-playing-black-sex.⁸

Frith's main point is that no listener would have conceived of Jagger or Lewis as black, although listeners would claim this is what they would have wanted them to do. Taking on the fantasy of the characteristics of another's voice, and blending it, through quotation, into your own personality describes a common technique in pop music. How then does one read the songs from *Justified,* and work out what they are telling us about masculinity, and, moreover, how do we go about assessing J.T.'s mannered way of controlling the tone of his voice and attitude?

Not surprisingly, exaggerated gestures and camp gestures have been an integral part of many boy bands' repertoire, which are located in a contemporary meterosexual urban landscape. Similarly, a spin off into the domain of gay culture via the carnivalesque of straight-talk and queer mannerism is discernible in sleek music recordings and glossy pop videos. At any rate, the ways that images and sound are disseminated by J.T. point to the continuity between male behavior and musical performance, providing important clues for working out the relationship among music, personality, and sex.

Shamelessly, he draws on the classic sounds and vocal idiosyncrasies found in Michael Jackson's legendary *Off the Wall* (1979) and Stevie Wonder's double album, *Songs in the Key of Life* (1976). Not surprisingly, the exaggerated gestures one finds in many earlier styles, an integral part of much pop music, are located in today's urban settings.

Queering Performance

What might seem odd is that the pop body, as transgressive carrier of countless sounds and images, is constructed around various cultural orders that inscribe differences at the same time they uphold dominant values. It is easy enough to spot the macho representation of the hard rock star or the effeminate camp image of the boyish twink pop artist. After all, the pop body is tightly controlled and commercialized to reaffirm the heteronormative ideals of social discipline. For many, however, the pop body has also become the site for a utopian vision of life, where the pain, anguishes, and despair of everyday existence is superseded by escapism and pleasure.[9] Nowhere do the politics of masculinity and music become more apparent than in MTV culture, where the display of male fantasy and conventions of heterosexual desire reign assured. There is a simple point here: the consistency of heterosexuality is dramatically displayed as a normative measurement of the real through the male who reveals the performative dimension of compulsive desire. Yet, in recent years numerous pop representations have deviated from the rigidity of heterosexual norms, with the emphasis falling on the theatrics of sexual subjectivity. I am referring to the queering antics and camped up performances of male and female artists who have set out to destabilize gender display and flirt with the dualities of sex, sexuality, and ethnicity.[10] Notably, straight performativity can denaturalize gender from its assured normativity through musical expression and animate fantasies in ways that tease out the incongruities of gendered normativity. But, of course, transgressive representations cannot just be taken at face value as they are often rooted in heteronormative norms that are linked to dominant inscriptions of conformity.[11]

From this perspective, performance strategies that shape the aesthetic display of pop idols can tell us much about cultural identification. Indeed, this is the context in which the visual display of pop secures a primacy of rules and ideological messages that describe the arrangement of heterosexuality. This naturally leads to J.T.'s performances and how they function as a basis for broader reflections on masculinity's construction. Perhaps most pertinent is how his brand of masculinity is appropriated through musical agency, and what makes this an expression of pop culture. In one respect, the display of masculinity emerges in the most spectacular of fashions in a queer time and space, where profit and commercial success become the main goals of certain performances. Take J.T.'s performances and songs: they function as indicators of the adjustments in male representations in recent years, demonstrating that social constructions are the result of changing social relations. My position on this matter is that *queer pop* has seeped into almost all areas of mainstream pop, designating new understandings of gendered identity that are enabled by the dynamics of cultural production. Judith Halberstam argues brilliantly in her study of the transgendered body that "the gender-ambiguous individual today represents a very different set of assumptions about gender than the gender-inverted subject of the early twentieth century." Halberstam characterizes gender flexibility as a "site of both fascination and promise in the late twentieth century,"[12] questioning the implications of this for other economies of flexibilities within a postmodernist space. On a cautionary note though, she points out that the neoliberal notions of uniqueness in queer urban settings need to be mapped against the "transmutations of capitalism in late postmodernity."[13] Halberstam further notes, "transgressive exceptionalism" is the by-product of local interpretations of neo-liberalism, and when it comes to masculinity, popular culture still guards the bond between masculinity and men, especially in the United States and England. Tracing the processes by which a performance becomes queer, she reveals the diffuse affiliation between the dominant and the marginal, which is discernible by "who becomes rich from certain performances of male parody and who never materially benefits at all."[14]

It is precisely here that we can begin to understand how sexual behavior is a central component for the organization of identity categories in pop expression. Yet, when it comes to linking sexual behavior to queering, the latter remains an excruciatingly difficult term to justify. For the process of identifying the act of queering necessitates a differentiation between what is meant by "straight" and what is "queer." And, simplified evaluations can all too easily exclude the discursive and linguistic disciplining of shifting spaces that explain transgression and subversion. More than ten years ago, queer theorist Alexander Doty attempted to define queer as something different from lesbian, gay, or bisexual in his groundbreaking book, *Making Things Perfectly Queer*. Positioned outside dominant cultural codes, queer would (ideally speaking) resist the gender-policing of assimilationist politics. To move beyond gender, Doty suggested that queerness might dissolve the binarisms that slotted people into fixed categories for living out their lives. Notwithstanding all its shortcomings, queer theory so far has had much to offer when it comes to a consideration of queer aesthetics in artistic expression.

Seen from another vantage point, the problematics of defining queer scripts bear strongly on the reporting, documenting, and performing out of gender, all of which are tightly associated with how the media has elevated the body beautiful as the prime determinant for marketing pop. On this matter, Chrys Ingraham has researched into how sexuality becomes the dominant category within a commodity culture. This point is exemplified by the media's obsession with Michael Jackson's supposed sexual transgression.[15] That the media reportage of Jackson's behavior coincided with G. W. Bush and Tony Blair's first debriefing in England of their conquests in the Middle East is not necessarily a coincidence. Not only was the focus on Jackson's body, but also on his sexuality and race, which became a global focal point of intense cultural and social debate. In one of the rarest examples of scopophilia in Western media coverage, Jackson's body, having turned the whitest shade of pale, became a battleground for sexual condemnation and discrimination. Coinciding with the tragic developments in Iraq, the media's coverage of Jackson's trial became a lurid show of stories that dealt with indecent excursions into child molestation at his Californian ranch, Neverland.[16] It seemed that the images and writings surrounding the spectacle of Jackson's body and his gendered identity during this period were out to stigmatize the black male pop star, and call for his punishment, in what became little more than a cruel "freak show." Paradoxically, Jackson's public ridicule and the repeated images of his frail, imperfect, and emaciated body, would serve as a reminder that in a world of multiple choices a loathing for transgressive males is more constitutional than optional. Thus, at all levels of representation, the radicalized and sexualized male body in pop culture raises critical concerns that deal with the ideology of physical appearance and the politics of stereotypical representation.

Fashioning Masculinity

In spite of recent trends to queer the "body spectacular," males in the majority of pop videos are still selected on the basis of rigid criteria that are restricted to norms of facial beauty and muscularity. The continuation of these ideals which have been around since ancient Greece, predicated

on over seven thousand years of patriarchy, pander to a mainstream heterosexual culture where straight men (and the acceptable Other males) are
compelled to check their bodies the whole time. Muscular and hairless,
the ideal male body today continues to be defined in terms of sex roles and
gender relations that ultimately market a product. Add to this pop music,
which is airbrushed, modified, and "rectified." There is an important historical framework here.

At the same time that digital technology arrived, the new male of the
1980s signaled a watershed in advertising as men started shopping for
themselves and spending a lot more time on their appearance as a new
brand of masculinity was marketed. Male nudity was suddenly ubiquitous, selling everything from fragrances to music. Calvin Klein's perfume "Obsession" pushed forward the boundaries for the nude male body,
while Levi's commercial of a male stripping down to his boxer shorts in a
launderette heightened the homoerotic gaze. No matter what was being
sold—cigarettes, watches, underwear, perfume, cars—representations
of beautiful, lean, and muscular men abounded. Popular culture in the
last decades of the twentieth century was predicated on a proliferation of
men's magazines and aggressive advertising campaigns that spotlighted
the changes in the male body. Right through the 1980s and 1990s MTV
became a visual medium for many of these trends, selling pop music in a
way never seen before. Gradually the "male look" became as important as
the sound. Identifying this tendency in his book, *Behold the Man,* Edisol
Wayne Dotson accounts for how it was the look as much as the music that
turned pop and rock musicians into superstars:

> An overweight or wimpy singer was fine in the days when maleness
> and masculinity were not measured in physical appearance and in
> the days when music came in the form of sound over the radio or
> stereo and not as visuals from a television screen.[17]

With little exception, male pop stars, like their counterparts in film and
football, have become visual celebrities as their bodies have been compelled to meet all the requirements of the advertising industry. Dotson
makes the claim that viewers in the closing decades of the twentieth century demanded that male musicians were good-looking and muscular to
the same degree that the pressure has always been on women. This now
extends to male backing singers and dancers where "P and A (pecs and
ass) have become as popular as T and A (tits and ass) in music videos."[18]
Intended for the queer as much as hetero gaze, MTV continues to thrive on
the spectacle of the body as an object of desire by offering its spectators a
narrow range of stereotype body-types that seldom verged from culturally
defined norms of beauty.

Musically speaking, the fashioning of masculinity through pop certainly raises questions linked to performance and the aesthetics of recorded sound. In the spirit of camping it up, how sound and style function is most vital to record sales. I would suggest that it is the unique combination of the visual display of the body and its sound through vocal articulation that holds the clue to why certain pop stars succeed. Moreover, stereotypical associations with boys "being emotional" through singing and playing musical instruments is largely recognized as unmasculine, unless of course the boy is singing or playing to the girl in one of those intimate, but rare moments. It is well known that the regulation of emotional display through all forms of artistic expression determines the tightly regulated behavioral patterns in males. Yet, not all emotions have to be restrained. As David Plummer asserts, anger and happiness are permissible because they stand for strength and therefore do not threaten the primary order of masculinity.[19] Justification for this is found in all the familiar categories of strength and weakness that are subject to all forms of social scrutiny. In contrast to sportsmen, male musicians in pop are often defined by transgression and fluidity, best demonstrated through the flimsiness of rigid boundaries. From an early age virtually all males quickly learn that ignoring the rules, those that do not "behave like a man" run the risk of alienation, which can easily result in being a target for homophobic scorn regardless of sexual orientation. Plummer has insisted that the agency of boys is completely influenced by "the management of these dynamics, and (that) a variety of mechanisms is available to modulate their risks."[20] By stigmatizing gender fluidity as perverse, and positioning it in opposition to hegemonic masculinity, homophobia seeks to polarize male sexuality, becoming a regulator for what is acceptable or unacceptable. Young men who do not uphold the dominant forms of male behavior are highly prone to exclusion, bullying, and contempt, where derogatory labels such as sissy, faggot, mummy's-boy, follow them everywhere. Despite its somewhat egalitarian and queer façade, MTV is a regulator of homophobia and misogyny through many of its programs, in which there is great pressure on boys to verify their heterosexuality. Indeed, the purpose of the majority of pop videos is to validate masculinity and delineate the social boundaries that conform to peer pressures. Overtly, then, pop songs are persuasive carriers of hegemonic norms. Let us further explore this with reference to J.T. and his conscious decision to play queer.

Boy-Talk!

Telling stories is a competitive activity among the majority of males.[21] Pop stars use this as a mechanism to boast about their successes and conquests and bemoan their struggles and failures. Jonathan Rutherford has described how Bruce Springsteen's songs generally "allude to a sense of loss, a time in men's lives, before adulthood, when we were authentic and complete."[22] In many ways, Springsteen's championing of an American blue-collar, Levi-jeans-type machismo expresses the "broken promises of patriarchy" and the intangible goals of masculinity that can never be realized. Rutherford insists that Springsteen seeks to "feel at home in his sexual identity rather than change it,"[23] and that the ultimate result of this is failure and disappointment. If we take J.T.'s songs, from the *Justified* album, there is strong evidence of a similar type of narrative content that stakes out the artist's heteronormativity. Instantly what strikes one is that all his songs are first-person narratives that conform to gender expectations. They engage directly with the internal world of the young male and his relationship to women. Adhering to conventional gender norms, J.T.'s songs are about competition, achievement, control, and emotional restraint. At this point, I wish to avoid oversimplification by stressing the binary distinctions of boy/girl, masculine/feminine, straight/queer, all of which can circumvent the underlying complexity of male behavior. Although J.T.'s songs, on the surface, appear to establish a straightforward narrative underlay, they constitute useful representations for considering the implications of "boy-talk," and, moreover, appeal to emotions and values that are important for people. In the song, "Right for Me," the sexiness in the funk-style performance is derived from a Prince-like vocal style. Constructing an all-male fantasy musically, by teasing out the erotic qualities of falsetto and animated vocal inflections, J.T. tells the girl in the song that she should know "what is right for *him*." Cheekily, the male protagonist is positioned in a dominant way, securely aligned to what is deemed acceptable for the male. In the middle section of the song a male rapper further assists J.T. to perform out his male desires. If we dwell on the type of response rapping evokes, delivered in a register considerably lower than J.T.'s affected, nasal falsetto, we might conclude that it signifies a macho element that contrasts with the artist's own identity. Lasting no more than twenty-four bars, this rap break, underpinned by an intense bass riff, focuses on the male's problematic relationship to girls, idealizing heteronormativity. With a deft resistance to the more poignant emotions of J.T., the rap passage evokes sentiments that convey a different form of masculinity. Structurally, rapping fulfils the function of a responsorial fill, intensifying the density of the arrangement by enhancing the interplay between J.T. and the backing vocal and instrumental parts.

Quivering in a Jackson high-pitched, breathy close-up mic'd melodic strand, J.T. tells us in the track, "Never Again," that he is half the man he used to be because *she* doesn't love him nearly enough. We learn that his heart will never mend, as the girl will never get to love him a-a-a-again. Throughout this ballad, musical clichés abound. For example, a piano part carries the sentiments of the lyrics with characteristic accents on strong beats, all neat and tidy, while the guitar fills that escort the piano lines are delicate and unobtrusive, with a noticeable absence of drum-kit parts. The turn-the-lights-down-low mood of this song seems perfectly shaped as J.T. affirms his gendered identity through the motions of heterosexual gesture and claims of lost love. Emphasizing his pain, he explores a range of emotions that typify the male's despair at not getting what he wants, a fitting example of how gender distinctions can be maintained in ballads. Indisputably, male desire is at the core of this song as J.T. labors the point of his heartache in a well-worn narrative that suggests sex is easier attainable than love, something he had little qualms in telling Barbara Walters in a national televised interview when he disclosed personal information concerning his girlfriend at the time, Britney Spears.

Another song stacked with an abundance of romantic disillusion is "Cry Me a River" (not to be mistaken for a hit with the same title by Arthur Hamilton from 1955, originally performed by smoldering chanteuse, Julie London, in the rock 'n' roll movie *The Girl Can't Help It* from 1956). Allegedly, J.T. wrote this song about Spears when the couple broke up in 2002, and the song is his side of the story, where the girl cheats on the boy, wrecks the relationship, at which the boy moves out. Distressed by *his* rejection, she cries *him* a river.

Starting with a mournful operatic countertenor voice in mock-recitative style in a harmonic minor mode, there is a sample of gushing water (as in waterfalls of tears) in the background. Throughout the song, the protagonist laments his lost love in a series of clichés that tell the girl that she was his sun, his earth, his entire existence, and that when she told him she loved him he believed her. One distinctive feature in the music that helps extract these sentiments lies in Timbaland's original production: the precise edits and compression in the mix of the ad lib rap underpin the tightly controlled and stuttering phrases of J.T. In the climactic reiterative loop, "cry me, cry me," he proclaims the trauma of loss, as his voice trembles and blurs the distinction between tough male and enfeebled wimp. There is a sense that J.T. denaturalizes masculinity through the excess of emotional outpouring and parody. In a song in which the title hook is repeated about thirty times, singing becomes both a public and intensely private act. Notably in the glossy promo video of "Cry Me a River," J.T. is filmed getting involved with and worked up by a stereotypically sexy girl. On his girlfriend entering, who has a striking resemblance to Spears, everything has been set up so that she will see the tape. The video leaves little doubt that it is a message to Spears.

Pleasure in J.T.'s songs and performance is largely derived from playfulness between the sexes that frequently probes at traditional masculine values. Musically, his white-boy sound is assisted enormously by the hip-hop and R&B style of the Neptunes and Timbaland. The character he portrays in his videos and live appearances is constructed along the lines of the cool, sexy, pretty young boy pop idol. Like Robbie Williams, he has been afforded leeway by the industry to misbehave, as demonstrated by his staged groping of Kylie Minogue's backside at a Britpop Awards appearance and the tearing off of a part of Janet Jackson's costume, baring her large, right breast, during the halftime show of Super Bowl in 2004. Not unlike Christina Aguilera, Minogue, and Spears, J.T. has been intent on discarding his former squeaky-clean image for a dirtier, street cred persona. At the same time, there is always evidence of a queer spectacle, most discernible in his style of dancing and dress codes. His nifty dance routines certainly typify a new generation of so-called meterosexuals, best exemplified by celebrities such as football player David Beckham, one of the greatest media icons of all time. Decidedly on the side of queer, Beckham's mannerisms and features, polished nails, make-up, jewelry, skirts, and the frequenting of well-known gay bars, have aroused much attention. Meterosexual celebrities who play out queerness, however, are very different from the group of males who are queer and display similar differences. As an essential part of media-hype, celebrities like J.T. and Beckham hardly express attitudes that put them at risk as they still contribute to the dominant system by spelling out their underlying heterosexuality. All too often, it seems that the women in their lives, their girlfriends, wives, mothers, are made-up larger than life to endorse their heteromasculine identity. As an acceptable alternative to heteronormativity, straight celebrities who play queer fit comfortably into the category of *stylistic straight-queers*.

In a fascinating study that theorizes "straight-queers," Robert Heasley has developed a typology of masculinities that captures the ways in which the characteristics of heteromasculinity are queered. Indisputably, J.T. is part of a select group of males who have consciously taken on a stylistic mode of representation that is associated with gay male culture. Heasley examines the strategies of such males, writing:

> These "stylistic straight-queers" allow themselves to develop and display an aesthetic, such as stylish haircuts and clothes, having facials and pedicures. In so doing, they are attracting the attention of gay men, as well as those straight males who can identify with border crossing identities. They also get the attention of straight women who find themselves attracted to what is perceived as a "gay" aesthetic or a "gay" sensibility.[24]

While identifying the risks that straight-queers subject themselves to, in terms of rejection, Heasley emphasizes the commercial and sexual gains of this category. There are huge benefits in appropriating gender-bending strategies (as evidenced by generations of rock and pop stars) as "border crossing" and the appeal of this within popular culture is ever increasing. In his conceptualization of straightness, Heasley insists that to behave outside the idealized framework of the heteromasculine is always going to be problematic. He refers to how psychologists often label straight identified males who border cross as "latent homosexuals" or "homos in waiting." According to Heasley, such practice is predicated on a reductionist perspective of human sexuality that rather conveniently classifies people as hetero-, bi-, or homosexual. Despite all the developments and writings about "gender trouble" in recent years (scholastically and in the popular press), hetero-masculinity is still legitimized as a normal way of being, and affirms the category of sexuality that historically has been understood as "normal" or traditional. Because of this the nontraditional male "presents an unknown,"[25] where his differences demand *justification*. As for the queer male, his isolation by the dominant group is a stark reality, where there is little space for *justifying* nontraditional masculinity.

Characterizing oneself as different has always been problematic, not least for male musicians. For instance, because queer-straights elect queer masculinity as a means of liberating themselves, the idea of them "thinking straight but acting queer" requires rearranging the boundaries of sexual identity. Take icons such as Marc Almond, David Bowie, Prince, and Jarvis Cocker, who have flirted with queerness in a world of show business where it is relatively acceptable. Assuming the characteristics of singing, dancing, dressing up and putting on makeup, these artists queer their pitch for the purpose of entertaining and not necessarily for social or political justification. Historically, flamboyance has been a strategy for letting go of inhibitions and profiling oneself. Interestingly then for those pop personalities who do border cross, their performativity can be likened to drag, which gains much more credibility when there are beautiful young girls in the background. It is as if these males can present themselves outside the boundaries of normative masculinity because, in another sense they are secure from inside. In other words, these boys are not compelled to conceal what they do (as many gay males are), for they are most unlikely to add a "sexual component" to their status as straight-queer.

Emerging from this are many issues worth exploring that deal with moving in and out of heteromasculine spaces. After all, we might ask: does J.T.'s queerness privilege straightness at the expense of the Other? And, if so, what are the implications of his queer display in a white homosocial space and to what extent does he give voice and legitimacy to new hetero-masculine norms?

Concluding Points: Rocking the Body

Queer pop generates a smooth and logical progression that "rocks the body" more than necessarily rocking the boat. Affirmation of sexual preference must be fairly obvious for a range of differences to be carried out in queer fashion. From his *hautcontre* vocal techniques to his body spins and quirky limb mannerisms, there is this sense that J.T. befits all the stereotype notions of queer, with one exception: his biography.

The possibility of his success relies on two important issues: first, the background information all his fans have access to from the outset, and second, the storytelling that goes on in his songs. Following his career climb from his childhood stint on the U.S. show, *Star Search,* when he became a member of the teenage variety show, *The New Mickey Mouse Club,* to joining the all boy band, *NSYNC, stories of girls have accompanied every press release.[26] Promo videos, interviews, and live performances have featured a string of beautiful girls, including Aguilera, Spears, Janet Jackson, Minogue, Cameron Diaz, and many others. Playing safe, J.T.'s queering has redefined the bounds of acceptability and transgression, all of which is elegantly tailored by his boyish masculinity. As I have attempted to point out by reference to various tracks, his songs primarily function as carriers of heteronormativity. All his songs are first-persona narratives that construct a world that includes female characters in romantic and sexual terms. Not only do these stories verify the conditions of the internal world of men and how masculinity depends on encounters with women, but they also document the musical pleasures historicized by social changes. What matters here is that J.T. constructs himself in a way that produces specific pleasures. Convincingly, he performs out his gender on a level that mobilizes all sorts of reactions and attitudes. Songs such as those off the album, *Justified,* probe at the question "what it is to be a young male," and all the debates connected to a new era of identity performance.

Blatantly prosthetic, J.T.'s style comes over a lot more queer and dandified than others of his peer group. In contrast to the macho styles of rap, R&B, and hip-hop, J.T.'s recordings suggest that, in the end, his brand of white-boy masculinity might just be a parody. In many ways, his appropriation of African-American music and musicians creates a space for his heterosexuality and whiteness to comfortably bridge the gap of homosociality. Performatively, the spectacle of J.T. with artists such as Snoop Dogg and the Black Eyed Peas, rapping, twisting, and dancing, registers the meanings and practices associated with straightness, race, and sexuality.

Moreover, his live performances and videos offer an insight into the operation of institutionalized heterosexuality: its materiality, its straightness,
and most of all its concealed contradictions. J.T. demonstrates how queer
performativity alongside white heterosexuality is crammed with paradoxes as he invites us to listen, enjoy, and dance within the hypnotic haven
of the gaze. As a result, his performances tempt us beyond the parameters of fixed representation. Because of the complex construction of the
mix between masculinity and queering, there is a tendency to praise and
applaud difference. Yet, the hype of queering offers a "twist of the straight,"
a cunning way of modernizing patriarchy and dramatizing tensions rather
than resolving them. If we consider there are countless genders, if not sexes
around, becoming queer is in constant flux, enacting fantasies, desires,
dreams, and experiences. In this sense, the straight-queer signals a refusal
to be normalized. The pronouncement, "I am quirky, camp, and perfectly
cool!" might be perceived as a step towards embracing a transgressive politics that offers strategies of resistance to an audience by exposing cultural
control. It seems then that the ambiguity of transgressing gender norms
through pop music comes with a price. Most of all, mainstream queering
reflects an avid preoccupation with a specific kind of aesthetics, an aesthetics that offers a performative site for transposing many of the conventions that have been imposed on us for far too long.

Notes

1. *Justified* debuted at number 2 on the Billboard Top 200 album chart, selling
   over three million copies in the United States alone and over seven million
   copies worldwide. *Justified* (Jive ROD9198), 2002.
2. The production team behind an artist determines everything when it comes
   to success. The African-American influence on J.T.'s debut album has a
   major role in establishing the artist's style and would explain why his mode
   of performance is frequently linked to Michael Jackson, Prince, and Stevie
   Wonder. In addition, the influence of the black producers, Timbaland and
   the Neptunes, on his "sound" cannot be underestimated. Born Timothy
   Z. Mosley, Timbaland has emerged a leading hip-hop and R&B producer
   and rapper who has had a profound influence on popular music from the
   mid-1990s onwards. Likened to producers such as Phil Spector and Norman
   Whitfield, Timbaland has redefined the sound of an entire genre through
   an immediately recognizable production style and unique sense of rhythm.
   Like Spector and Whitfield, Timbaland's production sometimes overshadows the credited performer, as he becomes the actual "star" of the song. In
   collaboration with Missy Elliott and songwriter Steve "Static" Garrett, Timbaland has produced a wide range of hits, which include singles for Timberlake, Aaliyah, Ginuwine, SWV, Total, and 702. The Neptunes, consisting of
   the duo Pharrell Williams and Chad Hugo, emerged at the turn of the century as highly sought after producers of rap. In 2001 they crossed over from

rap to pop, producing hits such as Britney Spears' "I'm a Slave 4 U," Usher's "U Don't Have to Call," and *NSYNC's "Girlfriend." Continuing to produce rap hits for artists such as Nelly, Busta Rhymes, LL Cool J, and Bow Wow, they formed their own rap-rock group, N.E.R.D. In 2003, the release of their debut album, *Neptunes Present . . . Clones,* confirmed their crossover success as, at the same time, they continued to produce hits for huge stars, such as Snoop Dogg, Jay-Z, and Justin Timberlake.

3. This use of this term and its conceptual framework comes from Christopher Small's groundbreaking discourse on the act of musicking, which occurs through a set of relationships that are located not only between organized sounds that are "conventionally thought of as being the stuff of musical meaning" but also in the relationships between "person and person, between individual and society, between humanity and the natural world and even perhaps the supernatural world." Christopher Small, *Musicking: The Meanings of Performing and Listening* (Hanover, NH: University Press of New England, 1998), 13.

4. Wayne Koestenbaum, *The Queen's Throat: Opera, Homosexuality, and the Mystery of Desire* (New York and London: Poseidon Press, 1993), 164.

5. Ibid., 65.

6. Ron Smyth, Greg Jacobs and Henry Rogers, "Male Voices and Perceived Sexual Orientation: An Experimental and Theoretical Approach," *Language in Society* 32 (2003): 329–350 (347).

7. Simon Frith, *Performing Rites: On the Value of Popular Music* (Oxford: Oxford University Press, 1996), 198.

8. Ibid., 198.

9. For Mikhail Bakhtin the social complexities of the body politic are made expressive through the disorders and inversions of the carnivalesque, which permits all types of possibilities. Mikhail M. Bakhtin, *The Dialogic Imagination,* ed. C. Emerson and M. Holquist, trans. V. W. McGee (Austin, TX: University of Texas Press, 1981). Understanding the transgression of established orders through Bakhtinian application has been taken up in my earlier studies. See for example, Stan Hawkins, *Settling the Pop Score: Pop Texts and Identity Politics* (Aldershot, Hampshire: Ashgate, 2002).

10. For example, see my discussion of identity politics in the case of pop stars, such as Annie Lennox, Madonna, Morrissey, Prince, and the Pet Shop Boys. Hawkins, *Settling.*

11. See for example: Judith Halberstam, *In a Queer Time & Place: Transgender Bodies, Subcultural Lives* (New York: New York University Press, 2005); Hawkins, *Settling*; Gilad Padva, "Heavenly Monsters: The Politics of the Male Body in the Naked Issue of *Attitude* Magazine," *International Journal of Sexuality and Gender Studies* 7, no. 4 (2002): 281–292.

12. Halberstam, *Queer,* 18.

13. Ibid., 19.

14. Ibid., 127.

15. Chrys Ingraham, "Introduction: Thinking Straight," in *Thinking Straight: The Power, the Promise, and the Paradox of Heterosexuality,* ed. Chrys Ingraham (London and New York: Routledge, 2005), 3–13 (3).

16. Jackson has admitted that he preferred the company of children, often inviting them to stay at his Neverland Ranch and enjoy the playground that had

been built there. In 1993, he was accused of molesting a 13-year-old boy who frequented Neverland. A media frenzy and savage witch-hunt ensued.

17. Edisol Wayne Dotson, *Behold the Man: The Hype and Selling of Male Beauty in Media and Culture* (New York: Harrington Park Press, 1999), 82.
18. Ibid., 83.
19. David Plummer, *One of the Boys: Masculinity, Homophobia, and Modern Manhood* (New York: Harrington Park Press, 1999).
20. Ibid., 219
21. In an insightful study of what men's talk is like, Jennifer Coates draws on a wide range of conversational material to examine the intersection between masculinity and language. In particular, Coates considers how gender construction works through men's stories, pointing out how they are generally characterized by emotional restraint. The suggestion here is that in the company of other males, men tend to exaggerate the masculine and deny the feminine. Jennifer Coates, *Men Talk: Stories in the Making of Masculinities* (Oxford: Blackwell, 2003). See especially chapter 5 (107–141).
22. Jonathan Rutherford, "Who's That Man?" in *Male Order: Unwrapping Masculinity,* ed. R. Chapman and J. Rutherford (London: Lawrence and Wishart, 1988), 21–67 (56).
23. Ibid., 54–55.
24. Robert Heasley, "Crossing the Borders of Gendered Sexuality: Queer Masculinities of Straight Men," in *Thinking Straight: The Power, the Promise, and the Paradox of Heterosexuality,* ed. Chrys Ingraham (London and New York: Routledge, 2005), 109–129 (121).
25. Ibid., 115
26. I would suggest a useful link between Timberlake's early success in the Mickey Mouse Club and the content of his songs from *Justified,* which in true Disney fashion bring much pleasure to children, teenagers, and adults. Yet, as Carrie Cokely has pointed out, to derive pleasure from Disney films "one must be firmly situated within the dominant ideologies of heterosexuality and patriarchy," which set out to establish and reaffirm identities. Cokely's critical approach draws attention to the "heterosexual imaginary" of the Walt Disney Company and how animated fantasies secure heterosexual romance as true love and institutionalize this as a ruling order. Carrie L. Cokely, "'Someday My Prince Will Come': Disney, the Heterosexual Imaginary and Animated Film," in *Thinking Straight: The Power, the Promise, and the Paradox of Heterosexuality,* ed. Chrys Ingraham (London and New York: Routledge, 2005), 167–181 (177).

11

"Not with You But of You"

"Unbearable Intimacy" and Jeff Buckley's Transgendered Vocality[1]

SHANA GOLDIN-PERSCHBACHER

I wish I had gotten the chance to sing with Jeff Buckley. The combination of our voices would have turned any straight boy gay.[2]

Rufus Wainwright's playfully campy suggestion might not have appealed to Jeff Buckley (1966–1997), who, unlike Wainwright, was straight and did not joke about "turning people gay." However, Buckley's vulnerable-sounding voice and penchant for singing women's songs in a female vocal range may seem queer to many listeners. Such behavior overloads the circuits of our oversimplified binary gender system and its attendant "types" of sexuality.[3] As far as I know, Jeff Buckley did not "turn straight boys gay," but his vulnerable, affecting music coaxes male fans to connect with what many of them refer to as their "feminine side," a set of identifications and behaviors they attribute mainly to women and gay men. Being emotionally receptive to another sensitive male, one who happens to be singing with an ambiguously gendered voice, would seem to present a serious threat to one's heterosexual manhood. This chapter deals with Buckley's "transgendered" performances and the sometimes uncomfortable relationship that his music invited with listeners.

Certainly much popular music invites intimacy. It eloquently expresses common experiences in moving ways, while at the same time sensually pleasuring listeners with its aesthetic beauty. Popular culture sociologist Simon Frith argues that "we enjoy music . . . because of its use in answering questions of identity. . . . [Another] function [of music] is to give us a way of managing the relationship between our public and private emotional lives."[4] Buckley's music serves these purposes while also complicating them—his earnestly transgressive gender and sexuality performances contribute to the way many fans understand their own identities. Yet his performance aesthetic could seem, to some, too private for public performance. The relationship between Buckley and his listeners was so intense that it felt metaphorically, if not literally, sexual, in terms of privacy, pleasure, and self-discovery. Feminist musicologist Suzanne Cusick asks, "What if music is sex?"[5] For Cusick, sex "is a way of expressing and/or enacting relationships of intimacy through physical pleasure shared, accepted, or given."[6] Consequently, "like good sex, [musicking] is an experience that re-teaches me how to relate to the world, how to have the nerve to open myself to it."[7] If music is, in these ways, sexual, how does one interpret the intimate relationship between fans and Buckley, a straight man who queered his gender by identifying with and emulating his favorite female singers and the vocal characters they created? This is a question that his fans often ask themselves. As one male listener says of his relationship to Buckley's music and his own sexuality, "I'm not gay, but if Jeff Buckley wasn't dead, I would kiss him on the lips."[8] Neither the listener nor Buckley defines himself as gay, yet their musical intimacy evokes a sensual connection between listener and singer that cannot be described by traditional notions of gender and sexuality.

Until his untimely death, Jeff Buckley provocatively challenged the norms of 1990s white boy rock. With his unusual vocal range he fluidly performed a wide variety of gendered and sexual personae, imbuing each with an earnest sense of identification. Covering at least four octaves, Buckley was capable of a coordinated head voice into the falsetto range (in addition to a true falsetto), chest alto voice, and full lower tenor range.[9] Not only his vocal range, but also his persona and performance style were based on multiple and changing gender identifications. Because of his wide vocal range, it was possible for him to cover songs written for the ranges of both male and female singers. He sang songs made famous by Nina Simone, Judy Garland, Edith Piaf, Billie Holiday, and Janet Baker, and sang them in the female performers' vocal ranges (higher, in Simone's case). Even more unusually, most of the time he did not change gendered pronouns, singing "The *Man* that Got Away," "*I Loves You Porgy*," and *Queen* "Dido's Lament" from Henry Purcell's opera *Dido and Aeneas*; he also sang as a betrayed wife in "The Other Woman."[10]

Identification with the gendered personae of the songs was important to his performance aesthetic. He said that he chose to cover certain songs that "I really respected, and all the experiences within them that I really admired, and identified with them."[11] The particular female singers he chose to emulate are interesting for their own vocalized genders and sexualities. The beautiful but tortured Garland was the favorite of a generation of gay men, who identified themselves as "friends of Dorothy." Piaf's strong chesty voice sounds almost masculine to French listeners despite her emotional songs.[12] Simone, the "High Priestess of Soul," sang black feminist songs in an androgynous register. Janet Baker often played operatic trouser roles. Holiday used her limited registral range with raw, intense expressivity. And Yma Sumac, another favorite of Buckley's, created campily exotic vocal extremes with her huge vocal range and palate of vocal colors. Buckley's identification with female singers went so far as calling himself a "male chanteuse" or "a chanteuse with a penis."[13] These identifications suggest a multiply gendered vocality, one in which the torchy, emotional expressiveness and even vocal ranges of (these) female singers is embodied by a man.

It is not that Buckley disavowed his biological maleness or social performances of it, but that he was not limited by white middle-class heterosexual American standards of it. This traditional notion of masculinity depends, by definition, on *not* being a woman and *not* being gay. White, straight, middle-class masculinity is performed most successfully when one is in control, not out of control, is strong, rather than vulnerable, and takes possession, rather than showing need. Buckley, though, did not enforce these standards in his own performances, which, as my examples will illustrate, were often vulnerable and sometimes seemed out of control. And he did not cling to his dominant identifications at the expense of identifying with women, black or queer people, or their music.[14]

Buckley's identification with women and widely ranged gendered singing styles suggest a kind of transgendered vocality—a vocality that resists identification with his biological sex.[15] I use the term "transgendered" to describe Buckley's voice, knowing that, for the most part, he was recognizable as a heterosexual male. Thus, unlike many transgendered people, he did not face the everyday oppression and dangers of living in between genders, or having crossed over "untouchable" boundaries. However, his gender transgressions were and continue to be noticeable and defining to almost everyone who hears him, disturbing notions of rock masculinity and influencing listeners' conceptions of their own identities. Since Buckley went so far as to claim that he identified with and emulated the vocal styles of the female roles of the songs he sang, my use of the term "transgendered" is not entirely metaphorical.

Not all scholars praise Buckley for his diverse musical identifications. Some hear Buckley's practice of singing covers of female performers' songs in terms of "iconoclastic mimicry" and "hetero camp."[16] Literary critic Oliver Lovesey argues that:

> In his relentless and doomed search, in a postmodern context, for an original genre and an authentic voice to give full expression to his gift . . . Jeff Buckley sometimes became narcissistic and mannerist in his shape shifting, seeking to camouflage or even symbolically murder his iconic voice, the inherited signature of his father, in hybridized ambiance and postmodern pastiche.[17]

Buckley's work, through its wide variety of affiliations, communicated meaningfully to its audiences (as my later discussion of fans' comments will reveal). Unfortunately, Lovesey, following Fredric Jameson's theories, dismisses Buckley's broad musical tastes as "postmodern pastiche" or "depthless parody," an ignorant masquerade lacking humor and anything but superficial meaning.[18] What Lovesey fails to consider is that Buckley may have actually identified with these singers and the different genres of their songs, as well as having had a sense of humor about their passionate, sometimes eccentric music, and his (at times, unusual) relationship to it.[19] Buckley's covers seem "absurd" to Lovesey because they are often influenced by other singers' covers of the songs.[20] For example, it is true that Buckley was most inspired by John Cale's rendition of Leonard Cohen's song "Hallelujah." Yet, it is Lovesey's standards here that seem absurd, demanding that songs are covered in an artistic vacuum, where an artist is not allowed to be influenced by any of the other versions of the song previously recorded, except the original. Like these "covers of covers," "hetero camp" seems to Lovesey to be an artificial and meaningless copy of gay camp, which itself might seem, to outsiders, to be an inauthentic simulation, as in drag's parody of gender.[21] However, if Buckley's covers were evidence of his "search for an original genre," why would he have committed to record such a broad array of musical genres while so many white male musicians in the nineties were focused on grunge?[22] Buckley appears to have confidently identified with many styles of music, regardless of their gendered or sexual connotations, or their perceived authenticity by the rock world. Critic Ann Powers argues that it is Jeff Buckley's defiance of category that allows him to successfully utilize his unusual voice. Powers argues that in contrast, Tim Buckley, Jeff's father, took such efforts to remain part of the free jazz movement that his attempts at crossing genre sound "tortured" and his music more wedded to the movement than the "musicality."[23] Jeff's unconventional gender related perfectly with multigenre affiliation, as genre, like gender, is an invented category intended to police borders and advertise identity.

Jeff Buckley's choice of cover songs was not simply to exercise his vocal capabilities or to find a single genre with which to identify, but rather aided his exploration of the boundaries of his musical and gender identities. That his search entailed sexual and musical identity was no coincidence, for these facets of his persona were closely related. Buckley explained:

> In my early shows, I wanted to put myself through a new childhood, disintegrating my whole identity to let the real one emerge. I became a human jukebox, learning all those songs I had always known, discovering the basics of what I do. The cathartic part was in the essential act of singing. When is it that the voice becomes an elixir? It's during flirting, courtship, sex. Music's all that.[24]

Buckley believed that his "true" identity came out through singing, replacing his old identity, developed during childhood. Singing not only offered an emotional outlet but also rid him of characteristics with which he did not identify. He mysteriously referred to the voice as an "elixir," perhaps envisioning the emotional catharsis of singing as creating a musical love potion, since emotional sharing often brings people together. Like Cusick's sense of musicosexuality, Buckley's voice conveyed his identifications and his feelings, and seduced his listeners, seeming to entice them into an intimate relationship with him.

Two musical analyses will help illustrate both the transgendered nature of his singing as well as the intimacy it invited. Buckley used his voice uninhibitedly as part of his musical aesthetic of raw, spontaneous expression. His song "Mojo Pin" (which he wrote with his early collaborator, guitar virtuoso Gary Lucas) serves as an unusually vulnerable opening for a 1990s alternative rock album. Buckley's high, gentle voice enters imperceptibly from within intricate, delicate guitar movement. Wordlessly, he warms into the song, as if he were one of the Sufi singers he so greatly admired.[25] When he finally uses lyrics he immediately calls into question his own safety—a decidedly unusual introduction for a male rock singer: "I'm lying in my bed / The blanket is warm / This body will never be safe from harm." Vulnerability also exudes from this record's unusually high level of audible consonants and extraneous sound-forming declamation. Buckley refused to clean up the recording with a "de-esser"—thus the presence of tongue and mouth sounds (especially singing the words "touch my skin") makes him appear to be very close (close to the microphone and thus to the listener) and reveals the source of the words and sounds emerging from his body. Using a vulnerable voice to remind listeners of the excesses and uncontrollability of the body is certainly an unusual way to evoke masculinity in popular music.

Later in the song he sings about being submissive to a sexual partner, "The welts of your scorn, my love, give me more / Send whips of opinion down my back, give me more." The wordplay of his lyrics suggests that the lover's aggressive words have a physical effect on Buckley, who seems to be playing the submissive partner asking to be dominated. "Mojo Pin" in performance could be a mixture of quiet vulnerability and intense sexual passion, and also, at times, a tribute to women's sexuality—in the live performances of this song that he called the "Chocolate" version, he added a verse about performing oral sex on a female partner: "Love turn me on / Let me turn you all over with my thumb on your tongue / Rest your heel on my shoulder / Your love is like chocolate on the tongue of God."[26] Because the song is cyclic and keeps shifting from one section to the other, the more aggressive musical sections of "Mojo Pin" always transform into the vulnerable again, thus seeming like contained outbursts of anger or strength within an otherwise delicately beautiful environment. "Mojo Pin" illustrates the appealing but risky relationship between desired intimacy and the danger of vulnerability, which is a crucial aspect of his performance aesthetic, and one to which fans are particularly drawn.

What does it mean to have a "vulnerable" voice? Must it feel vulnerable to the singer or is it a controlled performance by a calculating artist trying to evoke a certain feeling among his listeners? Does it matter? In her book about Buckley's album *Grace*, Daphne Brooks analyses "Mojo Pin" to argue that Buckley's vocal vulnerability was actually created through what she calls "a controlled spectacle of artfully losing control with the voice."[27] However, audiences often felt that Buckley was taking both himself and listeners to a shared space of vulnerability. In other words, they really felt that he was at times losing control too, and this encouraged them to go there with him. Another example, one of his improvisations, will help explore this issue.

Buckley's cover of Van Morrison's "The Way Young Lovers Do" could sound uncomfortably out of control, to the point of almost falling apart, going out of tune, or sounding ugly. Compared to Van Morrison's short and straightforward verse-and-chorus performance in a traditionally masculine lower register, Buckley improvises in a scat-inspired style for ten minutes, sprinkling his performance with fragments of Morrison's song. His apparent goal is spontaneous expression, risking everything, even the performance almost falling apart, for devotion to the moment. He pushes his voice in extreme directions: he exerts extra control by vibrating in a tight, purposely ugly way. He lets his voice go past its normal boundaries, until it shudders as he descends past where he can sustain the sound, and he reaches up high, either soft and trembling, or, in a rare moment, he pushes right out of his normally high register into an extreme upper register, one which few female singers can reach. His voice builds wordlessly as if he was going to open up Sufi-style like the beginning of "Mojo Pin," but instead he holds on, tightening. His delicate trembling and shuddering first seem like nervousness.[28] For fans, the exquisite revelation is that these vocal irregularities are more than nerves—through spontaneity and vulnerability he seems to be singing as if he were the fragile young lover himself and this expression is almost too much to bear. This identification seems to be confirmed when he steps back from the intense wailing at the end and moves inward, adding his own gasping, yearning verse about the young lovers before his frenzied end.

For fans, Buckley seemed both brave for taking risks and attractively vulnerable and open as a performer. One female fan explains:

> I love that he was such a risk taker vocally. Even at the cost of making a total ass of himself. I love how he pushed and explored forfitting [sic] his ego . . . you know singing from a woman's point of view. . . . I love that there were times where he would just take it completely over the top . . . . [S]ometimes his voice wouldn't quite make it where he wanted to go or he'd slip unintentionally out of key. No matter, you know he was giving it his all. Then there are times where he just goes off . . . out there . . . and no one seems to know just where he's going and then he pulls it back into place and it just fucking stuns you.[29]

She enjoys Buckley's risk taking even when or perhaps *because* it brings him to vocally uncontrollable places and places where he seems to abandon traditional masculinity for a wider range of expression. To the fan, Buckley seems to lose his ego by doing this. Part of the thrill is that he seems to lose control, going in unknown directions, being open to making mistakes, and then being able to "pull it back into place" again. Fans, as they listen, sometimes feel that they are surrendering to such moments. They describe the intense experience of having hidden feelings drawn from them. One fan, Nessa, writes:

> Its [sic] a bit of a love/hate relationship that I have over those over-whelming moments. . . . I hate how deeply they affect me (I already, quote, "feel too deeply, think too much") but then I love that it can touch me so much. Its [sic] amazing when you find something that can so deeply touch you in so many ways . . . art that can reach out and grab you . . . something that can even change you (how you think, feel, what you do, whatever).[30]

Nessa's feelings are mixed. The music overwhelms her, but somehow it positively changes her, and she appreciates this and seeks the experience. But it can feel invasive and sometimes fans take a break from listening to his music regularly. Another female fan explains:

> putting *Grace* on after a break is like diving into deep sea water. It is such a sensory overload, familiar and all-encompassing. It is a little bit scary in the emotions it can elicit from deep within me, I know

they lurk there, like shadows out of the corner of my eye, just waiting to show themselves. There are such moments of intense joy and
sadness there . . . .[31]

One gets the sense of an intimate relationship fans have with this music
and Buckley's persona in the many (somewhat unexplained) fan testimonies of having his music draw hidden feelings to the surface of their consciousness. The adjective "intimate" suggests "familiarity," is "indicative
of one's deepest nature," refers to something "private," or is related to a
"sexual relationship."[32] Fans continually discuss Buckley's music and the
relationship they feel that they have with him on these terms. One young
male fan, who calls himself "juvenescentboy," posts to an online journal
Web site:

Jeff speaks to me and tells me things about myself that I have always
known, but have been afraid to discover. . . . Every note that escapes
Jeff's guitar right now was played with me in mind. His words exist
only as I want them to. . . . The living sounds that fill the room echo
off the walls. The soft light is part of the sound. The gentle noise of
my fingers striking keys meshes with the music in my head, adding
to the feel. All is part of the sound of the guitar. The thoughts in my
head are calm, yet inspired. The breeze from the fan brings me closer
to the music. My apple juice tastes like a symphony. He is a trusted
friend, when others have let me down or aren't there. . . . The feeling
of loneliness that I deal with constantly is both richer and deeper, as
well as less worrisome. I may have no one, but the music is here.[33]

This intimacy propels the listener into his deepest nature, guiding him in
a familiar, friendly way to accept difficult aspects of himself. This listener
suggests that he has a choice in his interpretation of Buckley's music, so
that he is allowing himself to discover, through this music, certain fright-
ening aspects of himself that he would not want to address "alone," perhaps including issues of sexuality, depression, or mortality.

Such intimacy can feel almost sexual, as one fan, a 30-something
American mother, chatted on the *Jeff Buckley Board* (www.ezboard.com)
with a female 40-something Scottish freelance writer and musician:

That version of "I Woke Up in a Strange Place" is the most intense
music I've heard in a long time. The first time I heard it I was almost
ashamed to listen because he reavealed [sic] so much. . . . It's one of
my most favorite Jeff songs—a peak [sic] into his raw soul.[34]

The Scottish fan responded, "I know exactly what you mean. . . . That feeling
that you're eavesdropping, playing Peeping Tom. But you're not, you know

. . . he's giving himself freely." To fans, it appears that Buckley intended to be this open, so it feels appropriate to return that openness, even if it feels strangely sexual (which is why one would feel like a "Peeping Tom" rather than just a spy). The first fan then continued:

> Through his music and other mediums, I know more about . . . how he felt about his life than I do about people close to me. . . . I don't want to know things about people that I don't want to reveal of myself. But I suspect that if I ever would have met Jeff, I would have revealed all. Because when I listen to his music, especially certain songs, I analyze myself. Some things people can't face about themselves so they stock it away hoping it will never resurface. Jeff's music brings up all that stuff for me. Makes me face my own reality and deal with it some-how. Either make it alright or make it a part of who I am.

Buckley's unusual level of intimacy in his performances might have made some feel like "Peeping Toms" unless they were also open to revealing some of themselves (even if it was only to themselves). For this fan, this level of intimacy is something she reserves for her relationship with Buckley, as opposed to those "close to [her]."

Jeff Buckley's songs, which were often about intimacy with another person, were intended to create intimacy between him and his listeners. He said "tender communication is so alien in our culture, *except* in per-formance."[35] In this comment he values performance for allowing "ten-der communication." He wanted to challenge himself and his audiences to experience this intimacy, later reflecting on his days playing at the tiny New York café called Sin-é, "I figured if I played in the no-man's land of intimacy, I'll learn how to be a performer."[36] In this loud diner regular patrons were not always prepared for Jeff's intimate performances (that is, until word spread about him and crowds flocked to Sin-é). He liked the challenge of singing in a restaurant and choosing a key that worked with the hum of the dishwasher and still creating riveting musical moments despite the distractions. Parker Kindred, the second drummer to play with the Jeff Buckley Band, said that "a lot of people want to sit, drink beer, and not feel. Jeff's music forced them to feel."[37] Kindred said that he could tell, even within a concert, how this music changed people in the audi-ence. Bandmate and guitarist Michael Tighe said that Jeff intended to force people to contend with the intimacy that he compelled through his perfor-mances and to face themselves as a result, an experience that people seek from live music.[38] Although Buckley was skilled at creating this intimacy with strangers in his audience, it could also feel fleeting and one-sided.[39] In 1994, the year he released *Grace,* his first album, he remarked:

I'm still not comfortable with what I do. Every time I get home after a show, I feel really strange—like when you wake up in the morning and you realize that you went out the night before, got high, and told some stranger all the most intimate details of your life. It's kind of embarrassing.[40]

Buckley suggests a loss of control in performance, one in which he reveals too much. His description of performance sounds like the way people describe how they feel the morning after a one-night stand. Cultural theorist Lauren Berlant writes that "[intimacy's] potential failure to stabilize closeness always haunts its persistent activity, making the very attachments deemed to buttress 'a life' seem in a state of constant if latent vulnerability."[41] Berlant's comments seem intended for theorizing personal relationships, yet the very act of performing with intimacy that, in some ways, was similar to a relationship, suggests how powerful and unusual Buckley's musical performances must have been. Well into his tragically short career, he realized that his commitment to spontaneous, intimate, and widely ranged gendered expression would always leave him feeling vulnerable. He explained this tension over what an interviewer called his "exposing style," saying:

It's not really exposing. I mean it is, but . . . more accurately, for me, it's more like just speaking your heart . . . just things you've never admitted before and it feels great. . . . I . . . never get used to the feeling of having revealed some of myself, but I just get used to not getting used to it.[42]

This intimacy he sought with his audience could feel uncomfortable for both Buckley and audiences.[43] Critic Greg Kot writes:

There's a fine line between drama and melodrama, and Jeff and his musician father Tim Buckley both crossed that line more than a few times. I saw Jeff perform several times, and it was almost unbearably intimate at times. You either were pulled in or you brushed it off as self-indulgence. But there was no in-between. . . . [44]

Kot suggests that one must either allow Jeff, in his confessional, exposing performance style, to pull one in, or reject the whole performance. To allow passively such a performer to pull one in might have seemed a risk to some listeners' heterosexual, masculine identities. To maintain their masculinity, these listeners assure themselves that Buckley's transgendered, vulnerable performances are simply "self-indulgence," a common criticism (and one made by Lovesey when he calls him "narcissistic").

Yet, what does it mean to call a performance "self-indulgent"? It may seem to some that singing in such a feminine, emotive way could only be a vanity project, because the singer is too involved in his own emotional world and is not attending to the audience. This may be all that Lovesey and others mean, but "self-indulgent" also suggests sexual connotations. Critic John Harris calls Buckley "masturbatory": "When he wants to, Jeff Buckley . . . can sing like a lovesick nightingale. Trouble is, he knows it—and the masturbatory, for-my-next-trick results are frequently unbearable."[45] Perhaps Harris uses the term because he thinks Buckley enjoys his own voice too much, singing as if he is sexually pleasuring himself, as if he cannot pull his focus away from his (feminine) "lovesick nightingale" warbling. If Buckley did not seem to notice or take pleasure in his own supposedly effeminate voice, then Harris might not have such a problem with it. It is Buckley's awareness of and pleasure in this voice that make it "masturbatory." Calling his singing "masturbatory" is obviously meant as an insult and a way to "brush off" Buckley's performance. To sing as though one is sexually pleasuring oneself seems indecent to Harris. Sexuality, as it seems to many, is meant to be shared with a partner of the opposite sex. Pleasuring oneself seems narcissistic, and as in Ovid's myth of Narcissus, liking oneself is too close to liking one who looks like you. In other words, masturbation may be too close for comfort to being gay.[46] Harris spells out the anxious straight man's fear here—Buckley's voice is expressive to the point of sounding effeminate, overly sexual, and perhaps even gay. Transgendered identification is often incorrectly conflated with homosexuality. Intriguingly, because of this masturbatory quality, Harris describes Buckley's recordings as "unbearable." While Harris uses "unbearable" as a clear criticism, the "unbearability" that Kot describes is a challenge, one that fans seek: they desire and return this intimacy and musical experience of sensuality, even at the cost of, or perhaps purposely *because* the intimacy can become unbearable. For fans, the pleasure of intimacy is mingled with pain of self-examination and feeling exposed, as suggested in some of the testimonies above. An orgasm can be an "almost unbearable" sexual experience (because of the tension, the wait, the extreme intimacy if it is shared with a partner, or even the intimacy with oneself). Listening to Jeff Buckley, it seems, can be overwhelming to one's sense of emotional control in a similar way to having an orgasm.

The setup of Buckley's band and their performance aesthetic tells us more about this almost sexual style of performance. Because of the vulnerability and intimacy that Buckley required of his performances, his construction of a band was slightly unusual, at least for a musician of his skill and status (who either would have been expected to have grown an organic band based on musical interests and talent before signing a contract, or who would be expected to choose the most skilled performers possible). For Buckley, who put together a band after he was signed to a major record label, choosing bandmates had more to do with their character than their musical experience. All of the friendly, open bandmates he chose were inexperienced—especially compared to Gary Lucas, who had wanted Jeff to continue playing with him). Matt Johnson, original drummer of Buckley's band, explains that in his audition:

> there was a moment when we were playing and Jeff came up in front of the drum kit and closed his eyes and threw back his head and almost smiled. It was as if he had made a realization within himself that it felt right, like he was getting the okay from his intuition. After we were done, he said "I want to play with you."[47]

This story suggests a bonding experience almost sexual in nature. If his performances felt almost sexually intimate, choosing the right male musician friends to share and support these moments would have been very important. In fact, Jeff once suggested to an interviewer the similarities between his body position when singing and when making love: "'some of the pictures that have been taken of me onstage have brought back a couple of happy memories when I look at them—y'know, head thrown back, jaw locked, sightless eyes. . . .' Jeff does his orgasm face."[48] Merri Cyr's photograph of Jeff singing and playing air guitar (Figure 11.1) beautifully illustrates the sexual and musical feeling of cathartic release that he describes.[49]

Buckley also described the similarities between singing and orgasm in the positive feeling of losing control in the moment:

> I try to make my music joyful—it makes me joyful—to feel that music soar through the body. It changes your posture, you raise your chin, throw back your shoulders, walk with a swagger. When I sing, my face changes shape. It feels like my skull changes shape . . . the bones bend. "Grace" and "Eternal Life" are about the joy that music gives—the, probably illusory, feeling of being able to do anything. Sex is like that. You become utterly consumed by the moment. Apparently orgasm is the only point where your mind becomes completely empty—you think of nothing for that second. That's why it's so compelling—it's a tiny taste of death. Your mind is void—you have nothing in your head save white light. Nothing save white light and "Yes!"—which is fantastic. Just knowing "Yes."[50]

Buckley describes a musical and sexual gendered identity here that identifies partly as traditionally masculine and partly feminine. Singing seems to have made him feel as though he is moving in an assertive, manly way. He

Figure 11.1 Jeff Buckley by Merri Cyr. Used with permission.

feels powerful, as though he can do anything. But the only way to feel this power is also to give up control, to be "consumed by the moment," to feel "a tiny taste of death," which makes him feel vulnerable, feminine, and orgasmically joyful. Consequently his feeling of being powerful comes from allowing the music to "soar through the body," a willful loss of control that gives "the, probably illusory, feeling of being able to do anything." Singing, for him, combined aspects of musical performance that have, traditionally, been labeled either masculine or feminine:

> Words are really beautiful, but they're limited. Words are very male, very structured. But the voice is the netherworld, the darkness, where

there's nothing to hang on to. The voice comes from a part of you that just knows and expresses and is. I need to *inhabit* every bit of a lyric, or else I can't bring the song to you—or else it's just words.[51]

He describes a gendered opposition between masculine, structured words and embodied voice, which comes from a place in his body "where there's nothing to hang on to," a place that perhaps seemed less controlled, more feminine compared to the structured, controllable "masculine" words. Roland Barthes makes a similar distinction between vocal performance that not only enunciates words but also captures the embodiment of voice and language (as opposed to more "clean" singing which would try to cut out the "extraneous" bodily sounds).[52] Seemingly in concurrence with Barthes's theory, Buckley said that his music was "about the voice carrying more information than the words do."[53] Barthes also suggests that the "grain" of the voice opens up for its listeners the experience of "*jouissance*," a kind of musical orgasm, similar to what Buckley describes.

Thus, it may be Buckley's effeminizing willingness to lose control, to reach inside himself to a place that feels feminine, and to share something so private that it seems sexual and perhaps inappropriate, that may cause discomfort for some. However, these same qualities attract many fans, who willingly identify with him and his multigendered persona and cherish his music as a means of relating across boundaries. One female fan, an art historian, identifies with him seemingly because he transcends gender boundaries:

jb [Jeff Buckley], like prince [sic] and pj [P.J. Harvey], is/was the kind of musician i [sic] always wanted to be; technically proficient, emotionally honest and expressive, sexually and spiritually aware. they [sic] are all defiantly individual and androgynous and open to the darkness and light in humanity. they [sic] strive and challenge, change and grow. i [sic] have always experienced jb's music as sublime—it touches you in very specific places and then provides a conduit to our vast sameness.[54]

And what about the straight male fans who have some explaining to do about why they would want to kiss him? How has Buckley's music affected the way in which they understand straight masculinity? Mike Webb, a musician and critic, gives an interesting example of the discomforting appeal that straight male fans might encounter. He says of his first Buckley concert:

He was awe-inspiring. I described it as Ella Fitzgerald meets Jimmy Page, and I actually (if not accidentally) went up to him after the show and hugged him. I'd never met him, and didn't really mean to, but it was a very moving gig, and he was kind of drained, and we just did that manly "right on B" kinda hug.[55]

Although Webb gives exalting praise to the performance, the hug is the focal point of this story because of the challenges it poses to each man's masculinity. White straight American men do not often hug each other, especially not strangers. He has to explain the hug because it seems like a surprisingly emotional thing to do to this man he does not know. He is not sure if he did it on purpose or accidentally, but the performance moved him and Buckley seemed "drained," sort of vulnerable. Maybe the hug was as "manly" as Webb describes with his masculinizing black slang ("right on B[rother]"), but it was strange enough that it stood out to him and was worth qualifying. For any fan, it is unusual to approach a performer you do not know and hug him after a performance: such behavior seems to cross a line between appreciating that an artist's work moves you and actually feeling as though you have a relationship with that artist. Many fans feel as though Buckley's music fosters that sort of imagined or ambiguous relationship. Buckley's former tour-mate Brenda Kahn points out the unusual and potentially risky nature of this relationship: "There was something insanely vulnerable about him, which made him really attractive to people."[56]

Some have been so attracted to this vulnerability that they aspire to a different kind of masculinity. One male listener writes:

As a musician I am inspired beyond words with his openness and emotional range . . . his fearless expression of his feminine side. Growing up the typical Southern California youth where your "manliness" was a measure of your social status and being into bands like Iron Maiden and Metallica typified this way of thinking, discovering Jeff opened a whole new world for me . . . one that allowed me to dig deep into myself and find the full range of who I am.[57]

Again, Buckley's music does not push the listener to be like him, or like any other singer, but rather the listener feels that he is finding "the full range of who [he is]" by Buckley's example. Buckley's arguably most surprising influence has been on actor Brad Pitt. Voted by MTV Movie Award voters as "Most Desirable Male" in 1995 and 1996, Best Supporting Actor in a Motion Picture by the Golden Globe Awards in 1996, and "sexiest man alive" by People magazine in both 1995 (after starring in the movie Troy) and in 2000 (after his marriage to Friends star Jennifer Aniston), Pitt was one gauge of what masculinity meant in the 1990s. In a BBC documentary about Buckley, Pitt testifies:

For me, the thing that distinguishes him the most is that he was about love. He had no shame with addressing the subject of love. I wouldn't think it was brave for him, I think it was something he was led to do. But you look around and most of us are trying to be tough guys, trying to be de Niros, and here was a guy that went the complete opposite direction, in the middle of the '90s. I have a lot of respect for that 'cause I have this feeling at the end of the day when all's said and done that's all that's going to matter, isn't it?[58]

Allegedly, Pitt has even asked to play Buckley in a biographical film, an uncharacteristically transgressive gender role for him.[59] Why would Brad Pitt, whom one critic called "the utopian dick," admire and want to play in a movie the "chanteuse with a penis"?[60] It may be that this music reveals possibilities that some men did not realize were available to them and makes these possibilities feel organic, as though they have always existed within themselves. In one of the songs Buckley was working on for his second album, he sings "I'm not with you but of you." For fans, this kind of extreme intimacy is valuable, even at the cost of its unbearability, or perhaps because of it.

Notes

1. Thanks to Fred E. Maus, Susan Fraiman, Nadine Hubbs, Rose Theresa, Mary Simonson, and Loren Ludwig, who commented helpfully on earlier drafts and presentations, and to the members of *A Jeff Buckley Board* at www.ezboard.com, whose fan community offered much insight.
2. Rufus Wainwright, comments from his performance at Wolf Trap Center for the Performing Arts, Vienna, Virginia, August 3, 2005.
3. Eve Kosofsky Sedgwick lists many aspects of attraction, fantasy, and sexual behavior overlooked by a solely gender-based system of labeling sexuality. See Eve Kosofsky Sedgwick, *Epistemology of the Closet* (Berkeley: University of California Press, 1990), 25–26.
4. Simon Frith, "Towards an Aesthetic of Popular Music," *Music and Society,* ed. Richard Leppert and Susan McClary (Cambridge: Cambridge University Press, 1987), 133–149 (140, 141).
5. Suzanne Cusick, "On a Lesbian Relationship with Music: A Serious Effort Not to Think Straight," *Queering the Pitch: The New Gay and Lesbian Musicology,* ed. Philip Brett, Elizabeth Wood, and Gary C. Thomas (London and New York: Routledge, 1994), 67–84 (78).
6. Cusick, "On," 70. Feminist and queer theorization of sexuality has reinterpreted sex such that reproduction is but one element.
7. Cusick, "On," 75. The term "musicking," coined by Christopher Small, refers to any aspect of musical performance or reception, such as listening, dancing, humming, or playing an instrument, as important aspects of creating musical events. Christopher Small, *Musicking: The Musical Meanings of Performing and Listening* (Hanover, NH: University Press of New England, 1998). While Cusick does not use this word, it captures the broad range of activities she has in mind.
8. Thanks to Oren Magid for sharing his thoughtful paper, in which he quotes his friend. "The Vulnerability, Androgyny, and Music of Jeff Buckley," unpublished manuscript (December 19, 1998). This fan is certainly not

alone. On *A Jeff Buckley Board* (www.ezboard.com), another fan posted in a forum about compatibility with Jeff, "As a guy who 100% loves the ladies over the gents, and with official documentation to prove it, I would've kissed him!" (June 20, 2005).

9. Thanks to Kim "Mirko" Wilkins from the University of Queensland for her analysis of Buckley's vocal range. http://jeffbuckley.com/rfuller/buckley/faq/07vocals.html.

10. Like the film narrator or the news reporter, the universal voice of rock can be said to be male. Women can cover male singers' songs and they are not subject to the same imperative to change the gendered pronouns, because they clearly are not men—their versions of male-narrated songs can be seen as connecting to the "universal" perspective. Men, on the other hand, do not so often sing female-narrated songs without changing the pronouns, because it would be more noticeable (and arguably more transgressive) for a man to sing as a woman, since he would be taking on the "subordinated" gender position. Jeff Buckley ignored this common practice.

Although the lyrics of "The Other Woman" do not predicate the singer representing the betrayed wife (rather than an outside narrator), listeners can easily identify a female singer as the wife, singing heartbreakingly about her cheating husband. Buckley's performance of this song during his recording sessions for his album *Grace* (Sony Legacy C3K 92881), 2004, is tender and vulnerable, in a higher register and more quiet and trepidatious than Nina Simone's performance. The most poignant moment comes when he sings a line where the wife seems to be reconciled that her husband is now the other woman's "old man." This line, "and when her old man comes to call," is sung with so much emotion that it seems to be coming from the wife's point of view. Buckley sometimes changed the gendered pronouns, singing Simone's "Be My Husband" as "Be Your Husband," but the gender pronoun shift was not enough to overcome the feminized subject position of the narrator who offers to cook and sew if his partner will only marry him.

11. Kylie Buddin, "Jeff Buckley," *You Could Do Worse Zine* #3 (1994–1995), http://www.jeffbuckley.com/rfuller/buckley/words/.

12. This opinion about Edith Piaf was expressed by French Jeff Buckley fans in their twenties whom I interviewed in Paris in July 2004. I would like to thank Benoit, Véronique, Neyra, and Muriel for giving generously of their time, memories, and ideas about Buckley and his music.

13. That he used these terms to describe himself is well known and discussed among the listening community. However, the direct source for this quotation is, at the time of press, unknown. During an interview included on a DVD with the Columbia Legacy Edition of *Grace,* Buckley says, "I wanted to be a singer, a chanteuse!" Biographer David Browne refers to him as a "male chanteuse." David Browne, *Dream Brother: The Lives and Music of Jeff and Tim Buckley* (New York: Harper Entertainment, 2001), 146.

14. Rebecca Kane writes: "Some artists who left an impression on Jeff included Nusrat Fateh Ali Khan, Edith Piaf, Judy Garland, Nina Simone, MC5, Miles Davis, Duke Ellington, Led Zeppelin, Rush, Genesis, Weather Report, Rolling Stones, Pink Floyd, The Who, Patti Smith, The Cocteau Twins, Elvis Costello, Lou Reed, Merle Haggard, Aretha Franklin, The Pixies, David Bowie, Sebadoh, Stevie Wonder and Louis Armstrong.

"An early 'guitar chops' hero was Al Dimeola. Also high on his list were Jimi Hendrix and Robert Johnson, as well as Joe Pass. Songwriting influences included Joni Mitchell, Carole King and Bob Dylan. Jeff's vocal style was greatly influenced by Nusrat Fateh Ali Khan, as well as Mahalia Jackson, Ella Fitzgerald, Robert Plant and Freddie Mercury." http://jeff-buckley.com/rfuller/buckley/faq/09influen.html.

15. A transgendered person's gender is often either ambiguous or passes as the "opposite" sex. The term "transsexual" is reserved for those who choose sex reassignment via hormones and/or surgery. During the 1990s, "transgender" was the celebrated identity of queer studies (inspired by Judith Butler's *Gender Trouble* [London and New York: Routledge, 1990]). Embraced for its performative ambiguity, transgender seemed to be a state of flux that exposed the constructedness and oppression of the binary gender system, a system that, according to Butler, supports and naturalizes heterosexuality. (Transsexual operations, on the other hand, are sometimes interpreted as reinforcing the binary gender system. For example see Janis Raymond, *The Transsexual Empire: The Making of the She-Male* [New York: Teachers College Press, 1994]. For a counter-argument see Jay Prosser, *Second Skins: The Body Narratives of Transsexuality* [New York: Columbia University Press, 1998].)

16. Oliver Lovesey, "Anti-Orpheus: Narrating the Dream Brother," *Popular Music* 23, no. 3 (2004): 331–348 (340).

17. Ibid., 333.

18. Ibid., 347, n.8.

19. Buckley would do comic impressions of Rush—"Squeakor," the Rat King—or imagine what the members of Led Zeppelin would sound like performing "Kashmir" on speed. These comic interludes, regularly performed between songs throughout his career, suggest an intimate knowledge of these performers in what might have seemed to his audiences to feel like a fan-star relationship (where Buckley identifies with his audience for also being a fan of Led Zeppelin). This humor suggests that Buckley realized how over-the-top some of his favorite music could seem at times. However, he was also serious about covering the performers that he loved. In the *Live at Sin-é* Legacy Edition released by Sony, one can hear Buckley's cover of famous Sufi singer Nusrat Fateh Ali Khan's "Yeh Jo Halka Saroor Hai," complete with Urdu singing, which at first garners a comic reception from the audience, until Buckley continues with what is clearly a serious, lovingly devoted cover version of music that he wanted to share with his fans. Audiences respected his musical influences and I regularly hear, at *A Jeff Buckley Board,* of fans trying to learn more about Sufi music, Led Zeppelin, Edith Piaf, and other music that Buckley loved.

20. Lovesey, "Anti," 341.

21. Delight in artifice and celebration of androgyny are important aspects of camp, as Susan Sontag writes in "Notes on Camp," *Partisan Review* 31, no. 4 (Fall 1964): 515–530.

22. Lovesey argues that the covers and multigenre search were in part a way for Buckley to avoid sounding like his father. It is true that Jeff Buckley struggled with identity issues related to his father. Buckley biographer David Browne makes a convincing case that Jeff's semifamous folk-rock performer

father Tim Buckley's abandonment of Jeff before birth and Tim's early death of a heroin overdose, left Jeff with conflicted feelings about identifying with his father or as a singer with a similar voice as his father (Browne, *Dream*, 108). However, I do not agree with Lovesey that Buckley's wide range of musical interests via cover songs was evidence of his attempts to "murder" his "inherited" voice, which Buckley considered a voice that had been in his family long before his father had.

23. Ann Powers, "Strut Like a Rooster, Fly Like an Eagle, Sing Like a Man: Emotionally Immediate Male Vocalists Take Flight," *Revolver* (May-June 2001): 122.

24. Interview with Matt Diehl, "The Son Also Rises: Fighting the Hype and Weight of his Father's Legend, Jeff Buckley Finds his Own Voice on *Grace*," *Rolling Stone* (October 20, 1994): 68–70, (163).

25. He owned four hundred cassettes of Sufi *qawwali* singing, more than any other kind of music in his collection. On the recently released Legacy edition of *Live at Sin-é* one hears Buckley gush about his adoration of Nusrat Fateh Ali Khan's singing, followed by Buckley's stunning rendition of one of his songs. These Sufi songs tend to build slowly, almost warming up with simple phrases, building into words and more frenzied musical drama.

26. Daphne Brooks, in her book about this album, argues that Buckley plays both lovers in "Chocolate" versions of "Mojo Pin," as he "morphs this performance into both sex partners as they hit the pinnacle of wordless ecstasy in song." Daphne Brooks, *Grace* (New York: Continuum, 2005), 90.

27. Ibid., 92, 74, 77. As I understand it, Brooks's use of the word "spectacle" means "performance." However, in film and opera studies, "spectacle" has a more specific meaning as an elaborate and dramatic display, often freezing the narrative, from which audiences could feel safely distanced (as opposed to "narrative," where audiences identify with a main character who is experiencing the development of a plot). A musical number within a musical theater production would be considered a spectacle. While I agree that Buckley seemed, at times, to lose control purposefully, I do not think that audiences felt distanced as if they were watching this sort of "spectacle." For more on spectacle and narrative, see Rose Theresa, "From Méphistophélès to Méliès: Spectacle and Narrative in Opera and Early Film," *Between Opera and Cinema,* ed. Jeongwon Joe and Rose Theresa (London and New York: Routledge, 2002), 1–18.

28. In fact, he *was* nervous. The performance of this song that I describe was recorded in 1993 for his first short album (an EP), *Live at Sin-é*, which Columbia Records used to document (and test on larger audiences) his eclectic Monday night performances at the tiny New York diner Sin-é.

29. User "Jewelbox," thread "The Voice," *A Jeff Buckley Board* (June 13, 2002.)

30. User "MySpiritGenocide," thread "one of those nights when it sounds sooo good . . . ," *A Jeff Buckley Board* (July 10, 2002).

31. User "Shafm," thread "Grace revisited," *A Jeff Buckley Board* (March 19, 2003).

32. *American Heritage College Dictionary,* 3rd ed. (Boston: Houghton Mifflin Company, 1997).

33. User "juvenescentboy," http://www.livejournal.com (September 4, 2001).

34. Two anonymous fans, thread "New Lover," *A Jeff Buckley Board* (August 13, 2002).

35. Dimitri Ehrlich, *Inside the Music: Conversations with Contemporary Musicians about Spirituality, Creativity, and Consciousness* (Boston: Shambhala, 1997), 155.
36. Browne, *Dream*, 167.
37. Interview with the author, Richmond, Virginia, August 20, 2003.
38. Ibid.
39. And there is reason to believe that his love relationships could also tend towards both the very intimate and a more distant one-sidedness. Musician Elizabeth Frasier from the band the Cocteau Twins, who had a relationship with Buckley, said the following in the made-for-TV documentary *Jeff Buckley: Everybody Here Wants You* (dir. Serena Cross, 2002): "To meet Jeffrey was just like being given a set of paints . . . . I had all this color in my life again. I just couldn't help falling in love with him. He was adorable, he was lovely. I read his diary; he read mine. We'd just swap, we'd literally just hand over this very personal stuff, and I've never done that with anybody else; I don't know if he has. So in some ways there was a great deal of intimacy, but then there'd be times when I'd just think, 'I'm just not penetrating this Jeff Buckley boy at all.'"
40. Paul Young, "Talking Music: Confessing to Strangers," *Buzz Magazine* (1994), http://www.jeffbuckley.com/rfuller/buckley/words/interviews/buzz.html.
41. Lauren Berlant, ed., *Intimacy,* special edition of *Critical Inquiry* (Chicago: University of Chicago Press, 2000), 2.
42. Interview with Steve Harris in Japan, transcribed and posted as "Another Jeff interview transcription!!!!," *A Jeff Buckley Board* (August 12, 2003).
43. Lauren Berlant writes that "intimacy . . . involves an aspiration for something shared" but "the inwardness of the intimate is met by a corresponding publicness," in Berlant, *Intimacy*, 1.
44. Greg Kot, *Revolver* (May-June 2001), 120.
45. John Harris, "Jeff Buckley: *Live From the Bataclan*" (December 2000), http://www.q4music.com.
46. Freud (in)famously linked homosexuality with narcissism in his essay "On Narcissism," *The Freud Reader,* ed. Peter Gay (London, Vintage 1995 [1914]), 545–562. See also Eve Kosofsky Sedgwick, "Jane Austen and the Masturbating Girl," *Tendencies* (Durham: Duke University Press, 1993), 109–129, for a discussion of the reasons why masturbation, which used to function as a sexuality called "onanism," is, thanks to our binary sexuality system defined by the gender of one's object of desire, no longer socially acceptable.
47. See Browne, *Dream*, 203.
48. Caitlin Moran, "Orgasm Addict: There is No Name for the Places he or his Voice can't Go," *B-side Magazine* (Fall 1994).
49. I am grateful to Merri Cyr for generously allowing Routledge to reprint her gorgeous photograph here. For more of her professional photographs of musicians, see her book, *A Wished For Song: A Portrait of Jeff Buckley* (New York: Hal Leonard 2002) and her Web site, http://www.merricyr.com.
50. Moran, "Orgasm."

51. Interview by Ray Rogers, "Heir Apparent to . . . ," *Interview Magazine*, February 1994, http://www.jeffbuckley.com/rfuller/buckley/words/interviews/interviewmag0294.html.

52. See Roland Barthes, "The Grain of the Voice," *On Record: Pop, Rock, and the Written Word*, ed. Simon Frith and Andrew Goodwin (London and New York: Routledge, 1990 [1977]), 293–300.

53. Jeff Buckley interview with Aidin Vaziri, *Raygun* (Fall 1994).

54. Anonymous, thread "How Do You Connect With Jeff?," *A Jeff Buckley Board* (April 17, 2003).

55. Mike Webb, "When I met Jeff Buckley," *2Walls Webzine* (November 2000), http://www.2walls.com/MUSIC/music_jeff_buckley.asp.

56. Brenda Kahn quoted in Browne, *Dream*, 258.

57. Anonymous, thread "How Do You Connect With Jeff?," *A Jeff Buckley Board*, (April 17, 2003).

58. Interview with Brad Pitt filmed for a documentary about Jeff Buckley (BBC Four), http://www.bbc.co.uk/bbcfour/music/features/jeff_buckley.shtml.

59. According to Kimberly Brown, reporting for *The New York Times* (October 29, 2006), "Pitt, who at one point had called himself obsessed with Mr. Buckley's music, struggled for two years to make a film inspired by his life. But Ms. Guibert [Buckley's mother and executor of his estate] rejected the scripts he developed as straying too far from reality." There is considerable debate among Buckley's friends and fans as to whether Guibert's impression of Buckley's life is accurate, as the two were somewhat estranged at the time of his death, but the power to approve of a biographical film rests with her, his sole heir. At the time of publication, Guibert was working on her own biopic film, which she expects to release in 2008. The details of Pitt's endeavor are uncertain, but Buckley's influence on him remains noteworthy. See Brown, "Hollywood's Knocking but Mom Guards the Door," at www.nytimes.com.

60. Jonathan L. Beller, "Fight Club's Utopian Dick," http:// www.popmatters.com /film/fight-club.html.

12

"Some of Us Can Only Live in Songs of Love and Trouble"

Voice, Genre/Gender, and Sexuality in the Music of Stephin Merritt

MARK J. BUTLER

I was sitting in a piano bar, . . . and I had read earlier that day, Virgil Thomson I think, commenting on Charles Ives' songbook of 114 songs of all kinds . . . and I thought, I could do something like that. And I had been thinking it would be good to get into the world of musicals, and probably easiest to get into it through a revue of songs . . . The original idea was to have the singers be drag queens.[1]

With these remarks, New York City–based composer Stephin Merritt describes the genesis of *69 Love Songs*, the 1999 triple album recorded with his band The Magnetic Fields that won him widespread critical acclaim. As avatars of musical inspiration, the combination of Thomson, Ives, and torch-singing drag queens might seem unlikely. In Merritt's artistic universe, however, the creative spirits of these figures commingle comfortably. In fact, some of the characteristics they share are also striking features of Merritt's work. The first of these is a radical stylistic eclecticism, through which diverse musical references (including both "high" and "low" genres) mingle freely.[2] Second, both openly gay Merritt and his muses have used music—in sometimes very different ways—to foreground issues of gender and sexuality, and masculinity in particular.[3] Third, the work of all these musicians calls particular attention to "voice" as a bearer of identity. The following chapter addresses the striking ways in which these attributes coexist and interact in the music of Stephin Merritt. I begin by briefly presenting each theme separately in three short introductory sections, which also provide an overview of Merritt's activities as a creative artist. I then turn to an in-depth consideration of relationships among genre, voice, and sexuality within Merritt's work.

Genre: Or, Merritt's Multiple Soundworlds

Like Ives, Merritt has been a tremendously prolific composer. Since 1991, he has recorded approximately two hundred songs (on eleven albums, as well as a variety of EPs and singles), and in interviews he frequently describes additional songs that he has written but chosen not to record. Merritt has also conducted much of his career independently of "official" musical institutions: with the exception of his most recent album (The Magnetic Fields' *i*, 2004), all of his recorded output has been self-produced and released on indie labels such as Chapel Hill, North Carolina's Merge Records. He has recorded under several different names—The 6ths, Future Bible Heroes, The Gothic Archies, and The Magnetic Fields—though none of these are bands in a conventional sense; Merritt is the sole songwriter and principal instrumentalist, as well as the vocalist on a majority of tracks.[4] His music often reveals an interest in experimental traditions and has come to be celebrated by those who value such musical practices;[5] after the success of *69 Love Songs*, The Magnetic Fields were signed to Nonesuch Records, home of artists such as Steve Reich and Laurie Anderson.

Merritt's musical home, however, falls squarely within the domain of pop. His Web site, after characterizing him as a "bubblegum purist," notes that "Merritt credits much of his singular compositional ability to his early grounding in classic Top 40 pop, notably the shimmering structural perfection of ABBA (which he cites as his favorite band)."[6] The way in which Merritt has realized and framed his compositional activities in the form of "bands" also reveals a fascination with pop traditions. To those unfamiliar with his work, the simultaneous evocation of pop in its most commercially successful forms and avant-garde influences may seem surprising, for long-standing ideologies of artistic practice have conventionally positioned pop (in opposition to rock and other styles) as the nadir of authenticity and originality.[7] But in Merritt's work, extreme manifestations of "high" and "low" music coexist, rubbing against each other in productive and surprising ways.

Indeed, the stylistic breadth of Merritt's music is one of its most notable features; his songs encompass genres as diverse as punk, Tin Pan Alley, minimalism, country, and jazz. In combination with numerous direct lyrical references, these constantly shifting genres call attention to the history, institutions, and stylistic conventions of popular music, foregrounding it as a thematic element in its own right. In one segment of *69 Love Songs,* for instance (songs 49–52), we encounter "Busby Berkeley Dreams," in which Merritt sings lyrics that recall the poetic style of Cole Porter; then "I'm Sorry I Love You," which is rendered by Shirley Simms in a straightforward country style; third comes "Acoustic Guitar," sung by Claudia Gonson and strongly referencing the folk style of "women's music" (while also mentioning Steve Earle, Charo, and Gwar); and finally, "The Death of Ferdinand de Saussure," a ballad in which the Swiss semiotician, after proclaiming that "we don't know anything about love," is murdered to avenge the memory of Holland, Dozier, and Holland! While intertextuality is characteristic of popular music in general, the sheer number and range of genres involved in Merritt's music and the degree to which he treats popular music itself as a subject are exceptional.

Voice

The above list of songs also highlights the astonishing vocal diversity of Merritt's work. His *oeuvre* features a large number of soloists, both male and female, whose voices often differ remarkably in timbre, range, and delivery. Some of the more well-known singers with whom he has worked include Odetta, Gary Numan, and '60s folk singer Melanie (accompanied on the toy piano by new-music pianist Margaret Leng Tan).[8] Although Merritt sings the majority of his songs (see the Appendix for further information), he himself possesses more than one voice: most commonly he inhabits a baritone range, but he sometimes approaches a tenor register and at other times pushes his voice down into *basso profondo* depths.[9]

Paralleling this interest in unique vocal qualities is a fascination with diverse instrumental sounds. Merritt plays an extremely wide range of instruments on his recordings; *69 Love Songs,* for instance, lists a total of ninety-six different instruments on which he performs. These include twenty-three string instruments (e.g., mandolin, autoharp, multiple ukuleles, sitar), twenty-three keyboards (e.g., Moog Satellite, Juno 106, Wurlitzer electronic piano), thirty acoustic percussion instruments (e.g., xylophone, steel drum, thunder sheet), ten "rhythm units" (e.g., Roland TR-707), seven wind instruments (e.g., ocarina, pennywhistle), and three voice-modification tools (e.g., vocoder). To the extent that instruments function as a representation of the performer in popular music (in which many well-known musicians are strongly associated with a particular instrument), Merritt's use of multiple instruments represents a way of playing with identity that is clearly linked to the multivocality of his music. Notably, his most frequently used instrument is the synthesizer, itself a tool for the creation of diverse and often strangely unfamiliar sounds.

Gender and Sexuality

Most contemporary pop and rock performers or bands present the sound of a particular singer or group of singers as a consistent public "face." In contrast, the multivocality of Merritt's work subverts stable, direct mappings of the biological sex of the singer onto the gender of the character singing. Filtered through the lenses of gender, sexuality, and lyrical personae, the profusion of voices that populate his songs enables the articulation of a wide range of subjectivities. Interpretive issues related to sexuality emerge especially often in the music of The Magnetic Fields, whose members include Merritt, who is gay; Claudia Gonson, who is lesbian; and John Woo and Sam Davol, who are heterosexual. Both Merritt and Gonson have discussed their sexuality frequently in public contexts, and the characters that inhabit Merritt's songs express points of view that are frequently, but not exclusively, openly gay. These characters also present a multiplicity of gendered selves, revealing a keen awareness of dominant constructions while simultaneously illustrating alternative ways in which gendered subjectivities might be configured.

To summarize, Merritt's music articulates a complex space in which genre and voice intersect with gender and sexuality, and it is precisely this nexus that I wish to explore. By focusing on Merritt as an openly gay musician, I hope to show some of the ways in which music can articulate discourses of sexuality and gender in a contemporary American landscape in which both homosexuality and the forces attempting to control and police it are increasingly visible in public discourse. I will draw on a variety of scholarship theorizing gay male sexuality and its communicative conventions, though the majority of my argument will revolve around detailed considerations of the verbal and musical language of five songs. Each of these songs appears on *69 Love Songs*, which is widely regarded as Merritt's magnum opus. Although the features of Merritt's music that I have pointed out are realized in an especially clear and striking fashion on this album, they are also broadly characteristic of his work as a whole, as occasional references to other songs will reveal.

> Two characters been listening all night long
> For voices from Nashville above.[10]

Much of the existing research on gay male popular musicians has emphasized the ways in which their music participates in the discursive practices surrounding the closet, a cultural institution that is both characterized and supported by veiled communication and indirect language.[11] Fred Maus, for instance, has discussed the operation of "double-voicedness" and "deniability" in songs of the Pet Shop Boys. Describing how some listeners have strong perceptions of queer content in the Pets' music, while others see no particular associations with homosexuality, he notes that their music "describes situations and feelings that are basic to much twentieth-century gay life, but leaves out any fully determinate specification of sexuality."[12] As a result, "there are many songs in which gay listeners find strong evocations of gay lives about which, nonetheless, nothing can be proved."[13] Nadine Hubbs, meanwhile, has observed a similar phenomenon in Morrissey's songs with The Smiths:

> Morrissey has steadfastly refused to declare (or confirm) a gay subject position. But still he chooses to explore queer themes, in the most knowledgably "inside" of queer-insider language. This sign is abundantly meaningful to other insiders: for queer listeners, Morrissey's work is about queer erotics and experience. I know of no queer fan who perceives Morrissey's work or persona in terms at all straight. . . .
>
> I also know of straight fans who harbor no notion that Morrissey or his work has anything to do with queerness.[14]

Such dual functions are made possible through mechanisms of ambiguity and ambivalence, which both authors reveal in the lyrical and musical dimensions of these artists' songs as well as in their public personae. Hubbs, for example, highlights a textual dynamic in which erotic energy circulates around male figures whose status as objects of desire is articulated ambiguously, while female objects are defined more clearly yet desired ambivalently.[15] Maus, in turn, describes a number of songs that move between two different key areas without ever clearly specifying which is primary.[16]

Some of Merritt's songs also seem to reference these mechanisms of the "language of the closet." Consider, for instance, "The Luckiest Guy on the Lower East Side," excerpts from which are shown in Figure 12.1.[17] On its surface, the song appears transparently heterosexual: innocent references to candy and proms recall '60s teen-pop, and conventional indicators of female gender suggest that vocalist Dudley Klute is singing to a woman. Inverted, however, these signs of gender produce a song that is quintessentially camp. This double-voicedness is especially evident in verse 3, in which the singer twice invokes femininity as a feeling or quality that one might have. In so doing, he implies that his object of affection is neither a woman nor a little girl; his next reference, tellingly, is to secrets. More broadly, the text is also curious as a realization of the "list song," for what is enumerated, with poetic pleasure, is a series of men's names.[18]

Several musical and performative qualities underline the possibility of inversion. Vocalist Dudley Klute delivers the ostensibly straight lyrics in a manner that reads as effeminate: his singing is simultaneously breathy and refined, with quite precise diction; although he sings in a baritone range,

Vocalist: Dudley Klute

2. Harry is the one I think you'll marry,
But it's Chris that you kissed after school.
Well, I'm a fool, there's no doubt,
But when the sun comes out,
And only when the sun comes out,
[Chorus] [Bridge]

3. I know Professor Blumen makes you
feel like a woman
But when the wind is in your hair you laugh
like a little girl.
So you share secrets with Lou,
But we've got secrets too.
Well, one: I only keep this heap for you.
[Chorus]

© 1999 Stephin Merritt. Reprinted with permission.

Figure 12.1A "The Luckiest Guy on the Lower East Side."

Figure 12.1B "The Luckiest Guy on the Lower East Side."

his voice has some of the timbral qualities of a tenor. The most remarkable part of his performance begins at the end of the third chorus, where he sustains the "i" vowel in the final word for a full four bars. He then repeats the phrase "wanna go for a ride" three times, each time singing "ride" on a higher pitch and for an increasingly lengthy duration: first on an $F\sharp^3$ for approximately five bars, then on B^3 for another five bars, and then on a high $F\sharp^4$ for an astonishing ten bars. In contrast to the controlled and "natural" vocal presentation associated with dominant masculinity in most contemporary rock and pop,[19] this breakout from the song's carefully ordered structure seems ecstatic and performative.

The instrumental accompaniment, which consists of a ukulele, a saccharine violin line, and several vividly realized synth sounds (including a "splashy" or "squishy" percussion riff that articulates the beat), also seems at odds with the song's surface narrative. Indeed, this particular sonic configuration, while unique to this song, is typical of Merritt's work, in which the exemplars of rock are largely absent. Despite the extremely wide array of instruments he uses, electric guitars, loud kick drums, and prominent snare backbeats—which have been strongly associated with dominant constructions of masculinity in both popular and scholarly discourse[20]— are not standard elements in his songs.[21] Together, these features work to queer a song that is otherwise almost self-consciously conventional. Yet this reading remains completely deniable: in comparison to the semantic specificity of the lyrics, singing style and instrumentation signify in a more broadly defined expressive domain. In the end, the song *could* describe a man who wears gowns, but it could just as easily portray a teenage girl.

Hubbs and Maus have provided excellent illustrations of how such songs might be interpreted. For much of Merritt's work, however, theoretical models centered around the closet come up short, for many of his songs express same-sex desire in ways that are remarkably direct for today's popular music. In "When My Boy Walks Down the Street," for instance, the male vocalist specifies the gender of his beloved immediately, at the outset of the song (see Figure 12.2). More important, the space in which this song occurs—the street—is the *opposite* of the closet. It is a public space, and "everyone" is watching as this spectacle of love reveals himself. In contrast to the languorousness and inactivity that Hubbs associates with Morrissey's subjectivity,[22] this boy not only inhabits but also moves through his space. Rather than being controlled by his environment, the world itself is said to respond to his agency. The song also evokes a public space in musical terms: its principal instrument, the electric guitar, is distorted through a heavy reverb that strongly calls to mind the "arena" or "stadium" setting on an effects processor.

242 • Mark J. Butler

Vocalist: Stephin Merritt

2. The world does the hula-hula
   When my boy walks down the street.
   Ev'ryone thinks he's Petula
   So big and yet so petite.
   Butterflies turn into people
   When my boy walks down the street.
   Maybe he should be illegal—
   He just makes life too complete.
   [Chorus]
   [Bridge]
   [Repeat verse 1 and fadeout]

© 1999 Stephin Merritt. Reprinted with permission.

Figure 12.2A "When My Boy Walks Down the Street."

Melodic reduction

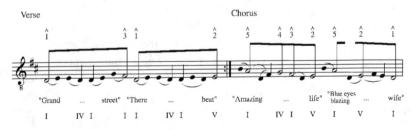

Figure 12.2B "When My Boy Walks Down the Street."

Queerness comes to the fore even more intensely in "Papa Was a Rodeo," presented in Figure 12.3. Desire, voiced directly and unambiguously, is both reciprocated and consummated. Significantly, the song's narrative is structured around a kiss: the first verse takes place in the suspended moment before the kiss (see especially bb. 17–20); the second verse leads up to it; and the third verse reveals the romance that followed it. In each case, the reference to a kiss occurs at a key structural moment, in association with musical characteristics that evoke a sense of suspended anticipation followed by completion. At the end of the first two verses, lyrics describing the impending kiss lead to a cadence on scale-degree 2 supported by dominant harmony (on the word "beer" in verse 1 and "now" in verse 2); the song's title line, supported by tonic harmony, follows immediately thereafter. Near the end of the chorus, the line "before you kiss me you should know" is set apart through a dramatic shift in register and a substantial caesura both before and after its delivery; it concludes with a cadence on scale-degree 3. The arrival on $\hat{3}$ prepares for a stepwise descent to $\hat{2}$ and $\hat{1}$ in the closing line—which, with its reiteration of the title in conjunction with a conclusive cadence on tonic, evokes the resolution that accompanies the kiss's completion.

The spectacle of two men kissing has, of course, been a sight around which homophobia has circulated with particular intensity. In 1994, for instance, a media brouhaha erupted in the United States over a planned kiss between the character Matt and his boyfriend on the show *Melrose Place*. The kiss was filmed, and news of it leaked to the press, but when the episode aired, the camera panned away.[23] In fact, a romantic kiss between men did not occur on primetime American television until 2000, on the program *Dawson's Creek*.

"Papa Was a Rodeo" is also transgressive in the way it claims the patriarchal genre of country music for queer expression. In a world of steers and guitars, the song's narrator is at ease—yet he and "Mike" also transcend the space in which the song is situated, leaving the "dive bar" for a lifetime together.[24] Of the various genres that Merritt employs, country is one of the most frequently recurring; in addition to its numerous appearances on *69 Love Songs* (e.g., "A Chicken with its Head Cut Off," "Sweet-Lovin' Man"), The Magnetic Fields' album *The Charm of the Highway Strip* offers a full-length treatment of its lyrical themes and stylistic markers.[25] This album, from a relatively early point in Merritt's career (1994), contains the song "I Have the Moon," which also presents a surprisingly direct portrayal of a male-male kiss. As in "Papa," the lyrical reference ("You have become like other men, but let me kiss you once again") occurs just before the song's refrain.[26]

Vocalist: Stephin Merritt

2. The light reflecting off the mirror ball
   Looks like a thousand swirling eyes.
   They make me think I shouldn't be here at all.
   You know, every minute, someone dies.
   What are we doing in this dive bar?
   How can you live in a place like this?
   Why don't you just get into my car,
   And I'll take you away;
   I'll take that kiss now, but
   [Chorus]

3. And now it's 55 years later.
   We've had the romance of the
   century.
   After all these years wrestling gators
   I still feel like crying when I think of
   what you said to me:
   [Chorus]
   What a coincidence, your
   Papa was a rodeo too.

© 1999 Stephin Merritt. Reprinted with permission.

Figure 12.3A "Papa Was a Rodeo."

Melodic reduction (sounds two octaves lower than written)

Figure 12.3B "Papa Was a Rodeo."

In comparison to these queer country songs, the relationship between sound-world and lyrical content in "When My Boy Walks Down the Street" appears less oppositional. The lyrics exhibit an interest in displaying a love object, and several musical features highlight other conventionally masculine qualities of self-presentation. The song is also rendered in a way that suggests ambivalence toward the act of singing: Merritt rarely sustains a vowel, but instead tends to move quickly to the following consonant; vocal range and rhythmic values are limited as well. At the same time, the gender reversals and surreal undertone of the text undercut these tendencies. In terms of genre, the use of a reverberant electric guitar persistently strumming out every quarter-note beat in combination with a limited harmonic palette and an emphasis on ascending-fifth progressions (D-A, C-G) evokes a straightforward alterna-pop style that is relatively nonchalant in affect; Merritt likens it to the Jesus and Mary Chain, an '80s and '90s "alternative" group known for their combination of distorted guitars and pop sensibilities (*69LS*, 30).

In spite of the obvious differences between "Papa" and "When My Boy," however, the latter song also suggests a political subtext in its own way. While undoubtedly humorous, the campy inversion of "he's going to be my wife" is just one of a number of instances in which Merritt claims marriage as a possibility for queer people.[27] Moreover, for some listeners a spectacular walk down the street may recall gay pride parades, at which the phrase "out of the closet and into the streets" is a staple chant. Ultimately, the song constructs an "out" gay subject whose behavior both draws upon and refracts conventional masculinity; this presents an intriguing symmetry to "The Luckiest Guy," in which a set of communicative conventions more traditionally associated with homosexuality (expressive behaviors and reversible language) are used to convey an effeminate masculinity.

The melodic construction of these songs reveals a twofold approach. In "Papa Was a Rodeo," for example, the verse is limited in range and material: in essence, it consists of one main melodic pattern, which oscillates around scale-degree $\hat{1}$ before cadencing on $\hat{2}$. This four-bar pattern occurs three times in measures 5–20 (see melodic reduction; compare with transcription[28]). The chorus, however, is much more active and goal-directed; from $\hat{5}$, the melody descends first to $\hat{3}$ (b. 22), then to $\hat{2}$ (b. 24), and then to $\hat{3}$ again (b. 26). It subsequently reaches up to a climactic high $\hat{2}$ (b. 28; here the melisma following the sustained A on "stand" is clearly ornamental) before returning to the lower register to descend to tonic. In fact, this contrast between a static verse and an active chorus is common to all of the songs considered thus far (see previous melodic reductions), including the double-voiced "Luckiest Guy" as well as those that express gay desire directly. An intensification of certain musical parameters in the chorus is undoubtedly a feature of many popular songs. Yet Merritt's music seems to manipulate this stylistic convention in a remarkably careful manner. In contrast to more common ways of raising energy to announce the arrival of the chorus, such as increasing the volume or thickening the texture, Merritt's precise control of melodic register suggests a conscious awareness of its effects; he uses the voice in a way that highlights its role as carrier of an increased affective charge.

The behavior of the verses resonates with observations Hubbs has made about Morrissey's vocal melodies. Specifically, she notes an avoidance of goal-directed motion and a "flatness of melodic contour"; her analyses reveal melodies that are limited in range, pitch content, and directionality, often beginning and ending on the same note and frequently repeating pitches or motives.[29] She reads these characteristics as a "mark of difference" in relation to the melodic norms of other singers and to Morrissey's more dynamic bandmates.[30] In Merritt's music, however, difference is constituted *within the songs themselves*. The relationship between verse and chorus suggests a particular dynamic, in which a constrained subjectivity articulated by the verse finds direction and freedom in the chorus.

> Who will mourn the passing of my heart?
> Will its little droppings climb the pop charts?
> Who'll take its ashes and singing, fling
> Them from the top of the Brill Building?[31]

The next song I will consider, "Reno Dakota," constructs its difference in the domain of rhythm and meter. As shown in Figure 12.4, its meter is pervasively hemiolic: recurring spans of six eighth-notes are consistently divided by the banjo into three groups of two and by the voice into two groups of three. Additionally, in measures 6–9, the two parts temporarily emphasize the weaker halves of their respective duple groupings; as shown by the dotted bar lines, the downbeat seems to shift to the middle of the measure. In measures 14–20, meanwhile, a series of jarring insertions of slower passages create approximate 2:3 relationships with the original tempo.[32]

The metrical identity of "Reno Dakota"—is it $\frac{3}{4}$ or $\frac{6}{8}$?—is fundamentally undecidable; there is equal evidence for either hearing. Pitch patterning, in concert with poetic meter, effects a clear $\frac{6}{8}$ in the vocal part, while the patterning of the banjo—the first sound heard, and one that returns several times as a solo instrument—articulates a clear $\frac{3}{4}$. The lyrical and vocal aspects of the song, meanwhile, enact a kind of indecisiveness with regard to gender and sexual identity. The subject of the song, Reno Dakota, is a real person, a queer filmmaker of Merritt's acquaintance who directed

Vocalist: Claudia Gonson

3. Reno Dakota, I'm no Nino Rota;
   I don't know the score.
   Have I annoyed you,
   Or is there a boy who?—
   Well, he's just a whore.
   I've had him before.
   It makes me drink more. [melody ascends to tonic: $\hat{5}\,\hat{5}\,\hat{6}\,\hat{7}\,\hat{1}$]

© 1999 Stephin Merritt. Reprinted with permission.

*This transcription was aided in valuable ways by feedback I received from graduate students in a spring 2005 seminar at the University of Pennsylvania.

Figure 12.4 "Reno Dakota."

the underground movie *American Fabulous*. Here he is the object of the singer's affection, although he does not return it—possibly because he is distracted by a boy, whom the singer jealously dismisses as a whore. In light of this common interest in boys, the song's first-person persona might be that of a gay man or a straight woman; further consideration of the lyrics actually deepens this ambiguity. In gendered terms, the protagonist behaves in ways that might alternately be understood as feminine, effeminate, or masculine: she or he cries, but finds comfort in beer; s/he uses campy, affected language ("alas and alack," "enthrall") to express a competitive attitude toward a love object. The vocalist, meanwhile, is the lesbian member of The Magnetic Fields, Claudia Gonson, who sings in a middle register that is shared by both men and women. Although her voice is clearly female, her singing is not especially "expressive": she uses little if any vibrato, maintains even dynamics, and (except in the latter part of the bridge) keeps the eighth-note pulse steady.[33] The instrumental voice is also difficult to place: there are no guitars, drums, or synths; only a traditional folk instrument (the banjo) that seems curiously at odds with the sophisticated play of words, rhyme, and gender in the lyrics. In these ways, "Reno Dakota" invites diverse identifications without specifying a definitive subject position for its voice; in its rejection of clear and fixed categories of sexuality and gender, it is characteristically queer.

"Papa Was a Rodeo," surprisingly, also challenges stable categories of sexual definition. After boldly establishing a narrative of gay desire and romance from its very first line, the song suddenly shifts in voice near its end. The third chorus is presented as a quotation: it is preceded by the lines "I still feel like crying when I think of what you said to me," and then is sung by a woman, Shirley Simms. Merritt joins Simms on the last two lines of the chorus, then sings two new lines ("What a coincidence, your Papa was a rodeo too") by himself to bring the song to a close.

The effects of these vocal shifts are unsettling. Having been charmed by a story of love between men that was highly unconventional for a pop song yet crystal-clear in its delineation, we leave the song feeling uncertain about who is loving whom. At first glance, the introduction of a possible male-female interpretation might appear to back away from the song's seemingly bold stance. As with "Reno Dakota," however, Merritt's play with multiple identities can be understood as a queer subversion of sexual classifications, both hetero- and homosexual. Hubbs also notes the significance such strategies can have for queer subjects:

> From both artistic and commercial perspectives, it's not difficult to imagine why Morrissey might wish to resist containment in the binary categories of contemporary sexual subjectivity—particularly when the one most eagerly offered (by the media) is that of homosexuality. Not all forms of subjectivity are equally containing, of course; such is the essence of difference, of Otherness. The neutrality that is ascribed to a normalized subject position (whiteness, maleness, straightness) carries with it the broadest range of possibilities for both empathic appeal and individual particularities. The Other's position is more circumscribed, and, significantly, less valent.[34]

Of Morrissey, Hubbs notes specifically that "presented with the standard sexuality ballot, he selects 'none of the above,' and specifies a write-in choice: celibacy."[35] In contrast, Merritt's approach to categorical subversion is quite different: he explores a full spectrum of sexual identities in his musical creations, while remaining quite clear about his own. In so doing, he also differs from other contemporary "out" gay male musicians. On the second album by Pansy Division (*Undressed*, 1993), for instance, every song is centrally concerned with gay male identity.[36] The work of Rufus Wainwright, while exploring a wider range of narrative personae, still preserves a certain stability of voice that is characteristic of the singer-songwriter tradition from which he emerged.[37]

It is also worth noting that the song's shift in voice may be explained more prosaically; the evidence for this explanation is intriguing, though anecdotal at best. On the Web page "Stephinsongs: Message of the Moment"[38] an archived message attributed to L. D. Beghtol appears. The message contains a quotation that is said to be from Merritt, in which he describes "Papa Was a Rodeo" as based on the movie *Wild Angels*. In this film, Lee Hazelwood and Nancy Sinatra played traveling alligator wrestlers, and Sinatra's character is named "Mike." The quotation goes on to note that "the song is heterosexual, with [a] homosexual tease because until Shirley sings you don't know Mike is a woman." From a listener's point of view, however, an association with a specific narrative on the part of the songwriter does not preclude diverse interpretations, for the majority of the song communicates a queer narrative that is only complicated near its end. Moreover, the statement attributed to Merritt reveals precisely the sort of interest in disrupting established sexual points of view that I have just described.

The shift in voice that occurs in "Papa Was a Rodeo" also places heterosexuality in a surprising position. If, as Foucault argued, modern sexuality is constructed as an asymmetrical binary, then "Papa Was a Rodeo" seems to reverse the usual structuring of this binary. A homosexual perspective constitutes the song's normative voice, and in relation to it, heterosexuality is contained in expression and marked as different. In short, the song positions heterosexuality as "queer."[39] Indeed, I would argue that a certain queerness is characteristic of many of the "straight" songs that appear on *69 Love Songs*: to cite several examples, the protagonist in "A Chicken with Its Head Off" is unable to rein in his affection; "Queen of the Savages" parodies the sort of ethnocentric voice that one might find in early anthropological writing; and "Yeah! Oh Yeah!" is a darkly humorous dialogue in which a husband murders his wife (sung by Merritt and Gonson, it is the only duet on the album).

But don't forget the songs that made you cry,
And the songs that saved your life.
Yes you're older now, and you're a clever swine.
But they were the only ones who ever stood by you.[40]

The last song I wish to consider returns to a more stable delineation of voice and is, like "The Luckiest Guy on the Lower East Side," more traditional in its articulation of a gay identity. As Figure 12.5 shows, the narrator of "My Only Friend" sings directly to Billie Holiday—or rather, to her recorded representation. The song creates a space in which only he and Holiday are present, and he identifies with her very strongly on a personal level, finding the possibility of salvation in her music. These themes of *living through* popular culture (here expressed literally) and intense, one-on-one identification with an icon who is known only indirectly resonate strongly with emphases noted by Eve Kosofsky Sedgwick in her work on the discourse of the closet; specifically, Sedgwick has revealed the importance of the "vicarious" and "identification through a spectatorial route" in various kinds of queer-inflected expression.[41] Highlighting camp and other traditions as ways of rehabilitating the "sentimental," Sedgwick takes care to point out that this attribute "inheres in the nature of the investment by a viewer *in* a subject matter."[42] The subject of this song is, characteristically, both flawed and fascinating, and the kind of investment it articulates is quintessentially camp.

Indeed, the identifications that camp expresses through popular music begin with and often return to the personal and the private, for these are the kinds of identifications that the closet affords. To put this slightly differently, we might imagine popular-music identifications to involve two possible aspects: first, identifications between a fan and a performer, and second, identifications among fans within a particular group.[43] The latter type of identification in particular is often expressed publicly and collectively—for example, at concerts, or through fashion. To the extent that the closet is operative, instances of the second type of identification that involve queer sexuality will be precluded, and the first type will receive a correspondingly greater emphasis. For queer individuals, group identifications typically become accessible much later in life than is the case with other kinds of difference, and even when they are achieved, the pervasive cultural dynamic of the closet continues to work as an isolating force.

Perhaps it is not surprising, then, that many examples of queer-affiliated music thematize the kind of identification described in "My Only Friend." The lyrics of The Smith's song "Paint a Vulgar Picture," for instance, are remarkably similar in this regard. Directly addressing a recently deceased musician whom the singer has idolized for years, this song also enacts a relationship with a star whose glamour has faded, known only from a distance and through recordings, and identified with most intensely in an

Vocalist: Stephin Merritt

[*Note: the overall pitch level of this track is about 30 cents higher than shown, presumably as a result of the way in which the piano sound that forms the accompaniment was programmed.*]

2. Billie, you're a genius,
    Enough to be a fool.
    A fool to gamble everything
    And never know the rules.
    Some of us can only live in songs of love and trouble.
    Some of us can only live in bubbles.
    [Chorus]

© 1999 Stephin Merritt. Reprinted with permission.

Figure 12.5 "My Only Friend."

enclosed space: "I walked a pace behind you at the soundcheck. You're just the same as I am: what makes most people feel happy leads us headlong into harm. So in my bedroom in those 'ugly new houses,' I danced my legs down to the knees." In another example, "Damned Ladies" by Rufus Wainwright, the protagonist sings to the heroines of a number of operas. Reflecting on the futility of his attempts to warn them about their bad choices, he asks, "Why don't you ladies believe me when I'm screaming? I always believe you."[44] More broadly, I would suggest that part of the power of drag for queer audiences lies in the way in which it performs these private kinds of identification publicly; in bringing them onto the stage, it allows them to become a basis of group experience.

> My sentimental melody,
> Like a long-lost lullaby,
> Will ring in your ears
> Down through the years,
> Bringing a tear to your eye.[45]

Throughout this chapter, I have emphasized the variety of voices populating Merritt's songs, the wide range of genres through which they speak, and the diverse subject positions made possible through the intersection of these two realms. I have also noted numerous ways in which Merritt's songs foreground popular music and its traditions. In relation to gender and sexuality, the examples I have discussed seem to enact a particular kind of involvement with popular music, one that can be understood in relation to gay cultural traditions. The dimensions of this involvement are threefold. First, as can be seen especially clearly in the final example ("My Only Friend"), Merritt's songs place a particular emphasis on personal, individual relationships with the styles and personae of popular music. Second, the subjects of these songs speak *through* popular music. They use genre itself as a kind of voice, one that complements the already broad palette of literal, poetic, and instrumental voices. Third, what these voices seem to seek in popular music is a liberative potential. In this regard "My Only Friend," a dark song about depression, is somewhat unusual, for in general these popular-music identifications are about creating rather than constraining possibilities.

Several of the songs I have discussed articulate this liberative potential musically through a particular verse-chorus dynamic: the chorus, the most emblematic representative of a song's identity, breaks free from the static oscillation of the verse, enabling the subject to find freedom of movement as well as a home. More broadly, the constant shifts in genre and direct expression of diverse sexual subject positions that characterize Merritt's work as a whole bring the double-voiced and camp qualities of songs such as "The Luckiest Guy" and "My Only Friend" into relief; they reveal the communicative conventions on which they rely to be one historically specific set of strategies within a range of possible ways of speaking. Merritt's songs clearly show an awareness of the continuing power of the closet to regulate discourse. Yet in subverting fixed categories of sexual identity and claiming a broad spectrum of genres for queer expression, his music shows that we can, in fact, make a home in any kind of song in which we might wish to live.

Appendix: Solo Vocalists on Stephin Merritt Albums

Year of Release	Title	Name of Recording Project	Solo Vocalist(s)	Number of Songs
1991	The Wayward Bus	The Magnetic Fields	Susan Anway	10
1992	Distant Plastic Trees	The Magnetic Fields	Susan Anway	10
1994	Holiday	The Magnetic Fields	Stephin Merritt	13 (+ 1 instrumental)
1994	The Charm of the Highway Strip	The Magnetic Fields	Stephin Merritt	9 (+ 1 instrumental)
1995	Get Lost	The Magnetic Fields	Stephin Merritt	13
1995	Wasps' Nests	The 6ths	Assorted: 10 male, 6 female (1 by Merritt)	16
1997	Memories of Love	Future Bible Heroes	Claudia Gonson (6), Stephin Merritt (5)	11
1999	69 Love Songs	The Magnetic Fields	Stephin Merritt (45), Claudia Gonson (7), L.D. Beghtol (6), Dudley Klute (6), Shirley Simms (6)	69 (includes 1 duet between Merritt and Gonson)
1999	Hyacinths and Thistles	The 6ths	Assorted: 5 male, 9 female	14
2002	Eternal Youth	Future Bible Heroes	Claudia Gonson	10 (+6 instrumentals)
2004	i	The Magnetic Fields	Stephin Merritt	14
13 years	**11 albums**	**3 bands**	**35 vocalists**	**190 (+8 instrumentals). Merritt sings 100, or 52.6%.**

Note: This listing includes albums only; the majority of Merritt's relatively small number of EPs and singles are no longer in print.

Notes

1. I wish to thank all those who have read and commented on this chapter, including Hilary Baker, Roger Grant, Monique Ingalls, Freya Jarman-Ivens, Fred Maus, and Timothy Rommen.

   This quotation appears on page 3 of an interview with Merritt that accompanies the box set of *69 Love Songs*. As this is by far the longest and most in-depth interview with Merritt available (and it includes commentary on each of the sixty-nine songs), I will refer to it frequently. Citations will appear in the text in the abbreviated format *69LS, #,* where # is the page number. (As no pagination appears in the source, I number pages consecutively with the inside cover page serving as "1.") Numerous additional interviews and journalistic profiles were also consulted in the preparation of this paper; for these sources, specific citations will be provided only in cases of direct quotation.

2. On Ives's use of wide-ranging musical sources, see J. Peter Burkholder, *All Made of Tunes: Charles Ives and the Uses of Musical Borrowing* (New Haven, CT: Yale University Press, 1995). In a recent monograph, Nadine Hubbs remarks frequently on Thomson's stylistic plurality, mentioning, for instance, "strikingly lucid tonal music neoclassically evoking Anglican chant in the same breath as Yankee hymns, and nineteenth-century American music-hall ditties alongside operatic gestures redolent of Mozart, Bizet, and Puccini." See Nadine Hubbs, *The Queer Composition of America's Sound: Gay Modernists, American Music, and National Identity* (Berkeley and Los Angeles: University of California Press, 2004), 24. Of drag performances, camp discrepancies between different strata of cultural expression are a quintessential component.

3. Hubbs, for example, writes convincingly about the ways in which Thomson, who was also forthcoming about his gay sexuality, created a musical language capable of expressing both queer sensibilities and an "American" sound, while Ives sought to counterbalance what he saw as effete tendencies in contemporary European music through the incorporation of "manly," forthright American styles. Hubbs, *Queer Composition.*

4. The Magnetic Fields, Merritt's most long-standing and active project, comes closest to a traditional band in its realization; it has always involved three to five members, and its current configuration has been consistent since 1995. No compositional collaboration is involved, however; the other musicians serve as performers. Merritt's other projects, in spite of what their names might suggest, are even less bandlike in conception. The 6ths features diverse guest soloists singing his songs, while Merritt is the only member of The Gothic Archies. In fact, Future Bible Heroes, in which Merritt contributes lyrics and melodies and Chris Ewen provides synthesized instrumentation, is the only project in which songs are co-written.

5. A number of tracks might be mentioned in this regard. On The Magnetic Fields' "Love Is Like Jazz," for instance, Merritt directed the performers to improvise on their own, in a single take, for two-and-one-half minutes, then combined and manipulated the results. After the vocals end in The 6ths' song "Oahu," the remainder of the track consists of a nine-second synthesizer loop that is subjected to extremely gradual timbral manipulation over

a duration of approximately twenty-five minutes. The Magnetic Fields' first two albums (*The Wayward Bus* and *Distant Plastic Trees*), which are currently released as a pair on a single compact disc, are separated by a silent "spacer" track lasting 4'32" (that is, exactly one second less than Cage's famous conceptual work).

6. http://www.houseoftomorrow.com/merritt.php.

7. See, for instance, Simon Frith, "Art vs. Technology: The Strange Case of Popular Music," *Media, Culture, and Society* 8 (1986): 263–79; and Simon Frith, *Music for Pleasure: Essays in the Sociology of Pop* (London and New York: Routledge, 1988).

8. These three performances occur on the album *Hyacinths and Thistles* by The 6ths.

9. As the majority of Merritt's songs explore the qualities of a particular voice, his multivocality is usually most noticeable from one song to another. However, several individual songs highlight his distinct registers in striking ways. Perhaps the most extreme example is "I Shatter" (no. 46 from *69 Love Songs*), in which Merritt sings the main melody (possibly with technological modification) on the unbelievably low notes of G^1–A^1, while periodically answering himself with short utterances using pitches from A^3 to D^4. Also noteworthy is "Epitaph for My Heart" (no. 41); this song begins in D♭ major with a madrigal-style introduction (Merritt uses multitracking to sing all parts) in which the lead melody falls mainly in the range of D♭³ to B♭³, and then abruptly shifts to A♭ major and a range of E♭²–D♭³.

10. "Two Characters in Search of a Country Song," The Magnetic Fields, *The Charm of the Highway Strip*, 1994.

11. For foundational theorizations of the dynamics of the closet, see especially Eve Kosofsky Sedgwick, *Epistemology of the Closet* (Berkeley and Los Angeles: University of California Press, 1990); and D. A. Miller, *The Novel and the Police* (Berkeley and Los Angeles: University of California Press, 1988), chap. 6.

12. Fred Maus, "Glamour and Evasion: The Fabulous Ambivalence of the Pet Shop Boys," *Popular Music* 20, no. 3 (2001): 379–393 (384).

13. Ibid. Secrecy, in the form of recurring themes of privacy and enclosed spaces, also plays a prominent role in a more recent article by Maus on the music of R.E.M. See Fred Maus, "Three Songs about Privacy, by R.E.M.," unpublished manuscript (2005).

14. Nadine Hubbs, "Music of the 'Fourth Gender': Morrissey and the Sexual Politics of Melodic Contour," *Genders* 23 (1996): 266–296 (285).

15. Ibid., 269.

16. See Maus, "Glamour," esp. 387–389. Although Maus's discussion focuses primarily on music written before singer Neil Tennant began to acknowledge his homosexuality publicly, he finds that indirectness of expression persists in the Pet Shop Boys' subsequent music (389–390).

17. All transcriptions are by the author. I will discuss the reductions appearing beneath the transcriptions shortly; for now, my arguments will focus on melody and lyrics.

18. Here I use the term "list song" to refer to a type of Tin Pan Alley song employing some sort of thematic list as a poetic conceit; two classic examples are Cole Porter's "Let's Do It" and "You're the Top." In reviews and other

journalistic sources, Merritt is often compared to Porter, perhaps because of the clever and sophisticated wordplay evident in both songwriters' lyrics. Merritt, however, more frequently associates himself with Irving Berlin, a connection that is in keeping with his interest in highly "commercial" styles of popular music. In the interview that accompanies 69 Love Songs, the following exchange occurs between Merritt and interviewer Daniel Handler (*69LS*, 13):

> Merritt: "The Luckiest Guy on the Lower East Side" was supposed to be an Irving Berlin song, but it didn't quite work out. The Lower East Side is the epicenter of songwriting history in the 20th century.
> Handler: It's lucky you live there.
> Merritt: It's why I live there.

19. For further discussion, see Suzanne G. Cusick, "On Musical Performances of Gender and Sex," *Audible Traces: Gender, Identity, and Music,* ed. Elaine Barkin and Lydia Hamessley (Zürich: Carciofoli Verlagshaus, 1999), 25–49 (see especially 34–36). Cusick's analysis highlights a number of ways in which masculine voices may perform issues of control (in particular, control of one's body and its borders) and exhibit ambivalence or reluctance toward the act of singing.
20. See, for example, Simon Frith and Angela McRobbie, "Music and Sexuality," *On Record: Rock, Pop, and the Written Word,* ed. Simon Frith and Andrew Goodwin (New York: Pantheon Books, 1990 [1978]), 371–389.
21. When these instruments do appear, they typically evoke a particular genre or effect, as occurs in the next song I will discuss.
22. Specifically, Hubbs argues that Morrissey's "visual, bodily, dramatic, and musical signs and gestures" convey difference through relative inactivity in a variety of expressive domains ("Music," 272–273). I return to consider the musical dimensions of her argument in more detail subsequently.
23. For a scholarly treatment that recounts these events and examines their discussion among a particular group of *Melrose Place* fans, see Paul Baker, "Moral Panic and Alternative Identity Construction in Usenet," *Journal of Computer-Mediated Communication* 7, no. 1 (2001), http://www.ascusc.org/jcmc/v017/issue1/baker.html.
24. The subject of "Papa" seems to anticipate a recent surge of pop-cultural interest in gay cowboys, illustrated by the success of the film *Brokeback Mountain* (dir. Ang Lee, 2005) as well as Willie Nelson's release in February 2006 of the song "Cowboys are Frequently Secretly Fond of Each Other" (written by Ned Sublette, and originally recorded by Pansy Division in 1995). In stark contrast to the successful relationship presented in "Papa," however, the lives of the male protagonists in *Brokeback Mountain* are destroyed by their inability to integrate same-sex desire into the conventionally masculine spheres they inhabit.
25. Of "Papa Was a Rodeo," Merritt has said that "the chorus for that has been sitting around since before *The Charm of the Highway Strip*. Clearly it belongs on *The Charm of the Highway Strip* but it wasn't finished nearly in time" (*69LS*, 48).
26. In this case, the kiss has an added resonance that is not present in "Papa," for

"I Have the Moon" is sung by a vampire to his lover. One of the subthemes of *The Charm of the Highway Strip* (along with travel), vampirism has a long history within homoerotic texts. For one of several sources addressing this tradition, see Richard Dyer, *The Culture of Queers* (London and New York: Routledge, 2002), chap. 6. Also see Maus's comments on the Pet Shop Boys' song "Vampires," in Maus, "Glamour," 289–290.

27. In discussing the song, interviewer Daniel Handler says to Merritt that "I think there will be people who hear this song [and] think that ' . . . and he's going to be my wife' is a gay marriage statement." Merritt replies, "Well, I suppose it is. It continues to mystify me that Death Row prisoners can get married, as a civil right, but gay people cannot" (*69LS*, 30). A related example is "It's Only Time," from the 2004 Magnetic Fields album *i*, in which Merritt sings a proposal—"marry me"—during the song's lyrical and musical climax. In this case there are no gendered nouns or pronouns within the song, although Merritt has recently discussed it as a "gay marriage ballad." See L. D. Beghtol, "Merritt's Multiple Tracks," *The Advocate* (May 11, 2004): 82–83 (83). "It's Only Time" is also noteworthy for its range: not only does Merritt cover G^2 to $F\sharp^4$, he also sings most of the notes within this span (rather than skipping between extremes, as in "I Shatter" and other songs).

28. The melodic reductions highlight stepwise patterns organizing the melodies of these songs. Empty noteheads with stems indicate the principal pitches involved, which are connected with beams and labeled according to scale-degree function. Of those notes that are not beamed, filled-in noteheads with stems indicate subsidiary pitches within the prolonged harmony, while unstemmed noteheads indicate embellishing pitches. Slurs connect pitches that are related through techniques of prolongation, such as passing motion, neighboring motion, or arpeggiation of a harmony. The reductions are informed by a belief that our ears tend to seek out anchor pitches and relatively simple, stepwise lines as a way of making sense of complex melodies. Although they are clearly influenced by the methods of Heinrich Schenker, they are not "Schenkerian" in any strict sense. I encourage readers to evaluate the reductions by playing or singing them with the recording.

29. Hubbs, "Music," 272.

30. Ibid., 272–273.

31. "Epitaph for My Heart," The Magnetic Fields, *69 Love Songs*, 1999.

32. According to Merritt, the banjo part was originally through-composed, but certain parts of the recording were lost and had to be recreated through sampling (*69LS*, 9). It appears, however, that he views the tempo changes as an integral part of the song; when I attended a concert by The Magnetic Fields in Philadelphia on April 26, 2004, their live performance of "Reno Dakota" closely paralleled the recording. Merritt has described "Reno Dakota," which is just over one minute in length, as "probably the song of the whole *69 Love Songs* that I spent the most time on" (*69LS*, 9).

33. Although certainly not butch, Gonson's performance in this song might be understood in relation to ideas of female masculinity (for the definitive exposition of this concept, see Judith Halberstam, *Female Masculinity* [Durham, NC: Duke University Press, 1998]). A related track on *69 Love Songs* is "Acoustic Guitar," in which Gonson repeatedly implores her guitar to "bring me back my girl." Both songs can be understood in relation to

a kind of modern troubadour tradition, coded masculine, in which a poet sings to an absent love object, though the latter is much clearer in its engagement with lesbian folk-music traditions. These songs are just two examples of the wide range of narrative voices suggested by Gonson's performances on *69 Love Songs*. Others include humorous narratives about straight marriages ("Yeah! Oh Yeah!"; "Zebra") as well as an ode to the virtues of men ("Sweet-Lovin' Man"). The complex interactions of Gonson's expressed gender and sexuality with the lyrical personae of Merritt's songs raise intriguing questions that could easily form the basis of another chapter; space prevents me from addressing them further here.

34. Hubbs, "Music," 286.
35. Ibid.
36. To be certain, Pansy Division are also involved in their own project of category refusal; their song "Anthem," for instance, presents the negative proclamation "we can't relate to Judy Garland" as well as the affirmative "we're queer rockers in your face today." (The latter theme is continued more explicitly in the chorus with the memorable lines "we're the buttfuckers of rock and roll / we wanna sock it to your hole.") For an exploration of Pansy Division's place within the punk tradition, see Cynthia Fuchs, "If I Had a Dick: Queers, Punks, and Alternative Acts," *Mapping the Beat: Popular Music and Contemporary Theory,* ed. Thomas Swiss, John Sloop, and Andrew Herman (Malden, MA: Blackwell, 1998), 101–120.
37. One notable exception is "The Art Teacher" (2004), sung from the perspective of a grown woman remembering a high school crush on a male teacher. One Magnetic Fields song that employs a similar maneuver is "The Night You Can't Remember," in which Merritt sings as a Rockette recalling a wartime tryst with a soldier. Such performances break long-standing taboos about "boys' songs" and "girls' songs" and who may sing them (see Hubbs, "Music," 274–277, for further discussion).
38. http://stephinsongs.wiw.org/msg.html.
39. My argument here addresses a broad level of signification involving the song as a whole. However, queerness also inheres in several details of a potential "heterosexual" reading: if the character "Mike" is understood as female, then she is in some respects a masculine woman who engages in activities such as alligator wrestling; furthermore, she loves a man who has a history with truckers.
40. The Smiths, "Rubber Ring" (1987).
41. Sedgwick, *Epistemology*, 150–151.
42. Ibid. Original emphasis.
43. I derive this schema from R. J. Warren Zanes, who in turn bases it on Freud's writings on group psychology. See R. J. Warren Zanes, "A Fan's Notes: Identification, Desire, and the Haunted Sound Barrier," *Rock Over the Edge: Transformations in Popular Music Culture,* ed. Roger Beebe, Denise Fulbrook, and Ben Saunders (Durham, NC: Duke University Press, 2002), 311–334 (300).
44. Although this song focuses on opera (traditionally thought of as a "high" cultural form), the fan relationships it describes can certainly be understood as instances of popular culture. Listeners may also notice some musical similarities between the openings of "My Only Friend" and "Mr.

Tambourine Man." Notably, the two songs share themes of musical power, the act of listening, and insomnia, but they differ in significant ways: the protagonist in the Dylan song does not identify with the musician, who is a mystical or symbolic figure rather than a real performer; he experiences the performance directly rather than through recordings; and instead of being enclosed, he follows the musician on a trip.

45. "My Sentimental Melody," The Magnetic Fields, *69 Love Songs,* 1999.

Contributors

Ian Biddle is the head of the International Centre for Music Studies and senior lecturer in music at the University of Newcastle upon Tyne. Dr. Biddle completed his PhD at the University of Newcastle upon Tyne in 1995, *Autonomy, Ontology and the Ideal: Music Theory and Philosophical Aesthetics in Early Nineteenth-Century German Thought*. His teaching includes music and cultural theory, music in contemporary culture, music and politics in Germany (1900–1945), and music, gender, and sexuality. He has also recently taught as visiting professor at the Institutionen för Musikvetenskap, University of Uppsala, Sweden. Dr. Biddle's recent and current research includes projects on music, masculinity, and the Austro-German Tradition (for a forthcoming single-authored book), a coedited book on world musics and national identities, and German electronic group Kraftwerk. He also convenes the University of Newcastle's Popular Music Research Group and organizes the Music Research Forum.

Mark J. Butler is assistant professor of music at the University of Pennsylvania. He received his PhD in music theory, with minors in ethnomusicology and music history, from Indiana University in 2003; his doctoral dissertation received the Wiley Housewright Award from the Society for American Music. Dr. Butler's research interests include popular music, rhythm and meter, music and sexuality, and the history of music theory. He is the author of *Unlocking the Groove: Rhythm, Meter, and Musical Design in Electronic Dance Music* (Indiana University Press, 2006) and is currently writing a book focusing on relationships between technology, improvisation, and composition in electronic-music performance.

Aaron Corn is a postdoctoral fellow in the Department of Music at the University of Sydney, where he leads an Australian Research Council Discovery–Project into the application of indigenous performance traditions from remote Arnhem Land to new media and performance contexts. He is a graduate of the Queensland Conservatorium and holds a PhD in music from the University of Melbourne where he also worked as a lecturer in anthropology and Australian indigenous studies. Corn's doctoral thesis explores tradition and innovation in the repertoires and activities of popular bands from Arnhem Land. He is secretary to the annual Symposium on Indigenous Performance at the Garma Festival of Traditional Culture, which is hosted by the Yothu Yindi Foundation at Gulkula in NE Arnhem Land, and maintains fruitful dialogues with Yolŋu leaders from NE Arnhem Land on the centrality of hereditary performance traditions to their social, legal, and intellectual institutions.

Shana Goldin-Perschbacher is completing her PhD in Critical and Comparative Studies in Music at the University of Virginia, where she has been teaching courses on gender and sexuality in popular music, women's studies, and classical music in contemporary culture. Her doctoral thesis, *Vocality, Listening, and Intimary: Gender Transgression in Popular Music, 1990–2005,* explores Jeff Buckley, Antony Hegarty, Björk and Meshell NdegeOcello's gender transgressions and their influence on fans' conceptions of their own gender and sexuality. This work offers some of the first extended analysis of the gendered sounds of popular singers' voices. The essay on Jeff Buckley in this collection won the Zora Neale Hurston Award and prize for the best graduate student paper on gender at the University of Virginia in 2006. Ms. Goldin-Perschbacher's paper, "Meshell NdegeOcello and Black Female Masculinity" won the US IASPM (International Association for the Study of Popular Music) award for best student paper at the society's national conference in 2004.

Jonathan Gruzelier completed his BA (Hons) in Popular Music and Recording at the University of Salford. His final-year dissertation explored the inner meanings of moshpit culture and the act of moshing. As an active practitioner of metal music, he plays lead guitar for a Manchester-based metal band, Gone Til Winter. Mr. Gruzelier intends to pursue a PhD, during which he will further investigate the position and meanings of moshing within popular culture.

Judith Halberstam is professor of English at the University of Southern California, where she is also the director of the University's Center for Feminist Research. She has been widely published and has had several articles translated into various languages. Her article "Oh Behave! Austin Powers and the Drag Kings" won the Compton-Noll Award for best LGBT essay in 2001, and her book *Female Masculinity* (Durham, NC: Duke University Press, 1998) was nominated for two Lambda Book Awards. She is also the author of *Skin Shows: Gothic Horror and the Technology of Monsters* (Durham, NC: Duke University Press, 1995) and *In a Queer Time and Place: Transgender Bodies, Subcultural Lives* (New York: New York University Press, 2005). Professor Halberstam is a renowned gender theorist, specializing in cultural studies, queer theory, and visual culture.

Stan Hawkins is professor of musicology at the University of Oslo, Norway. He is the author of *Settling the Pop Score: Pop Texts and Identity Politics* (Ashgate, 2004) and has coedited (with Sheila Whiteley and Andy Bennett) *Music, Space, and Place: Popular Music and Cultural Identity* (Ashgate, 2004) and (with John Richardson) *Essays in Sound and Vision* (Helsinki University Press, 2007). He has published numerous articles and contributed to major anthologies in the field of popular music, with specific focus on music analysis and gender identity. Professor Hawkins is editor-in-chief for *Popular Musicology Online* and editor for the Norwegian musicological journal *Studia Musicologica Norvegica* (2203–2006). From 1991 to 1993 he was the chair of UK IASPM (International Association for the Study of Popular Music), and from 1999 to 2004 the Norwegian chair IASPM Norden. He is currently working on his next book, *The British Pop Dandy: Male Identity, Music, and Culture* (Ashgate), which explores the ways in which masculinity is inscribed through performance.

Freya Jarman-Ivens is a lecturer in music at the University of Liverpool. She received her PhD from the University of Newcastle upon Tyne and her thesis explored ways in which identity is fragmented in late-twentieth-century popular musics, especially through use of the voice. Her research interests include queer theory and performativity, psychoanalytic theory, and discourses of technology and musical production. Dr. Jarman-Ivens works on a wide range of musical material, including easy listening, alternative rock, and late-nineteenth- and early-twentieth-century opera. Her teaching ranges from popular music analysis to the musical representation of character in the Austro-German operatic canon.

Richard Middleton is emeritus professor of music at the International Centre for Music Studies, University of Newcastle upon Tyne. His research interests lie in the fields of popular music and the cultural theory of music, and he has published numerous articles in these areas, as well as three books. Professor Middleton was a founder of the leading journal in his field, *Popular Music* and one of the editors from its conception in 1981 until 1996. He is associate editor for the *New Grove Dictionary of Popular Music,* and the *Encyclopedia of Popular Music of the World,* a major new reference work for which he has also written several articles. Professor Middleton has been working recently on "vocality," in particular, the popular voice, and is the author of *Voicing the Popular: On the Subjects of Popular Music* (London and New York: Routledge, 2006). In 2004, Professor Middleton was elected to a fellowship by the British Academy.

Henry Spiller is assistant professor of ethnomusicology in the Department of Music at the University of California, Davis. He earned a master's degree in harp performance from Holy Names College and a doctorate in ethnomusicology from the University of California, Berkeley. At Kenyon College, Dr. Spiller teaches courses in anthropology and ethnomusicology and directs a Sundanese gamelan ensemble. His work focuses on Indonesian music and dance, with which he has been involved as a scholar and performer since 1976, and his current project investigates twentieth-century encounters by North American artists with Indonesian performing arts.

Sheila Whiteley is chair of popular music at the University of Salford. She was the general secretary (1999–2001) of the International Association for the Study of Popular Music and is now publications officer for the association. She is a reader for Routledge, Blackwell and Ashgate publishers, and is on the editorial board of Ashgate's popular and folk music series. Professor Whiteley has also coedited (with Jennifer Rycenga) *Queering the Popular Pitch* (London and New York: Routledge, 2006), a new collection of essays, which reexamines lesbian and gay identity and their relationship to popular music. Her work in the field of popular music has led to invitations to present keynote addresses in Belgium, Finland, Australia, and the United States, as well as numerous international broadcasts, including Radio 4's *Woman's Hour* and Channel 4's *Top Ten Lead Guitarists.* Professor Whiteley is currently leading an ESF-funded research project in gender and the cultural industries.

Sarah F. Williams received a PhD from the Northwestern University School of Music, with a dissertation entitled *Now Rise Infernal Tones: Representations of Early Modern English Witchcraft in Sound and Music.* She has taught courses at Northwestern on gender and popular music, and rock music and media culture, and on women in music at DePaul University in Chicago. Dr. Williams has presented her research internationally on the acoustic properties of witchcraft, authenticity in American cowboy music, and technology and androgyny in 1980s New Wave music. She is also a freelance journalist and makes regular contributions to *Play Music* magazine, and currently resides in San Diego, California.

Index